AF477454

Frida Kahlo's Month in Paris

A Friendship with Mary Reynolds

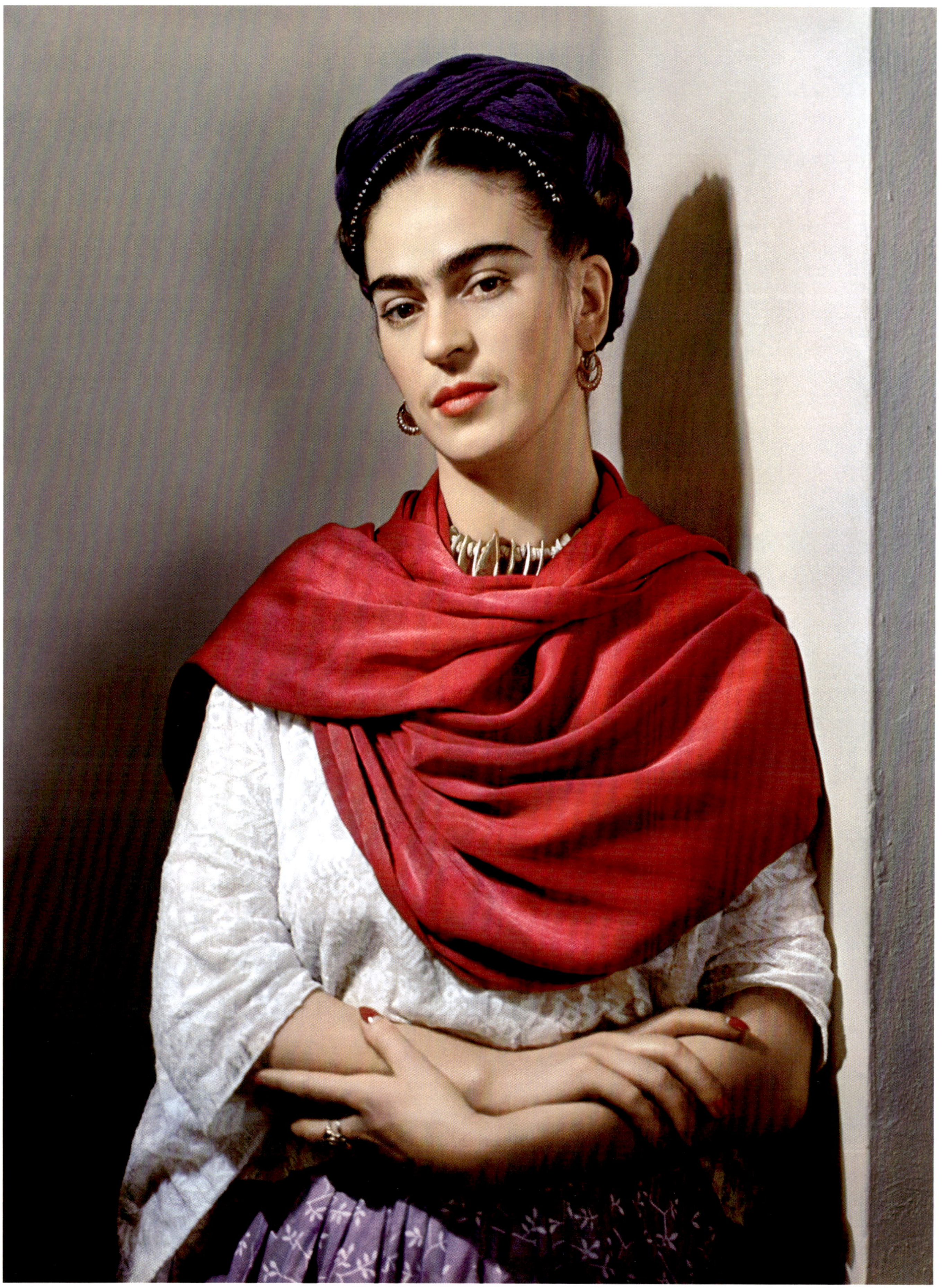

Frida Kahlo's Month in Paris

A Friendship with Mary Reynolds

Edited by Caitlin Haskell
with Tamar Kharatishvili
and Alivé Piliado Santana

The Art Institute of Chicago
Distributed by Yale University Press,
New Haven and London

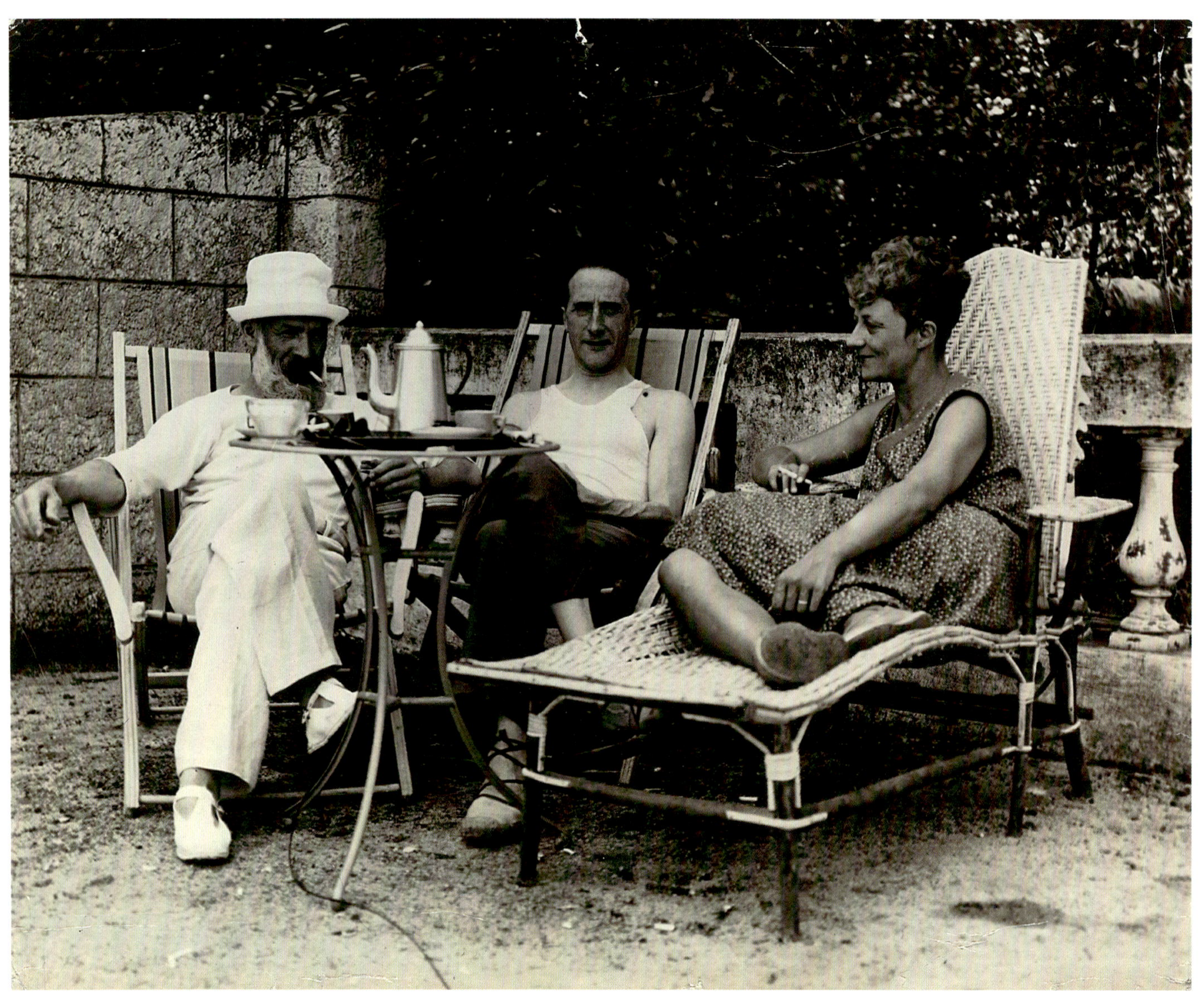

Fig. 1 Constantin Brancusi (Romanian, active France, 1876–1957). *Constantin Brancusi, Marcel Duchamp, and Mary Reynolds at Villefranche*, 1931. Gelatin silver print; 23.9 × 30 cm (9⁷⁄₁₆ × 11¹³⁄₁₆ in.). The Art Institute of Chicago, gift of Frank B. Hubachek, 1970.798.

CONTENTS

9 Foreword

10 Acknowledgments

---

13 **Frida Kahlo and Mary Reynolds:**
A Surrealist Drama in Five Acts
Caitlin Haskell

24 **Cast of Characters**
Tamar Kharatishvili and Alivé Piliado Santana

In order of appearance:

24 Julien Levy

25 André Breton

26 Jacqueline Lamba

27 Dora Maar

28 Diego Rivera

29 Nickolas Muray

30 Pierre Colle & Maurice Renou

31 Marcel Duchamp

32 Man Ray

33 Peggy Guggenheim

34 Walter Pach

35 Henri-Pierre Roché

36 Alexander Calder

37 Constantin Brancusi

38 Jean Cocteau

39 Raymond Queneau

40 Alfred Jarry

41 Manuel Álvarez Bravo

42 Wolfgang Paalen & Alice Rahon

43 Frank Brookes Hubachek

44 Artworks

96 **Lives in Parallel: A Chronology, 1891–1954**
Tamar Kharatishvili and Alivé Piliado Santana

---

109 Notes on Mary Reynolds's Bindings

110 Contributors

111 Photo Credits

Major support for *Frida Kahlo's Month in Paris: A Friendship with Mary Reynolds* is provided by the Zell Family Foundation, Pat and Ron Taylor, Constance and David Coolidge, The Donnelly Family Foundation, and Natasha Henner and Bala Ragothaman.

Additional support is contributed by Kathy and Chuck Harper.

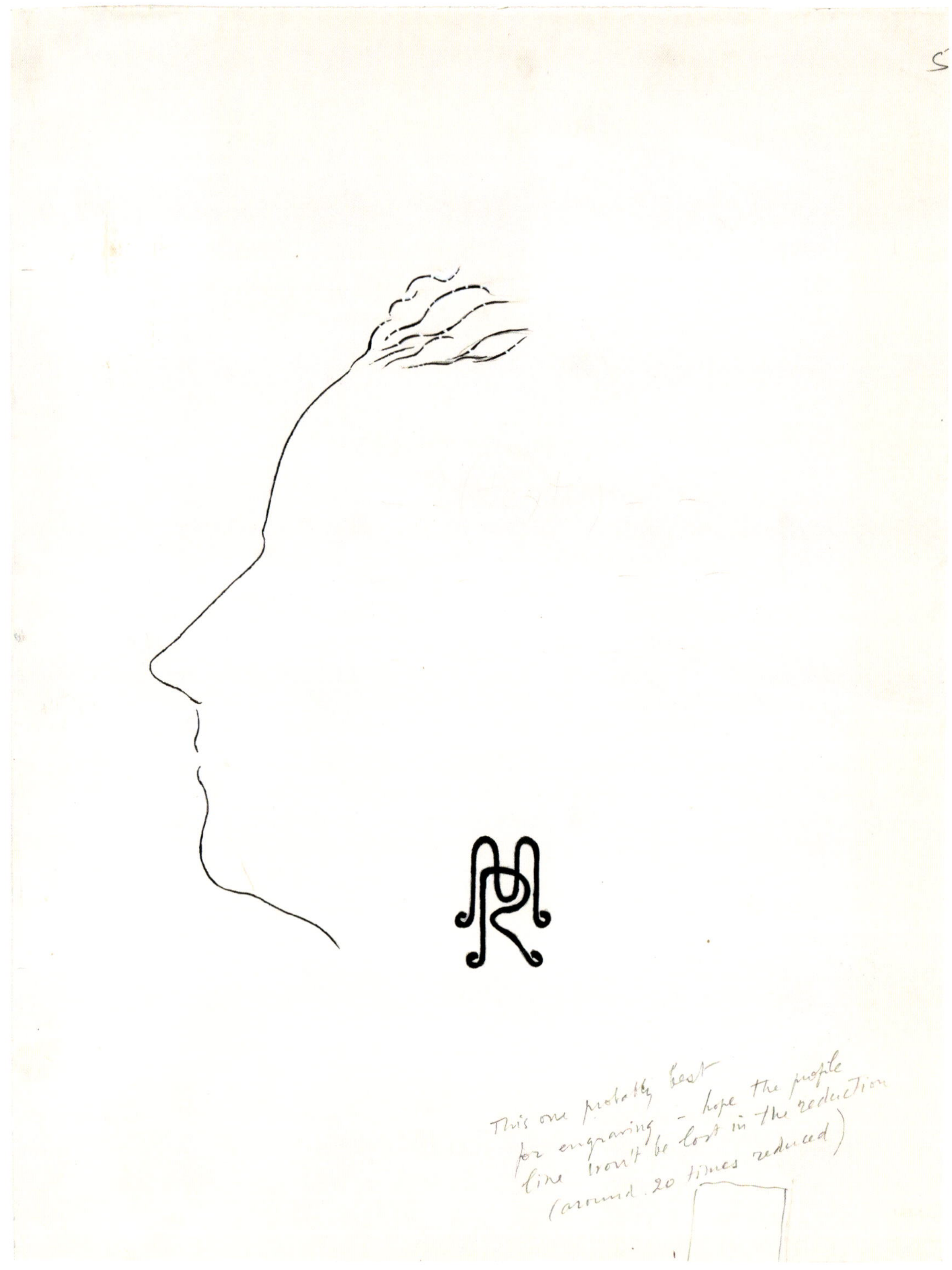

Fig. 2 Marcel Duchamp (American, born France, 1887–1968). *Bookplate Design for the Mary Reynolds Collection,* 1951. Pen and black ink, over graphite, with white gouache, on off-white wove paper; 34.7 × 26 cm (13 11/16 × 10 1/4 in.). The Art Institute of Chicago, gift of Frank B. Hubachek, 1974.923.

Foreword

The Surrealists believed that unplanned encounters had the power to redirect the course of life and the future of art. When artists Frida Kahlo and Mary Reynolds crossed paths in Paris in 1939 through a series of chance events, their lives already mirrored each other in meaningful ways both personally and professionally. Their serendipitous meeting during the weeks Kahlo spent in Paris in 1939 is a story that before now was little known. Yet it coincided with Kahlo's rise as an international artist, coming on the heels of her first solo gallery show, in New York. Kahlo's brief engagement with Surrealism brings new and necessary light to Reynolds, an avant-garde bookbinder who was socially central to the movement and yet is rarely mentioned in contemporary discussions. Considering Kahlo and Reynolds as artists—and as partners of artists Diego Rivera and Marcel Duchamp, respectively—reveals an enriched story of Surrealism in the Americas that also highlights a moment of cultural exchange between France and Mexico on the eve of World War II. For this reason, Kahlo and Reynolds are joined in this book by a cast of characters—artists, gallerists, writers, and friends—whose participation in the social group of Surrealism is also key to this story.

In presenting the history of Kahlo's one and only trip to Europe, we are fortunate to bring her paintings to the Art Institute of Chicago for the first time, situating them within the museum's own history as the steward of the Mary Reynolds Collection. This extraordinary trove of artworks, books, and archival materials created or collected by Reynolds came to the Art Institute after her death through the efforts of Duchamp and her brother, former trustee Frank Brookes Hubachek. Now, after seventy years of caring for Reynolds's archive, we are uniquely positioned to examine its original context in her home, which was itself a living work of art and a gathering place for artists. The resulting tableau invites not only a closer look at our protagonists' biographies but also a reconsideration of where and how Surrealism happened.

For conceiving this exhibition and catalogue, I commend Caitlin Haskell, the Art Institute's Gary C. and Frances Comer Senior Curator in Modern and Contemporary Art. Caitlin has been joined by two dedicated collaborators: Tamar Kharatishvili, Daniel F. and Ada L. Rice Research Fellow in Modern Art at the Art Institute, and Alivé Piliado Santana, curatorial associate at the National Museum of Mexican Art, Chicago. To tell this story, they have assembled rarely seen holdings from the Mary Reynolds Collection. They have also selected a key group of Kahlo artworks and archival materials from public and private collections across France, Mexico, and the United States that chart these exciting years of her career. For the loan of these treasured artworks, many of them icons of their home collections, we express deepest appreciation to the lenders. We are grateful to Reynolds's family, especially Scottie Walsh, for their continued support. This exhibition would not have been possible without major support from the Zell Family Foundation, Pat and Ron Taylor, Constance and David Coolidge, The Donnelly Family Foundation, and Natasha Henner and Bala Ragothaman and additional support from Kathy and Chuck Harper.

For the past century, the Art Institute has been at the forefront of collecting and exhibiting works by many of the Paris-based artists who came through Reynolds's home. Kahlo's arrival in our galleries is long overdue, yet we eagerly embrace this occasion to observe how her radiant art casts new light back on European Surrealism, illuminating not only its achievements but also its limitations and biases. This important chapter of the museum's engagement with Reynolds recognizes her accomplishments both as an artist and as a builder of community. Telling their story together reorients our understanding of how artists serve to inspire one another—through chance encounters and longtime friendships alike.

James Rondeau
President and Eloise W. Martin Director
The Art Institute of Chicago

Acknowledgments

Mary Reynolds's home at 14 rue Hallé in Paris enabled art to flourish, even when artists were not working there. Her residence was a frequent gathering place for the city's visual and literary avant-gardes, and, for a few weeks in 1939, it was also a refuge for Frida Kahlo. It has been our great pleasure to bring this encounter to life by placing key loans of Kahlo's artworks in conversation with the Art Institute of Chicago's Mary Reynolds Collection, containing Reynolds's extensive library of Dada and Surrealist publications, her art collection, her personal archive, and nearly the entire body of books she bound during her own artistic career. Our endeavor to present Kahlo's Paris sojourn within the unique context of Reynolds's home and to offer new insights on Reynolds's bindings was aided by numerous partners.

First, we thank the generous sponsors who enabled us to tell this story: the Zell Family Foundation, Pat and Ron Taylor, Constance and David Coolidge, The Donnelly Family Foundation, Natasha Henner and Bala Ragothaman, and Kathy and Chuck Harper.

Our museum's leadership championed this project from the outset, with strong support from James Rondeau, President and Eloise W. Martin Director, and Sarah Guernsey, Deputy Director and Senior Vice President for Curatorial Affairs. During the exhibition's genesis, Sarah was also interim Chair of Modern and Contemporary Art, and from this position she facilitated a powerful collaboration between this department and the museum's Research Center. As Vice President of Curatorial Strategy, Sarah Kelly Oehler joined James and Sarah in recognizing the project's urgency and, alongside Emily Benedict, Vice President of Campus Operations, enthusiastically shepherded it forward. The support of David Nacol, Senior Vice President, Philanthropy; Katie Rahn, Senior Vice President, Marketing and Communications; Amy Allen, Vice President, Engagement; and Aaron Anderson, Associate Vice President, Financial Planning and Analysis, has been equally crucial.

We express our deep gratitude to those who made this project possible by loaning prized works from their collections: Anne Helmreich, Archives of American Art, Smithsonian Institution, Washington, DC; Caty Cárdenas Ruelas, Alberto Gómez Alcalá, Carlota Romero Andrade, and Alberto Sarmiento, Banco Nacional de México, Mexico City; Cathleen Chaffee, Holly Hughes, and Janne Sirén, Buffalo AKG Art Museum, New York; Jeanne Brun, Laurent Le Bon, and Xavier Rey, Centre Pompidou, Paris; Verónica Chávez, Xochiquetzal González, and Perla Labarthe Álvarez, Museo Frida Kahlo, Mexico City; Beverly Adams, Glenn Lowery, Ann Temkin, and Anne Umland, Museum of Modern Art, New York; Christopher Bedford and Janet Bishop, San Francisco Museum of Modern Art; Kendy Genovese and Rowland Weinstein; and other lenders who wish to remain anonymous. We also thank Jill Bugajski, Kevin Salatino, and Matthew S. Witkovsky for generously providing works from the Art Institute's Ryerson and Burnham Art and Architecture Archives and departments of Prints and Drawings and Photography and Media, respectively.

Throughout exhibition planning and research, we received generous and gracious assistance from Matthew Affron, Aurelia Álvarez Urbajtel, Tere Arcq, Marie Aude, Mel Becker Solomon, Sheelagh Bevan, Fariba Bogzaran, Rosa Casanova, Rachel Cohen, Emmanuel Di Donna, Marie Difilippantonio, Erika Erdely Ruiz, Alberto Foncerrada, Paul B. Franklin, Kathleen Giblin, Jennifer Gross, Hannah B Higgins, Diane Miliotes, Jaime Moreno Villarreal, Hervé Motel, James Oles, Luis Santiago Vargas, Kate Seno Bradshaw, Angela Steinmetz, Ron Tyler, and Scottie Walsh.

Current and former colleagues in Modern and Contemporary Art at the Art Institute encouraged this work at every stage. Thea Liberty Nichols was a key research partner while the catalogue was being planned. When Paulina Pobocha joined the department as chair and curator in November 2024, she embraced the project and helped to see it forward, as did Joanna Abijaoude, Giampaolo Bianconi, Annika Bohanec, Jay Dandy, Susanne Ghez, Makayla May, and Tacy Wagner. Colleagues in the museum's Research Center were essential collaborators. Christine Fabian, Beth Iska, and Cecile Webster conserved Reynolds's bound volumes and constructed elegant supports for their display. Violet Jaffe, Anthony Morgano, and Nathaniel Parks tracked down crucial primary documents and helped navigate complex archival inquiries and interlibrary loan requests. Jill Bugajski and Leslie Wilson lent research support throughout the many months of exhibition planning. We also thank Bonnie Rosenberg and her team in Imaging, particularly Joe Tallarico and Juan Molina Hernández, for extensive new photography of Research Center holdings.

This book celebrating books was elegantly designed by Anjali Pala, who embraced the challenge of giving us an object worthy of Mary Reynolds. Publishing at the Art Institute, led by Katie Reilly, made this a beautiful and accessible volume of which we can be proud. Elizabeth Upenieks and Lauren Makholm skillfully oversaw the book's production. Josephine María Yanasak-Leszczynski managed images and rights. Kit Shields expertly steered the catalogue's editorial process with grace and intelligence, and Lisa Meyerowitz regularly provided valuable input.

Many additional talented colleagues at the Art Institute contributed to realizing our vision for the galleries. Our exhibition project team was helmed by the unflappable Megan Hurlbert, joined by CJ Lamborn and later by Becca Schlossberg. In Collections and Loans, led by Cayetana Castillo, we offer our gratitude to Tim Campos and Ariana Webber. Leticia Pardo created a compelling design, which Samantha Grassi realized with characteristic thoughtfulness. Under the leadership of Michael Neault in Experience Design, Salvador Cruz and Christine Zavesky created the exhibition's striking visual language and signage. In Interpretation, Emily Fry, Ginia Sweeney, and Loren Wright ensured that our exhibition didactics were informative and accessible. Kristin Best, Erin Fenton, and Kari McCluskey produced them with great care, and we are grateful to Eriksen Translations for their exacting Spanish translations. We are deeply indebted to Nicholas Barron and Christina Warzecha for their unparalleled expertise in art handling and installation. In Conservation, we are grateful to Megan Cramer, Haddon Dine, Sylvie Pénichon, María Cristina Rivera Ramos, Felice Robles, and Katrina Rush. Additionally, James Iska and Mardy Sears helped prepare many works on paper and photographs for presentation. Corey Burrage, Lucio Ventura, and the Protections Services officers ensured the artworks' safety and the visitors' comfort. For creating the exhibition's online presence and deftly spreading the word, we thank Shannon Burke, Nadine Schneller, and Lauren Schulz in Public Affairs. In Philanthropy, we are grateful to James Allen, Anna Maria Caravallo VanMeter, and Erika Lowe Mullins. Joe Maxwell and Meghan McCray were instrumental in welcoming visitors.

Finally, in this book about creative partnership, we want to acknowledge our own collaboration, begun at the Art Institute and completed with Alivé in a new role at the National Museum of Mexican Art in Chicago. We also wish to thank our own better halves, Kirk Nickel, Jacob Henry Leveton, and José Manuel Briseño Valenzuela, our collaborators behind the scenes who have supported this work in countless ways.

Caitlin Haskell
Tamar Kharatishvili
Alivé Piliado Santana

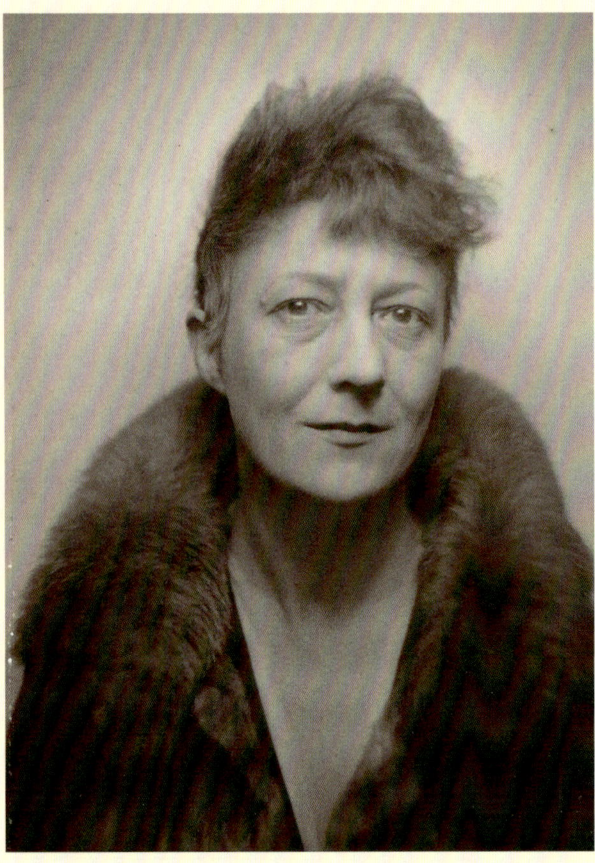

Fig. 3 *Mary Reynolds*, about 1935–40. Gelatin silver print; 5 × 4 cm
(2 × 1½ in.). The Art Institute of Chicago Archives, Mary Reynolds
Collection, gift of Marjorie Watkins, October 1992.

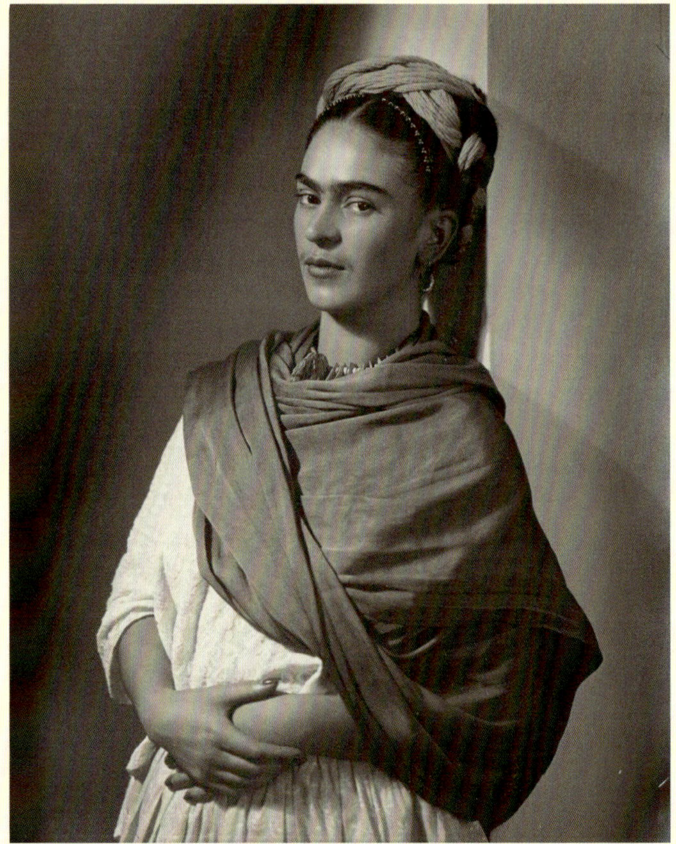

Fig. 4 Nickolas Muray (American, born Hungary, 1892–1965). *Frida
Kahlo (The Breton Portrait)*, 1938. Gelatin silver print; 24.1 × 19.1 cm
(9½ × 7½ in.). Private collection.

Frida Kahlo and Mary Reynolds: A Surrealist Drama in Five Acts

Caitlin Haskell

PREFACE

Mary Reynolds, the Minnesota-born artist and partner of Marcel Duchamp, "lived in France for twenty years because she was in love with it."[1] Frida Kahlo, the Mexican artist and partner of Diego Rivera, could barely bring herself to remain in the city for more than a few weeks. The unlikely intersection of their lives in the fourteenth arrondissement of Paris in February and March 1939—when Kahlo accepted an invitation to stay at Reynolds's home in the lead-up to the exhibition *Mexique*—illuminates a chapter in the history of cross-cultural exchange between Paris and Mexico City in the years 1938-40 that before now has rarely risen above the level of a footnote.[2] Typically, accounts of this history begin with André Breton's trip to Mexico in the spring and summer of 1938, when he and his wife, artist Jacqueline Lamba, were hosted by Kahlo and Rivera. If Breton believed that the aim of Surrealism was to find a meeting point of "life and death, the real and the imagined, past and future, the communicable and the incommunicable, high and low," then Kahlo's paintings presented him with a concept of art so fully integrated into the passions of daily life that these abstract polarities ceased to be oppositional.[3] For Breton, Kahlo's art held the potential of a new epitome of Surrealist painting, something he had been searching for, both within and outside his own milieu, for more than a decade. For Kahlo, the label of Surrealism was entirely unsatisfying, and she resisted it from the start.[4]

And yet Surrealist interest in Kahlo's paintings and their candid, existential subject matter was not without benefit to the artist. Ultimately, the liaison with Surrealism led to Kahlo's first solo exhibition, the first purchase of her work by a museum, and the rudiments of a body of critical writing on her oeuvre. It also made clear for Kahlo that her aims and those of Surrealism shared only a slim area of common ground. What she found in Paris, Surrealism's capital in these years, was a city where art was central to social life, if not social revolution. Even more, Kahlo found a compatriot in Reynolds, whose biographical circumstances mirrored her own and whose home realized the vital union of life and art in which Kahlo thrived.

The five acts that follow chart a brief history of two artists, Kahlo and Reynolds, whose ordinary lives were filled with the mystery and profundity that Surrealism sought to discover. Because artists are social, this is a social history, defined both by the figures our two protagonists encountered (presented in the Cast of Characters, **pp. 24-43**) and by the women themselves.

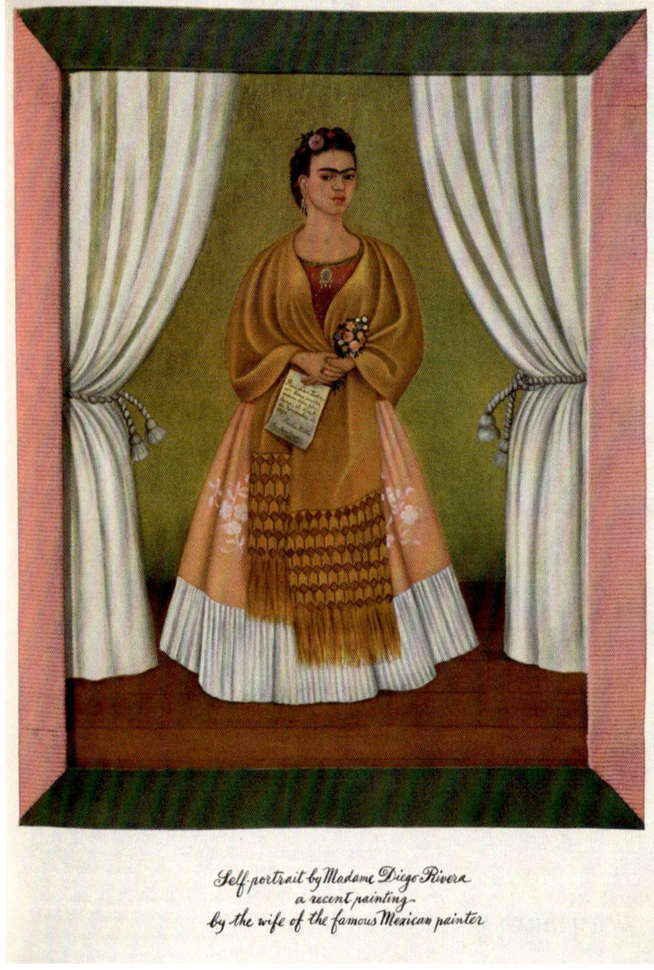

Fig. 5 Kahlo's *Self-Portrait Dedicated to Leon Trotsky* (1937; National Museum of Women in the Arts, Washington, DC) as it appeared in *Vogue*'s review of her first solo exhibition, November 1, 1938, p. 65.

ACT ONE: NEW YORK TO PARIS

Frida Kahlo's first solo exhibition took place in the fall of 1938, at the New York gallery of Julien Levy (**p. 24**). The newly designed exhibition space at Fifty-Seventh Street and Madison Avenue was then a hub of Surrealist art and social activity in the city. Levy presented twenty-five of Kahlo's works from November 1 to 15, and New Yorkers took note. The show received mention in *The New York Times* and reviews (mostly admiring) in *Art News*, *The New Yorker*, *Time*, and *Vogue* (see fig. 5), among others.[5] Several works sold to prominent collectors, and cultural and intellectual luminaries streamed through the gallery, both to see the art and to meet the artist herself. Kahlo was often present during public hours,

wearing a traditional Tehuantepec-style dress, and the high spirits recounted by attendees are apparent in Levy's photographs of the artist (see fig. 6). By all accounts, the exhibition succeeded in making a popular and commercial splash. Yet Kahlo's ties to Surrealism, as anything more than a lively and varied social group, were tenuous. Her own sense of her work's uneasy fit within the movement was quoted in the exhibition press release: "I never knew I was a Surrealist till André Breton came to Mexico and told me I was."[6]

Wary of Surrealist ideology and skeptical of the efficacy of its revolutionary rhetoric, Kahlo was nonetheless optimistic about the opportunities this context offered to present her artworks to a new audience. Within a few weeks of the New York exhibition's closure, Kahlo was en route to Paris to mount a French version of the show, which would introduce her work to viewers in Surrealism's capital. It would be her first trip to Europe and ultimately the only one she ever cared to make. Breton (**p. 25**), who had contributed a brief text for Levy's exhibition, was now the mobilizing force behind the Paris display.

With her paintings sent ahead to France and Breton awaiting her arrival, Kahlo set sail from New York aboard the SS *Paris* in mid-January 1939. She arrived in Le Havre, France, on January 21, her journey having been somewhat prolonged by rough seas. Kahlo was met at the harbor by Lamba (**p. 26**), whom she had befriended the previous spring and summer in Mexico. Now reunited in the depths of the French winter, Lamba escorted Kahlo and her luggage back to the apartment at 42 rue Fontaine where she and Breton made their home in Pigalle, one of the grittier areas of Paris. In the few weeks needed to mount her exhibition, Kahlo planned to stay with Breton, Lamba, and their three-year-old daughter. Whatever the painter might lack in creature comforts in the tiny apartment she would make up for with frequent opportunities to become acquainted with the Paris avant-garde. Such opportunities presented themselves from the moment Kahlo disembarked, as Lamba brought along photographer Dora Maar (**p. 27**) for company on the trip to and from Le Havre.[7]

After the long journey by ocean liner, described as one of the more treacherous crossings endured by the SS *Paris*, Kahlo would naturally have been eager to settle into her new residence and begin making herself at home.[8] But by the end of her first week in Paris, she had cut short her stay with Breton and Lamba.[9] She reserved a room at the Hotel Regina, near the Louvre, and that weekend (Saturday, January 28) began sending a flurry of letters and telegrams to Rivera (**p. 28**) and others expressing her displeasure with the city. She was furious with Breton for misleading her about the state of his plans for her exhibition, and she began to feel that the trip overall was ill-conceived. To Nickolas Muray (**p. 29**), who received Kahlo's most candid letters from Paris (see pp. 92-93, figs. 92-93), she confided: "I had the lousiest luck since I arrived . . . the question of the exhibition is all a damn mess."[10]

As Kahlo later explained to Muray, she spent her first weeks in Paris navigating a variety of crises, many of them matters she had assumed Breton would have resolved long before her arrival. First, her paintings were stuck in customs. Breton, it seems, had not applied for the proper permits when the works were sent from New York, and he was having trouble getting the crates released.[11] To make matters worse, a suitable gallery space still needed to be secured; Breton evidently had not mentioned to Kahlo that he did not have a space of his own. Among his preferred candidates to host the show was Pierre Colle (**p. 30**), who had deep connections to Surrealism and also, through his wife, ties to Mexico. Kahlo's account of meeting Colle conveys her displeasure in this fraught moment: "A pretty boy married to Carmen Corcuera, the most unfriendly and annoying I've ever seen in my life. He is Dali's dealer, but his gallery is worth shit because it's a filth-filled shack."[12] The frustration was in some ways mutual, although not on Colle's part; rather, his business partner, Maurice Renou (**p. 30**), who dealt primarily Impressionist and Symbolist paintings, initially found Kahlo's work too shocking to display. Furthermore, to create a more ambitious exhibition, Breton had added new material to the checklist, situating Kahlo's paintings in one of several sections in a thematic show. Naturally, Kahlo was unenthusiastic about the new direction, writing to Muray: "Now, Breton wants to exhibit together with my paintings, 14 portraits of the XIX century (Mexican) about 32 photographs of Álvarez Bravo, and lots of popular objects which he bought on the markets of Mexico—all of this junk, can you beat that?"[13] On top of this, the nineteenth-century paintings were not in exhibitable condition. Kahlo, exasperated, paid the bill for their restoration to keep the show on schedule.

The exhibition was not the only thing going awry. Kahlo's health, precarious since her childhood, had taken a turn for the worse in Paris, and she suspected that this, too, may have been Breton's fault. "I bet you

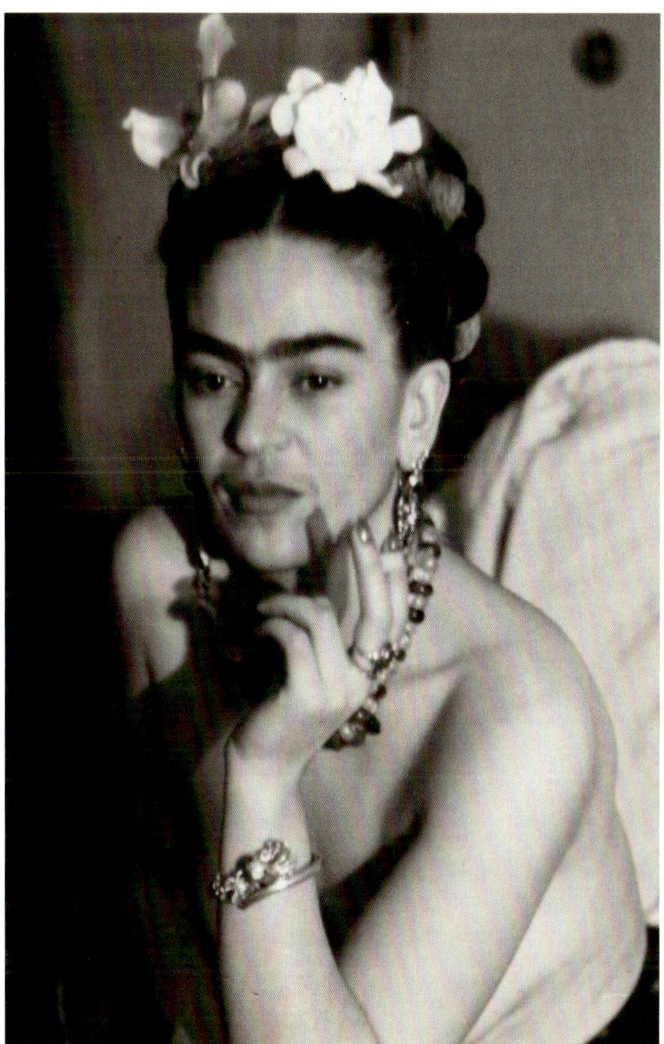

Fig. 6 Julien Levy (American, 1906–1981). *Frida Kahlo*, 1938. Gelatin silver print; 23.9 × 17.1 cm (9⁷⁄₁₆ × 6¾ in.). The Art Institute of Chicago, gift of Patricia and Frank Kolodny in memory of Julien Levy, 1990.565.40.

my boots," she wrote, "that in Breton's house was where I got the lousy collibacili. You don't have any idea of the dirt those people live in, and the kind of food they eat. It's something incredible. I never seen anything like it in my life."[14] Kahlo was in fact quite ill. In a matter of days, the bacteria caused a kidney infection that necessitated an extended stay in the American Hospital in Paris. The urgent need for medical care was recognized by Reynolds, virtually the only person in Paris for whom Kahlo spared a kind word in these early weeks. She, too, had recently dealt with a kidney condition and had been treated at the same hospital in 1937.[15] She knew the situation would not improve on its own.

ACT TWO: "A MARVELOUS AMERICAN WOMAN"

February 27, 1939: "Mary Reynolds, a marvelous American woman who lives with Marcel Duchamp invited me to stay at her house and I accepted gladly because she is a really nice person and doesn't have anything to do with the stinking 'artists' of the group of Breton. She is very kind to me and takes care of me wonderfully."[16] This is not the first reference to Reynolds in Kahlo's letters from Paris, but it is among the earliest mentions of her name. It also signals the nearly instant rapport between the two women, who connected as friends, as fellow artists, and also as partners of notable artists. Kahlo's earlier missives refer to Reynolds as the wife of Marcel Duchamp (**p. 31**)—a common enough mistake, although they were never married. The assertion that Reynolds lived with Duchamp was also somewhat inaccurate. Reynolds's house was her own, and although it seemed to most observers that Duchamp —"still the same charming clam"—was always there, he in fact kept a separate address, an attic studio at 11 rue Larrey, about thirty minutes away on foot.[17]

Reynolds had been living in Paris since 1921 and in recent years had developed a practice designing deluxe bookbindings, an art form known in French as *reliure* (see fig. 7). She specialized in avant-garde bindings of Dada and Surrealist publications, each a unique, non-editioned art object. Her home on rue Hallé in a quiet, tree-lined area of the fourteenth arrondissement was filled with different leathers and mechanical presses needed for her work. It also served as a gathering place for the artists and writers she and Duchamp most admired. Man Ray (**p. 32**), one of Reynolds's first and closest friends in Paris, described her home as "a little house with a garden . . . [where] many evenings were spent . . . with others who had been invited to dinner."[18] Another of Reynolds's earliest friendships was forged with Peggy Guggenheim (**p. 33**), and the two remained close for nearly thirty years following their initial meeting in 1922. Guggenheim and Reynolds both enjoyed fashion; when they traveled together to Egypt in 1923, they encouraged each other's penchant for eclectic earrings, which can be seen in photographs of these years (see figs. 8–9). Reynolds even opened her home to Guggenheim for two weeks when, like Kahlo, she briefly needed a place to stay. But compared to Guggenheim's, Reynolds's means were modest. She lived in Paris on a small trust established by her family and a pension she received as a "war widow." The need

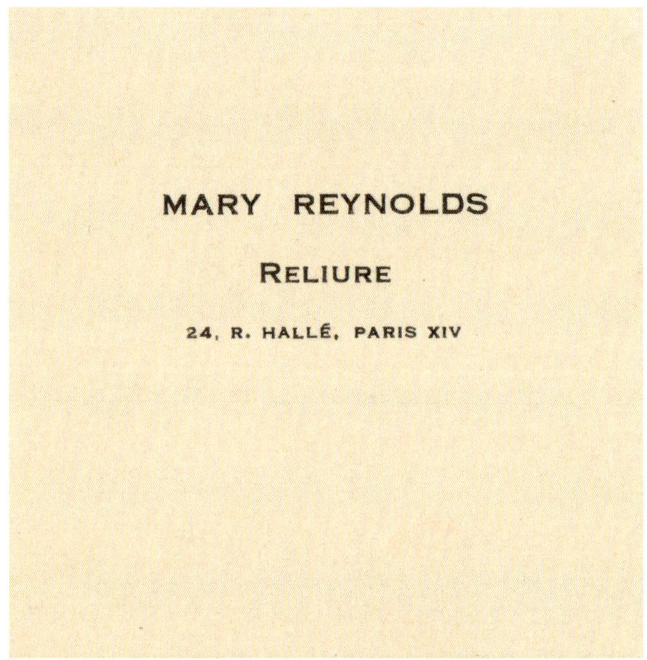

Fig. 7 Reynolds's business card, about 1934–37. The Art Institute of Chicago Archives, Mary Reynolds Collection, gift of Marjorie Watkins, October 1992.

to maintain this subsidy was one reason she never married Duchamp.

Reynolds's passion for her expatriate life in Paris was intensely felt and hard won, but a career in Europe was not necessarily something her family could have anticipated. Raised in Minneapolis, Reynolds (born Hubachek) graduated in 1913 from Vassar College in Poughkeepsie, New York, where she ran with the literary crowd. Her father was a lawyer, her mother a homemaker. Like Kahlo, she had a younger sibling, close in age, who was a valued friend. After college, Mary wed Matthew Reynolds and moved with him to Greenwich Village in New York, where they were happy and very much in love.[19] When the United States entered World War I, Matthew was called into service, and the life Reynolds envisioned met a tragic end. Stationed in France, Matthew contracted pneumonia and died abroad.[20] After two grief-stricken years, Reynolds decided to move to Paris, where she could feel closer to Matthew and perhaps carry on the vibrant cultural life they had enjoyed together in New York before the war. By 1932 Reynolds was a resident on the rue Hallé. She managed to secure two addresses—numbers 14 and 24—and divided her time between them personally and professionally until 1950.

ACT THREE: 14 RUE HALLÉ

It is unclear exactly when or how Kahlo and Reynolds were first introduced, but Kahlo was predisposed to enjoy her time at 14 rue Hallé. Even before she set sail for Europe, influential critic Walter Pach (**p. 34**) had predicted that Duchamp, "who spoke perfect English," would be a kindred spirit and useful ally as she worked toward her exhibition opening.[21] Reynolds proved to be extremely helpful too. As Kahlo was convalescing in the American Hospital and considering whether to remain in Paris, Reynolds extended the invitation to stay at her home, which Kahlo agreed would be far more pleasant than passing the days alone and frustrated in a hotel room. Reynolds collected her guest's belonging from the Hotel Regina, transported them to her house, and even paid Kahlo's hotel bill, including charges for cigarettes, drinks, phone calls, postage stamps, and telegrams.[22]

In Reynolds's house, Kahlo found herself returned to a place like her own family home in Mexico, where art and life comfortably coexisted. Reynolds's two-story house sat behind a gate with a flower garden in the front yard. The first-floor hallways led to a small kitchen and ample dining room with a large table for entertaining. Double doors in these rooms opened onto an enclosed backyard garden with established trees. Reynolds loved cats (see fig. 10), and they roamed the garden freely.[23]

More remarkable than the architecture and grounds, however, was the décor at 14 rue Hallé. The descriptions of Duchamp's room are perhaps most extraordinary, giving the impression of what today would be called installation art. The space was papered from floor to ceiling with Michelin road maps of France, randomly placed but "meticulously joined without gaps," suggesting recursive and overlapping itineraries from Paris to

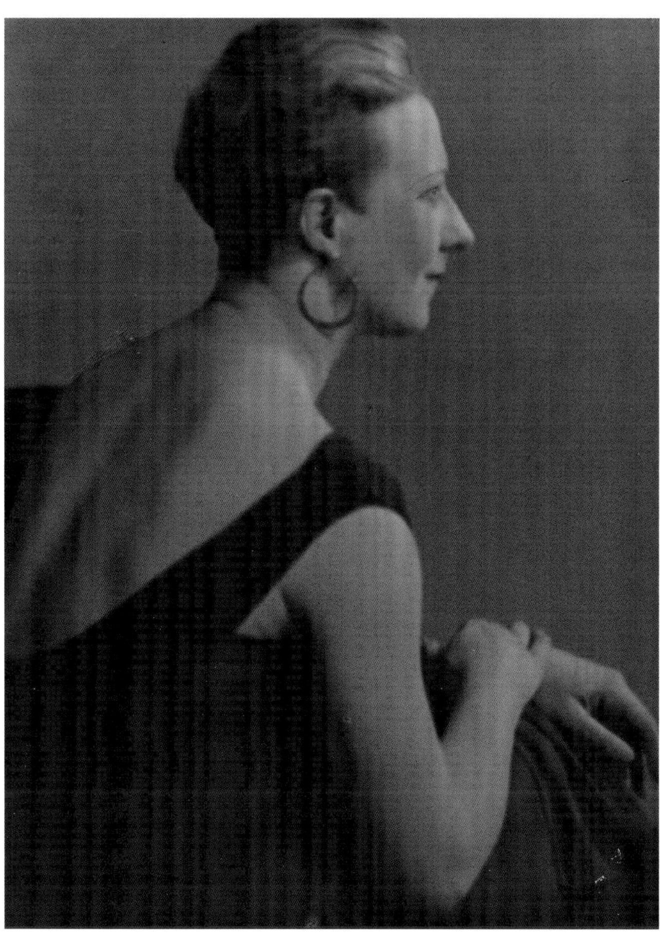

Fig. 8 Man Ray (American, 1890–1976). *Mary Reynolds*, 1930s. Gelatin silver print; 23 × 17 cm (9 × 6¹¹⁄₁₆ in.). The Art Institute of Chicago Archives, Mary Reynolds Collection, gift of Marjorie Watkins, October 1992.

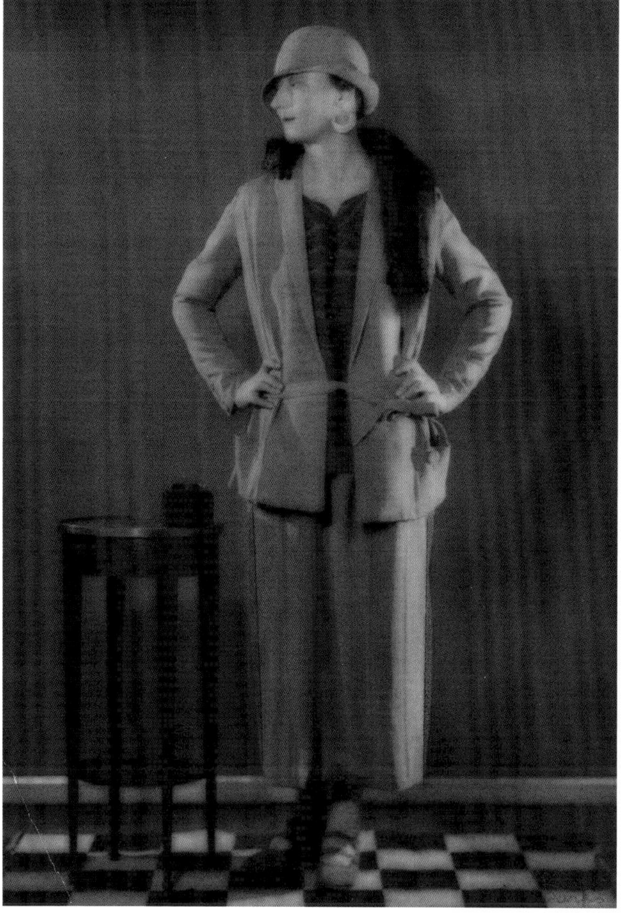

Fig. 9 Man Ray (American, 1890–1976). *Mary Reynolds*, about 1925. Gelatin silver print; 23.3 × 16.5 cm (9³⁄₁₆ × 6½ in.). The Art Institute of Chicago Archives, Mary Reynolds Collection, gift of Marjorie Watkins, October 1992.

Brittany, the Jura, and the Alps.[24] Duchamp made numerous interventions elsewhere in the house, "putting up curtains made of closely hung strings" and, later, studding the walls with unevenly spaced nail heads that functioned as nodes in string drawings.[25] String was also used on the stairway banister, suspending irregularly shaped pieces of glass to catch the light throughout the day.[26] Henri-Pierre Roché (**p. 35**), a frequent visitor, remembered the "beautiful uniform hue of the greenish wall paper" on the first floor. Elsewhere, white walls were adorned with Reynolds's collection of "pinned earrings going around the room," twinkling in pairs.[27]

What space remained, Reynolds and Duchamp filled with drawings, paintings, and sculptures by their friends, including reliefs by Jean Arp (see fig. 11) and mobiles by Alexander Calder (**p. 36**). In the garden, sculptures by Constantin Brancusi (**p. 37**) were occasionally installed, including *Two Penguins* (fig. 12); later, Reynolds hung large mobiles in the outdoor spaces, and panoramic scenes by Yves Tanguy (see fig. 13) hung on the walls inside.[28] This home, where Reynolds and Duchamp hosted "almost nightly" gatherings, was both "one of [their] most public collaborations" and a dynamic, constantly evolving reflection of the artistic community that lived, worked, and reveled together.[29]

During these years, Duchamp and Reynolds regularly worked together making art, jointly producing bindings and "boxes" (see p. 54, fig. 52, and p. 85, fig. 85), but they were far from each other's only collaborator.[30] The ideas of community and collaboration embodied at 14 rue Hallé also extended to Reynolds's expansive library, where Surrealist journals and printed matter were plentiful and literary works by her closest friends received considered responses in the form of her book-bindings.[31] Using a highly imaginative array of materials, from toad hides to teacup handles, Reynolds transformed retail copies of her friends' books into bespoke objects. Her earliest works most often explored allover pattern (see p. 49, figs. 45–46), using natural and synthetic materials decoratively to enhance the book's visual and tactile qualities, whether it was stored on a shelf or held in a reader's hands. With time, her passion for this "delicious" work became all consuming.[32] Reynolds bound so many texts by her close friend Jean Cocteau (**p. 38**)—twenty-five in total—that they could be identified by a single emblem, a star, appearing boldly on the cover of one volume (p. 57, fig. 55), discreetly on the spine of another (p. 63, fig. 62, not pictured), or as an array on end papers (p. 79, fig. 79). Cocteau, in turn,

regularly inscribed his appreciation for Reynolds's work with drawings and warm notes on the title pages (see pp. 62–63, figs. 60–62).

Bindings effectively became dialogues with the authors, with Reynolds serving as a visual and material interpreter, bringing aspects of a given text into the realm of sensation. Her work manifested the author's creative impulse in a kind of early twentieth-century hieroglyphics, encoding themes or episodes from the stories and poems concealed within her covers. Sometimes she achieved this kind of playful encryption with a readymade element, quickly apprehended and connecting to a conceit of the text—for instance, the kid gloves bound to the front and back covers of *Les mains libres* (Free hands; p. 58, fig. 56), a collection of Man Ray drawings accompanied by Paul Éluard's poetry, or the thermometer registering a perpetual 0 degrees Celsius that runs vertically down the spine of *Un rude hiver* (*A Hard Winter*; p. 77, fig. 77), a novel by her friend Raymond Queneau (**p. 39**).[33] In other designs, such as those

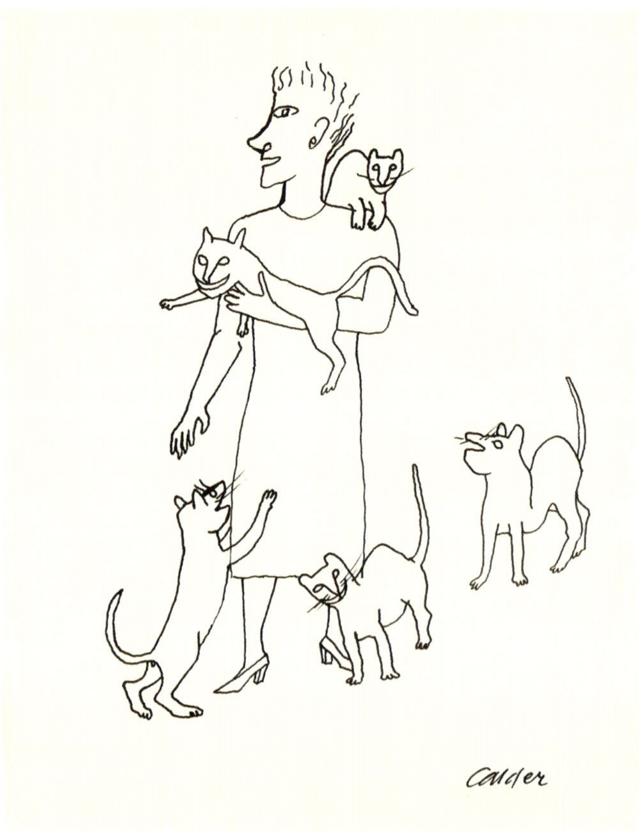

Fig. 10 Alexander Calder (American, 1898–1976). *Mary Reynolds with Her Cats*, 1955. Pen and black ink on white wove paper; 36.8 × 29.2 cm (14½ × 11½ in.). The Art Institute of Chicago, gift of Frank B. Hubachek, 1957.82.

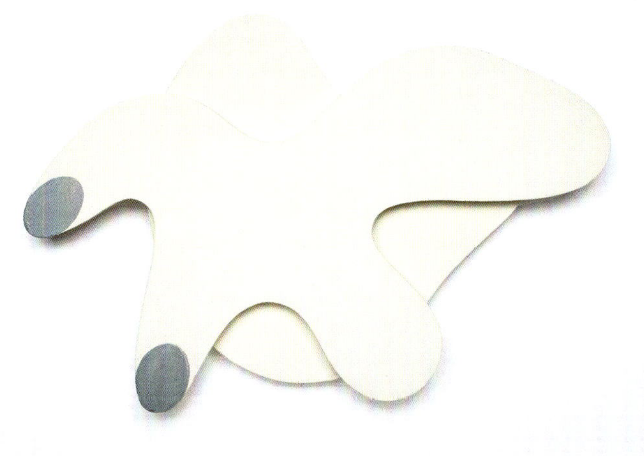

Fig. 11 Jean (Hans) Arp (French, born Germany, 1886–1966). *Manicured Relief,* 1930. Painted wood; 33 × 45.7 × 7 cm (13 × 18 × 2¼ in.). The Art Institute of Chicago, gift of Frank B. Hubachek, 1951.200.

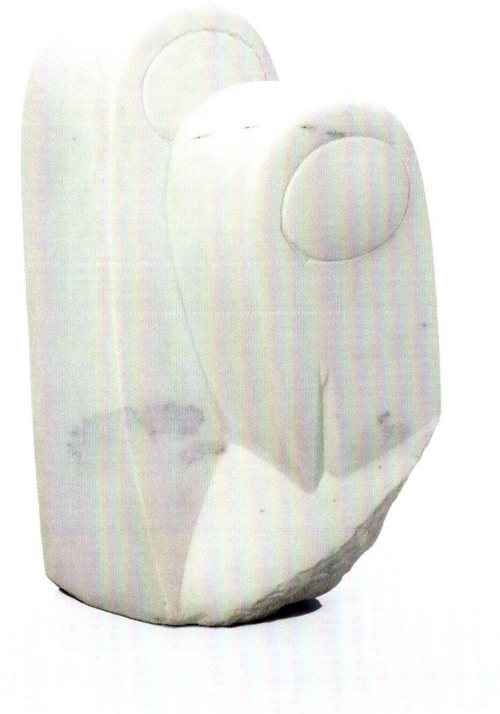

Fig. 12 Constantin Brancusi (Romanian, active France, 1876–1957). *Two Penguins,* 1911–14. Marble; 54 × 28.3 × 30.8 cm (21¼ × 11⅛ × 12⅛ in.). The Art Institute of Chicago, Ada Turnbull Hertle Fund, 1961.1115.

Reynolds made for the works of Alfred Jarry (**p. 40**), letters themselves inspired the shape and form of the book covers. Her binding for *Ubu roi* (*King Ubu*; fig. 14), designed in collaboration with Duchamp, sets the letters of the king's palindromic name in plane, with *U*-shaped front and back covers and a skinny *B* as the spine. In her binding for a later work in Jarry's saga, *Ubu enchaîné* (*Ubu in Chains*; p. 81, fig. 81), the same letters perform the title, interlocking in the voids of each *U* on the spine.

While some of Reynolds's inventive bindings could be enticements to pick up a book for the first time, others produce extended connections to symbols or narrative elements that become clear only by reading extensively into the text. The significance of the perforated copper sheets that cover Jarry's *Gestes et opinions du docteur Faustroll, pataphysicien* (*Exploits and Opinions of Doctor Faustroll, Pataphysician*; p. 50, fig. 47) comes into focus only in chapter six—"Concerning the Doctor's boat, which is a sieve"—with the realization that the punched metal alludes to the protagonist's skiff. Likewise, upon opening the cover of Antoine de Saint-Exupéry's *Night-Flight* (p. 53, fig. 51) the reader confronts a design by Duchamp—initially created for the journal *Minotaure* and later built upon in his Rotoreliefs—that evokes not only the action of airplane propellers but also the dizzying, quasi-ecstatic perceptual experiences recounted in the novel. Perhaps most evocative of all, Reynolds's design for Jean Desbordes's *Le vrai visage du Marquis de Sade* (The true face of the Marquis de Sade;

p. 76, fig. 76) presents the blood-red lines of a leather strap winding its way down the book's spine, suggesting both a whip and the slashes it might produce on a lover's body.

Whatever the design concept, from deadpan to masochistic, Reynolds herself was most often behind the scenes, applying her wit, warmth, and technical expertise to enhance the ideas of her interlocutors—their names appeared on the spine, while hers stayed out of view. A Reynolds work might have a signature look, but the designs were unsigned, and she rarely, if ever, created works for sale or exhibition; rather, she made them for her friends and herself to enjoy by living with them. Reynolds's ambivalence about self-promotion and her comfort outside the limelight may help explain why her work is not better known today. Prior to her engagement with the Surrealists, Kahlo held a similar attitude toward her own paintings, regarding them as personal

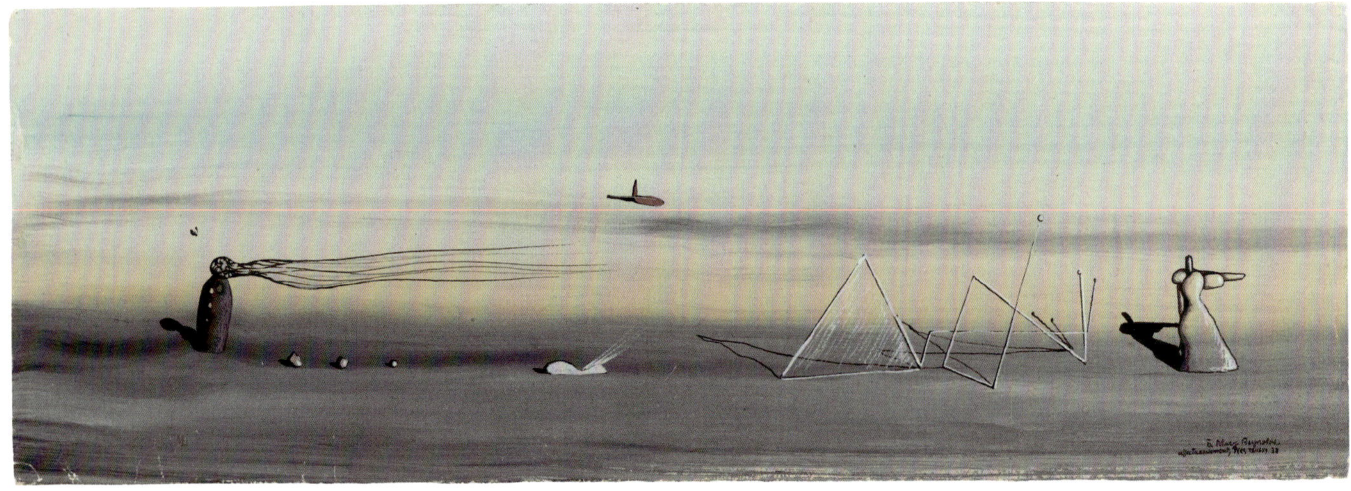

Fig. 13 Yves Tanguy (American, born France, 1900–1955). *Untitled*, 1938. Gouache, and pen and black ink, on off-white wove paper; 8.3 × 24 cm (3⁵⁄₁₆ × 9½ in.). The Art Institute of Chicago, gift of Mrs. Marjorie Hubachek Watkins in memory of her father Frank Brookes Hubachek, 2002.125.

expressions of her life and relationships that she preferred to offer as gifts to friends, only rarely selling them or showing them in commercial settings.[34]

ACT FOUR: *MEXIQUE*

Prior to meeting Reynolds, Kahlo threatened several times to leave Paris and effectively cancel her role in Breton's exhibition, which he ultimately chose to title *Mexique*. As she wrote to Muray, "I already have accommodations for the 'Isle de France' on the 8 of March.... In any case I won't stay here longer than the 15th of March."[35] Her desire to see her work thoughtfully presented won out, however, and she was persuaded to stay. Kahlo's paintings made their way out of customs, and Renou et Colle not only mounted the exhibition but also produced a catalogue (fig. 15) with an illustration of Kahlo's work, something Levy had not done. Their book featured a lightly edited version of Breton's earlier text on Kahlo that retained his provocative description of her art as "a ribbon around a bomb."[36] By the time the show opened, Kahlo was singing the praises of Colle's gallery as "one of the best here."[37]

Kahlo resided at 14 rue Hallé from February 22 to March 25, with the first half of her time there spent on preparations for *Mexique* and the second half occurring while it was on view, with the artist frequently in attendance to meet visitors, as she had been in New York. She had one painting still to finish before the exhibition, *The Suicide of Dorothy Hale* (1939; Phoenix Art Museum),

begun in New York as a commission. Not having a dedicated studio did not seem to hinder her, as she finished another commission, *Self-Portrait with Monkey* (p. 69, fig. 68), in her New York hotel.[38] By March 3 Kahlo was well enough to begin participating in the life of the home. She could join Reynolds and Duchamp for lunches in the garden when his siblings visited and came to make the most of the accommodations, getting to know artists and authors both personally and through their artworks. As she had done from the hospital and the hotel, Kahlo wrote letters regularly from 14 rue Hallé, now with a different tone: "I have enough [money] to stay here a month more. I have my return ticket. Everything is under control."[39] Photographs by Muray of her wearing a magenta rebozo (see p. 12, fig. 4, and p. 95, fig. 95), which she had been eagerly expecting during her time in Paris, finally arrived.[40] As she wrote to friends abroad, those who wanted to reach her could contact her at her new address: "F. K. c/o Mary Reynolds, 14 Rue Hallé, Paris."[41]

Mexique was installed as planned at Renou et Colle, 164 rue du Faubourg Saint-Honoré. Kahlo's portion of the checklist included eighteen works, and she was pleased with how they looked. Duchamp oversaw the hanging of her pictures, while Breton, assisted by Tanguy, installed the other areas of the exhibition. These included photographs by Manuel Álvarez Bravo (**p. 41**) and several objects Rivera lent from his collection of pre-Columbian and nineteenth-century Mexican holdings as well as his own work, represented by the image of *Communicating Vessels* that he created for Breton's lecture

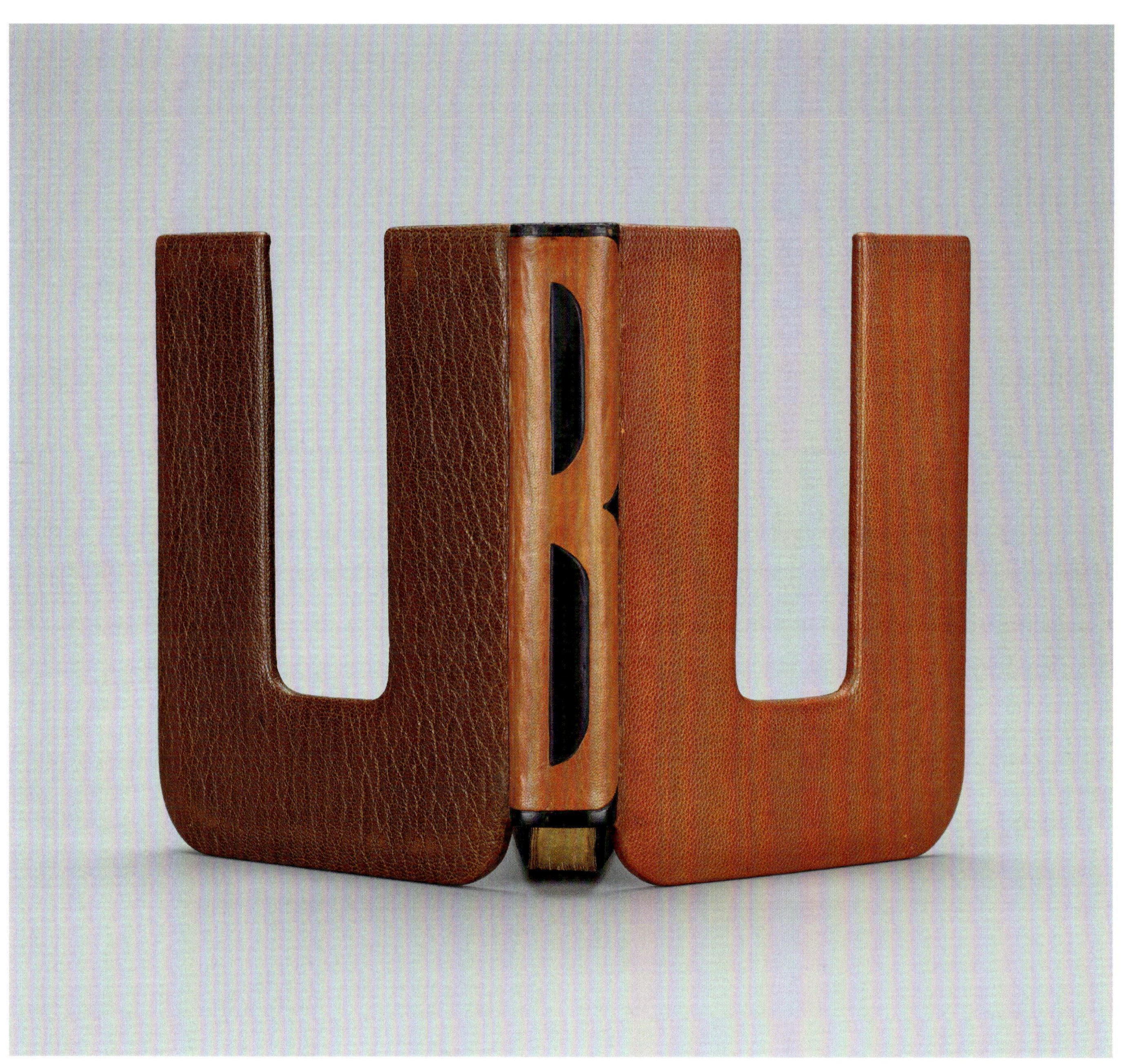

Fig. 14 Mary Reynolds (American, 1891–1950) and Marcel Duchamp (American, born France, 1887–1968). *Ubu roi* (*King Ubu*) by Alfred Jarry (Paris: Librairie Charpentier et Fasquelle, 1921), 1935. Full goatskin with onlay in the shape of a *B* and die-cut boards in the shape of a *U*. Black-silk endpapers with gold stamping and gilt edges; 16.8 × 13.5 × 2.8 cm (6⅝ × 5⅜ × 1⅛ in.). The Art Institute of Chicago, Ryerson and Burnham Libraries, Mary Reynolds Collection, 2019.180. See additional views on p. 52.

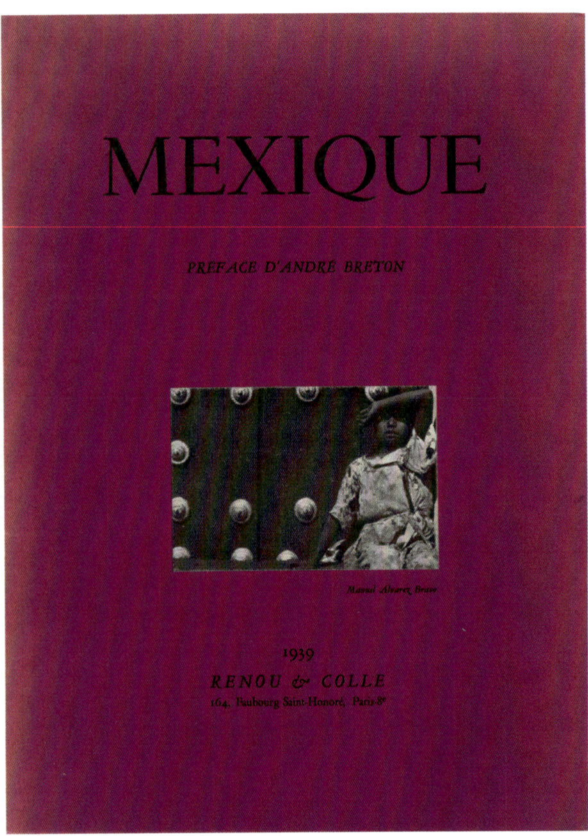

Fig. 15 Exhibition catalogue for *Mexique*, 1939. The Art Institute of Chicago, Ryerson and Burnham Libraries, Mary Reynolds Collection.

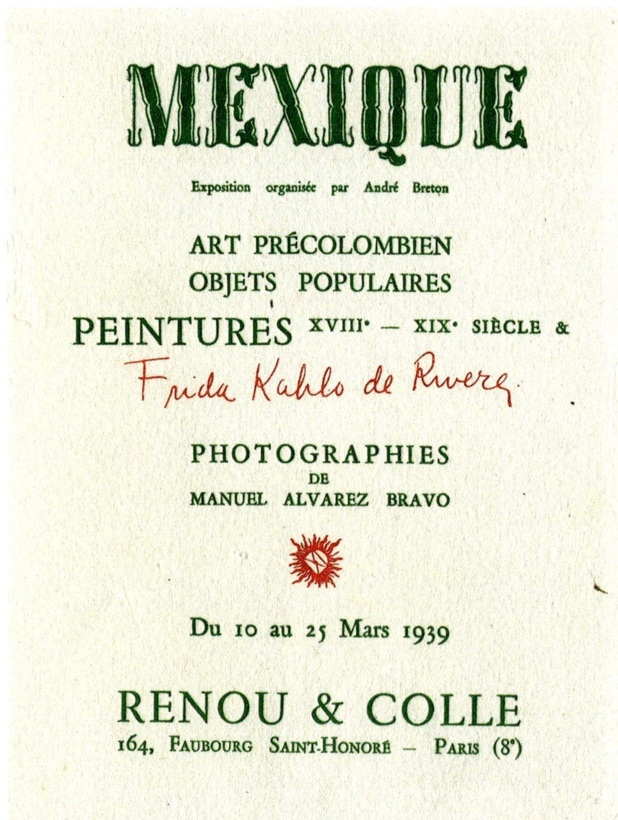

Fig. 16 Exhibition announcement for *Mexique* at Galerie Renou et Colle, March 10–25, 1939. Courtesy of the Museo Frida Kahlo, Mexico City.

series in Mexico.[42] Kahlo's contribution included a survey of pictures made in Mexico, San Francisco, and Detroit dating back to 1931. Three still-lifes, among them *Pitahayas* (p. 72, fig. 72) and *Food from the Earth* (p. 73, fig. 73), shared walls with self-portraits, including *The Frame* (p. 68, fig. 67), and other paintings with profound personal significance. The theme of life cycles—interpreted through botanical processes as well as existential events—united the different works, with Kahlo's own likeness or symbolic representations of her appearing in eight of the paintings.

As in New York, Paris's avant-garde turned out to celebrate Kahlo when *Mexique* debuted on March 10. The opening was attended by Joan Miró, who gave her "a big hug," and Vassily Kandinsky, who offered "great praises of my painting," as well as Pablo Picasso and Tanguy, who also conveyed congratulations.[43] Lamba was in attendance as well as Alice Rahon and Wolfgang Paalen (**p. 42**); Paalen's exhibition at Guggenheim Jeune in London had just closed the day before. Largely, the show went off as planned. The only deviation was that

Kahlo's pictures would have to be removed from the exhibition three days early so that she could ensure their satisfactory deinstallation before making her way to Le Havre on March 25, the day *Mexique* closed. "Overall," Kahlo confessed before leaving Paris, "I'd say that it was a success . . . . This whole thing turned out quite well."[44]

Despite having persevered through the challenges of her first days in Paris, Kahlo was not interested in prolonging her stay. The threat of war in Europe was increasingly palpable, even in France. While her exhibition was on view, news arrived that Germany had invaded Czechoslovakia. Guggenheim had offered Kahlo an exhibition at her gallery in London, but even with Duchamp's encouragement she rejected the invitation. The art market was no longer as favorable as it had been due to the situation in Europe, which was growing more concerning by the day. In her letters to Rivera, Kahlo wondered if there were ways the two of them could take action to assist others amid the growing crisis.[45]

ACT FIVE: DEPARTURES

On March 30 Reynolds typed a letter to Kahlo (p. 94, fig. 94) saying goodbye, which she sent along with mail that had arrived after Kahlo's departure. She and Duchamp were on their way to Orléans for a few days.

Kahlo, meanwhile, had made it to Le Havre to set sail for New York on the SS *Normandie*. As Breton predicted—although by means he could not have anticipated—Kahlo's home city soon became the next international gathering place of Surrealism, as artists, several of whom she had encountered in Paris, fled Europe. In 1940 Paalen co-organized an exhibition of Surrealism in Mexico City on behalf of Breton; both Kahlo and Rivera presented works. As Kahlo showed in several self-portraits (see p. 86, fig. 86), their marriage was strained, but together they became anchors of a community of Mexican and European artists making their home in the city both during and after World War II.

Kahlo's painting *The Frame* (p. 68, fig. 67) stayed behind in Europe, becoming the first of her works purchased by a museum.[46] A readymade of the most pragmatic type, the work began as a popular market item in Mexico, its red frame and decorative glass hand-painted for use as an ex-voto. Instead of the customary contents, Kahlo presented herself in the frame, painting her own image on an aluminum support. As a self-portrait, it was "the subject I know best," according to Kahlo, and it was also the work that Renou liked most.[47] It was purchased in July 1939 by the French state and accepted into the collection of the Jeu de Paume in Paris.

Reynolds, for her part, stayed at 14 rue Hallé as long as possible—dangerously long, to great personal peril— aiding in the French Resistance following the German occupation of Paris in 1940. After she was finally forced to leave in the autumn of 1942, her harrowing story was retold, with minor fictionalization, by her friend Janet Flanner in the three-part serial "The Escape of Mrs. Jefferies," which appeared in *The New Yorker* in the summer of 1943. Within six weeks of the Allied victory in Europe, Reynolds journeyed home to Paris, where she continued to pursue her creative endeavors. In addition to reliure, she served as a Paris-based editor for *View* magazine and worked informally as an artist's agent for Calder in the lead up to his 1946 exhibition *Alexander Calder: Mobiles, Stabiles, Constellations* at Galerie Louis Carré. When Calder needed help mounting his first postwar exhibition in Europe, Reynolds came to his aid,

receiving the works by mail and assembling them for installation in the show.[48]

In 1950 Duchamp heard that Reynolds was concerningly ill. Although she had always taken good care of others, it was not out of character for her to neglect her own health; by the time her cancer was diagnosed, it was too late for treatment. Her brother, Frank Brookes Hubachek (**p. 43**), paid for Duchamp to travel to Paris, and he was with Reynolds when she died. Her personal effects were not elaborate, but her library and collection of art needed attention, and there was no one better suited to the task than Duchamp.

Certain especially meaningful bound books were given to their authors as remembrances of Mary—for example Breton's *Anthologie de l'humour noir* (*Anthology of Black Humor*; p. 83, fig. 83) was gifted to the author. But Duchamp and Hubachek decided that, in the main, it was important that her collection remain together. Ultimately, they established the Mary Reynolds Collection at the Art Institute of Chicago, where Hubachek served as a trustee. With the placement of the collection, a few additional homages to Reynolds came to the Art Institute, by Calder, Cocteau, and Duchamp himself, who created the bookplate for the Mary Reynolds Collection (p. 8, fig. 2).

When the collection was published in 1956, Duchamp described Reynolds as an "eye-witness of . . . the birth of Surrealism," who through her friendships with artists "found the incentive to become an artist herself."[49] Our understanding of modern art today compels us to acknowledge that Reynolds held an indispensible role as a collaborator with artists and a catalyst for their creativity. A binder of books, Reynolds was also a binder of community, serving as a vital participant, advocate, and commentator, as well as a spectator. Kahlo's time at 14 rue Hallé gives us a glimpse into the everyday life that is needed to sustain artists' work. Part of Kahlo's resistance to her affiliation with Surrealism, even as her career and social life benefited from relationships with people in the group, was a resolute belief that life itself was the inspiration for her work: "I never painted dreams," she explained, "I painted my own reality."[50] Kahlo's work, confessional and intimate, required a space where her reality, in all its mystery and mundanity, could be experienced, day in and day out. For five weeks in February and March 1939, reality was 14 rue Hallé. Reynolds was happy to share it with her, "with love and thanks that we had you with us even a little while."[51] ◆

Cast of Characters

Tamar Kharatishvili and Alivé Piliado Santana

Characters are listed in order of their appearance in "Frida Kahlo and Mary Reynolds: A Surrealist Drama in Five Acts."

Julien Levy
Born New York, 1906
Died New Haven, Connecticut, 1981

Julien Levy opened his eponymous gallery on the fourth floor of 602 Madison Avenue in New York in October 1931 with the intention of championing photography. By the time he wrote to Frida Kahlo offering to mount a show of her work in 1938, his gallery had become the city's most prominent outpost for Surrealism in all media. It had also moved around the corner to 15 East Fifty-Seventh Street—a space noted for its unique design that included a curved wall in the main gallery.[1]

As he was laying plans for his gallery, Levy proclaimed Marcel Duchamp to be one of his "godfathers," and he was well connected within Mary Reynolds's Parisian circle.[2] Levy acquired many artworks on a trip to Europe with Duchamp in 1927, and he was a frequent presence at 14 rue Hallé whenever he was in town. Levy recounted how Duchamp split his time between his studio and Reynolds's home: "I could always find him in either place, as if he were in both at once. If I did not wish to climb to his rue Larrey studio I would shout up and he would meet me at the restaurant of a nearby Turkish mosque for coffee. Or, if I would visit Mary, Duchamp would also be there."[3]

Levy corresponded with Kahlo regularly throughout the planning of her 1938 exhibition, including to ask her preference regarding the display of her name. For the exhibition announcement, they agreed that Diego Rivera's fame would attract visitors and settled on "Frida Kahlo" printed in bold capital letters, with "Frida Rivera" set parenthetically below in smaller type (see p. 90, fig. 90).[4] Levy also gave Kahlo pointers on how to get her "strong" pictures, as he described them, through US customs from Mexico without issue. He sold six of her paintings to American collectors during the show.[5] —**TK**

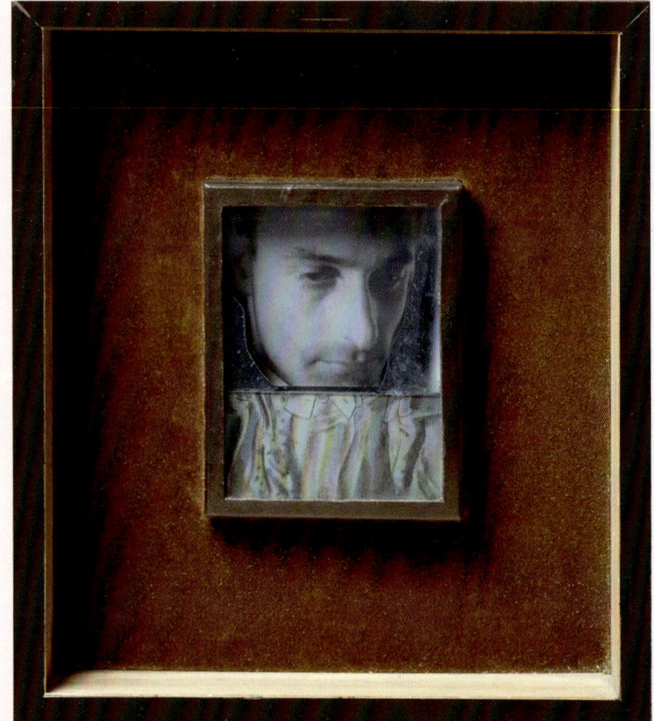

Fig. 17 Joseph Cornell (American, 1903–1972). *Portrait of Julien Levy, Daguerreotype-Object*, 1939. Assemblage of silvered glass, mirrored glass shards, black sand, gelatin silver print, and photomechanical print selectively glazed, in artist's frame; 27.9 × 25.4 × 5.4 cm (11 × 10 × 2⅛ in.). Philadelphia Museum of Art, 125th Anniversary Acquisition, The Lynne and Harold Honickman Gift of the Julien Levy Collection, 2001-62-1.

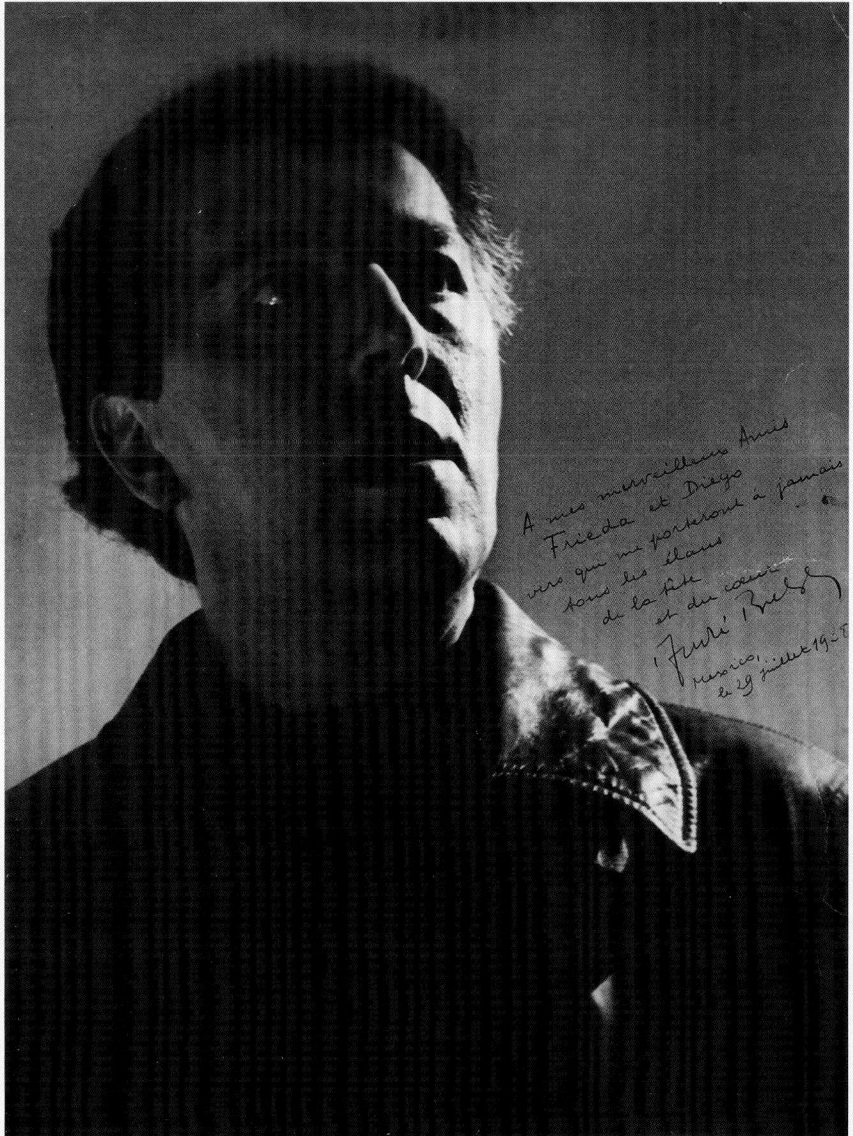

Fig. 18 Man Ray (American, 1890–1976). *André Breton*, about 1930s. Gelatin silver print; 38.2 × 28.7 cm (15¹⁄₁₆ × 11¹⁵⁄₁₆ in.). Museo Frida Kahlo, Mexico City.

André Breton

Born Tinchebray, France, 1896
Died Paris, 1966

> ## "The art of Frida Kahlo is a ribbon around a bomb."
>
> —André Breton, 1938[6]

In a 1938 interview in Mexico City, André Breton famously proclaimed Mexico "the surreal place par excellence."[7] By this time he had likewise proclaimed Frida Kahlo a Surrealist, having met the artist and her husband, Diego Rivera, earlier that year, when Breton and his wife, Jacqueline Lamba, stayed at their home in the San Ángel neighborhood from April to August.[8] Ever the entrepreneur, Breton offered to organize an exhibition of Kahlo's work in Paris once he returned home.[9] Ultimately, he displayed Kahlo's paintings alongside works he described as "Mexican curiosities" and objects from Mexica, Maya, Olmec, Tarascan, Toltec, and Zapotec civilizations, believing that the works would allow viewers to "stimulate their inventiveness" and find connections between these disparate art forms.[10] Breton's intense and, at times, essentializing engagement with Mexican art was brief, lasting from his first and only visit to the country in 1938 until the *International Exhibition of Surrealism* in Mexico City in 1940, which he organized remotely with the local help of artists Wolfgang Paalen and César Moro.

As the leader of the Surrealist movement and an editor of the journal *Minotaure*, Breton was acquainted with many of the same artists as Marcel Duchamp and Mary Reynolds. Reynolds's library included copies of Breton's books and magazines, and she created at least two binding designs for his publications: a bound set of his periodical *La Révolution surréaliste* (1929) and his book *Anthologie de l'humour noir* (*Anthology of Black Humor*; p. 83, fig. 83). Following Reynolds's death and the creation of the Mary Reynolds Collection, Breton kept a copy in his own library of *Surrealism and Its Affinities*, the first publication to catalogue her collection and work as a bookbinder.[11]—**APS**

Jacqueline Lamba

Born Saint-Mandé, France, 1910
Died Rochecorbon, France, 1993

When Frida Kahlo arrived in Paris, artist Jacqueline Lamba was one of her closest friends in the city. They first met in April 1938, when Lamba and her husband, André Breton, visited Mexico City and stayed at Kahlo and Diego Rivera's home in San Ángel for four months. Even after Kahlo decided she could no longer stay at Breton and Lamba's apartment, Lamba remained her unwavering companion, not only accompanying Kahlo on explorations of the Montparnasse neighborhood and the Louvre Museum but also visiting her regularly during her hospitalization.[13] In retrospect, Lamba admitted to Rivera that she and Breton "were not able to host her as we would have liked, since the financial situation of the surrealist group is of the most meager."[14]

Like Kahlo and Reynolds, Lamba was both an artist herself and the partner of a well-known figure in the art world, having married Breton in 1934. Few of Lamba's paintings and drawings from the 1930s survive, but those that remain demonstrate significant artistic prowess. Of Kahlo's work in *Mexique*, Lamba noted that "everyone has agreed in recognizing her paintings as the best that a woman has created so far," an assessment that esteems Kahlo while also acknowledging the limitations placed on women artists at the time.[15] In contrast to Breton's short-lived and sometimes transactional relationship with Kahlo, Lamba developed a lasting friendship with the artist. In 1944, after opening her first solo exhibition in New York as an exile during World War II, Lamba returned to Mexico—sans Breton—to visit Kahlo with her daughter, Aube.—**APS**

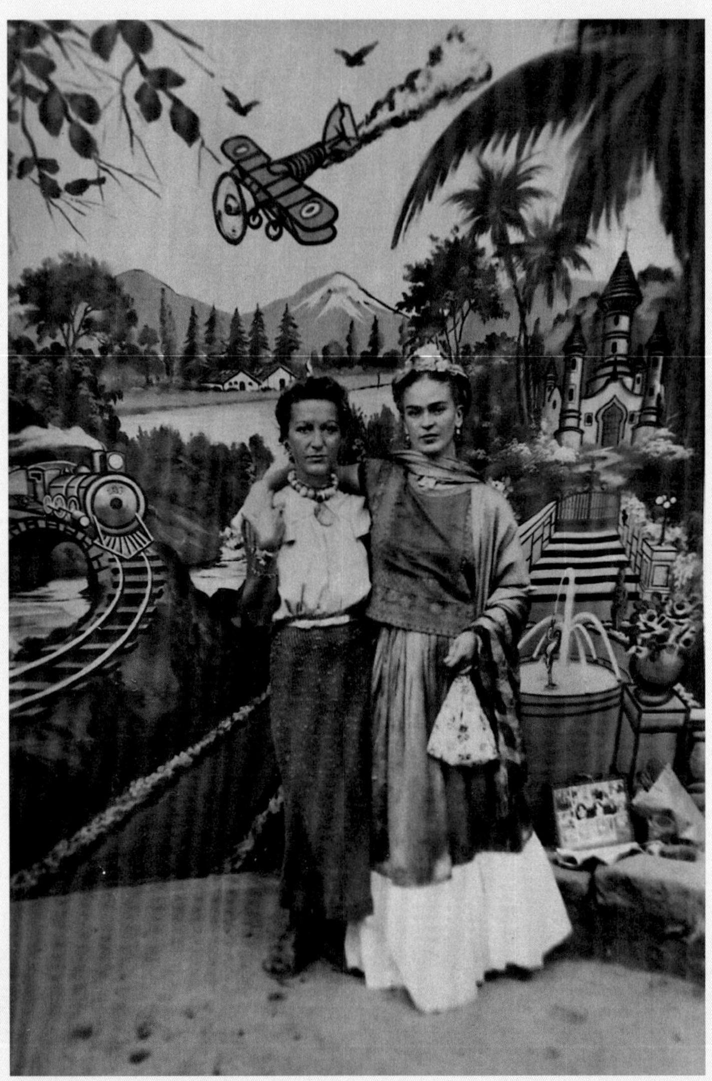

Fig. 19 Lamba and Kahlo in Pátzcuaro, Michoacán, Mexico, 1938. Courtesy of the Museo Frida Kahlo, Mexico City.

"Frida's brief appearance left everyone throbbing like a bunch of silkworms watching a speeding locomotive go by."

—Jacqueline Lamba, 1939[12]

Dora Maar

Born Paris, 1907
Died Paris, 1997

Dora Maar (born Henriette Théodora Markovitch) gained fame as a photographer among the Parisian avant-garde in the early 1930s. She started her career in a studio she shared with film director and set designer Pierre Kéfer, producing fashion and street photography and images for advertising. She opened her own studio in 1934, having joined the circle of Surrealists in 1933 and adopted a more uncanny style. Members of the movement appreciated the dreamlike scenarios and subtle evocations of the absurd in her photomontages.

Like Mary Reynolds, Maar engaged with Alfred Jarry's work,

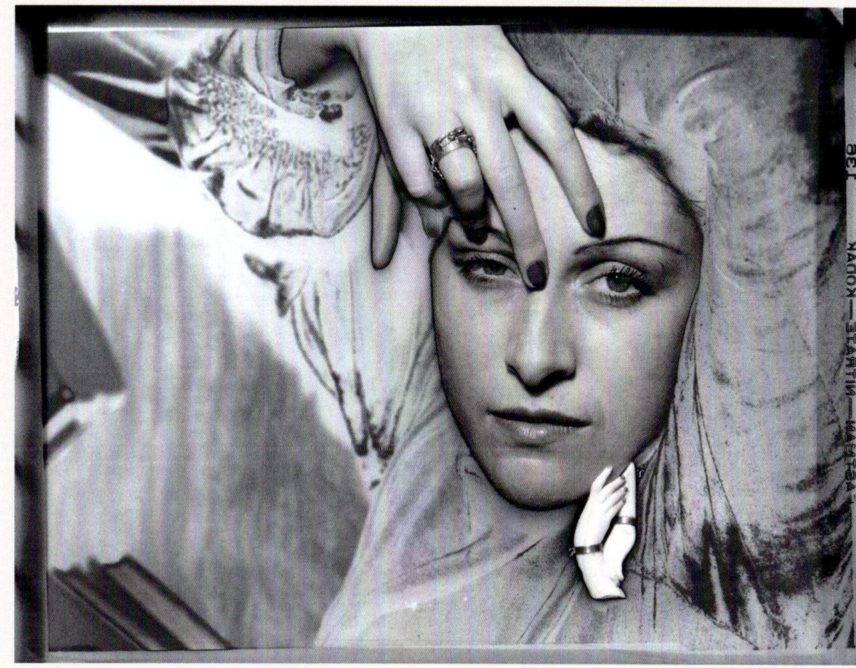

Fig. 21 Man Ray (American, 1890–1976). *Dora Maar*, 1936. Silver bromide gelatin negative on flexible cellulose nitrate support; 8.5 × 11.5 cm (3⅜ × 4½ in.). The Centre Pompidou, Paris, Cabinet de la photographie, AM 1995-281 (34).

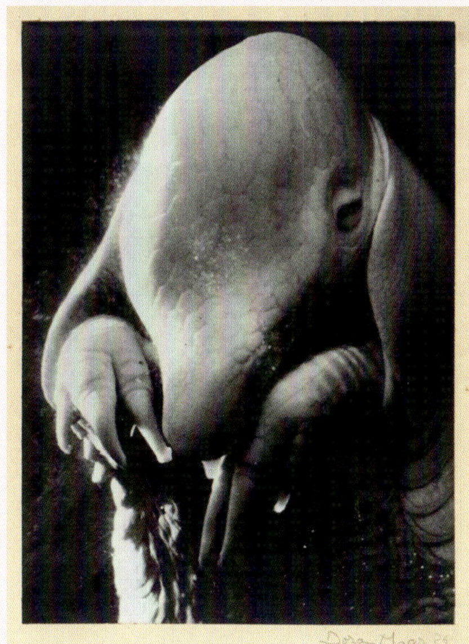

Fig. 20 Dora Maar, *Père Ubu*, 1936. Gelatin silver print; image: 39.7 × 29.2 cm (15⅝ × 11½ in.); mount: 64.7 × 49.5 cm (25½ × 19½ in.). The Metropolitan Museum of Art, New York, Gilman Collection, purchase, gift of Ford Motor Company and John C. Waddell, by exchange, 2005.100.443.

producing what has been called one of Surrealism's most "emblematic" photographs with her *Père Ubu* from 1936 (fig. 20).[16] And like both Reynolds and Frida Kahlo, Maar was in the sometimes difficult position of being partnered with a successful male artist—in her case, Pablo Picasso.

Maar was particularly close friends with painter Jacqueline Lamba. She socialized frequently with Lamba and her husband, André Breton, along with Surrealists Man Ray and Paul and Nusch Éluard, a group with whom she shared professional and political commitments.[17] Through her relationships with Kahlo, Lamba, Alice Rahon, and Reynolds, among other figures, Maar formed a network of women artists that both mirrored and provided a critical counterpoint to the male Surrealists' connections.[18]

Maar likely accompanied Lamba to welcome Kahlo's arrival by ocean liner in Le Havre, France.[19] Kahlo became friendly with Maar while she was in Paris, and Maar visited her often during her stay in the American Hospital.[20] Kahlo also posed for Maar for sketches and for the only known photographs of the painter taken during her stay in Paris (p. 97, fig. 97).—TK

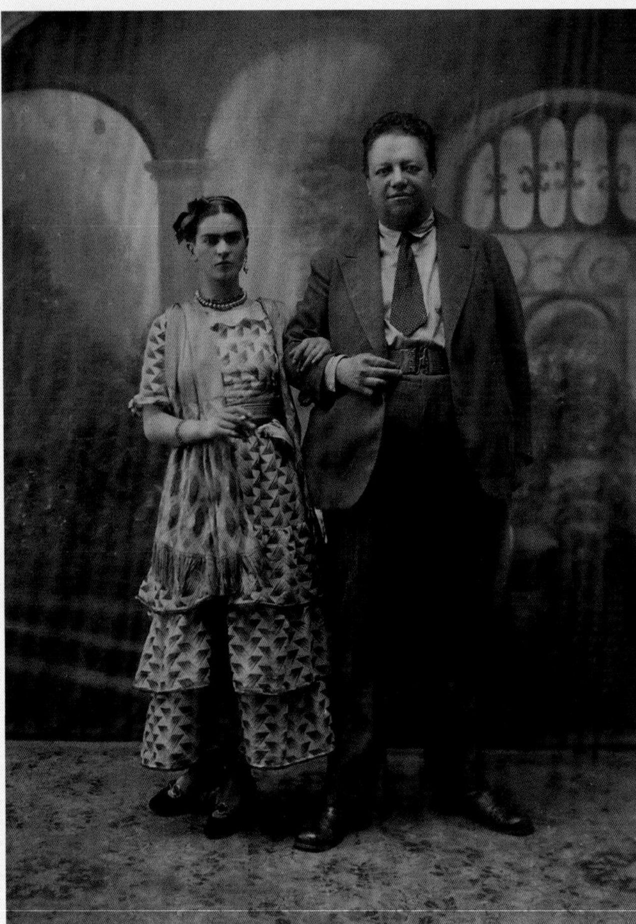

Fig. 22 Kahlo and Rivera on their wedding day at the Reyes Studio in Mexico City, August 21, 1929. Courtesy of the Museo Casa Estudio Diego Rivera y Frida Kahlo, Mexico City.

Diego Rivera
Born Guanajuato, Mexico, 1886
Died Mexico City, 1957

Before he married Frida Kahlo in 1929, Diego Rivera had lived in Paris from 1909 to 1921, and he was familiar with the city's cultural scene. Although he remained in Mexico the entire time Kahlo was abroad in New York and Paris, he helped facilitate many of the relationships she formed with artists and collectors in both cities. He also maintained constant correspondence with her, providing emotional and financial support during her travels. From Paris, Kahlo confided to Rivera her unvarnished opinions about the art-world luminaries she encountered as well as her frustrations with the Surrealists, especially André Breton and his cavalier attitude toward the preparations for her exhibition.[22] Rivera, in turn, expressed his concern for Kahlo's health but nonetheless encouraged her to make the most of her stay and, most importantly, to remain in France until *Mexique* closed. The show featured

a poster he illustrated for a lecture Breton gave in Mexico City, and he also lent four nineteenth-century Mexican paintings and one Olmec figurine. During this same period, Rivera fulfilled a special request from Breton to design an insert for the May 1939 issue of Surrealist magazine *Minotaure* (p. 71, fig. 71), which Breton edited.

At home in Mexico City, Rivera was involved in intense disagreements with Leon Trotsky, who was living there in exile. Their argument led Rivera to break from Trotsky politically, as he immediately communicated by letter to Kahlo. Trotsky also contacted Kahlo in Paris, requesting that she persuade Rivera to reconsider. Kahlo, however, defended Rivera, considering him the quintessential artist working for the revolution.[23]

Despite their profound respect for each other, Kahlo and Rivera's relationship was tumultuous, as she depicted in works such as *Self-Portrait with Cropped Hair* (p. 86, fig. 86), and he filed for divorce months after Kahlo's return to Mexico. They remarried a year later, in December 1940, in San Francisco. Rivera was then completing his mural *The Marriage of the Artistic Expression of the North and of the South on This Continent*, his largest in the United States. In it, he depicted Kahlo at work before her easel, having successfully established herself as an artist with an international following.**—APS**

Nickolas Muray

Born Szeged, Hungary, 1892
Died New York, 1965

Born Miklós Mandl, photographer Nickolas Muray met Frida Kahlo in Mexico in 1931 through their mutual friend, artist Miguel Covarrubias (see fig. 24). This encounter led to a lifelong friendship as well as a romance that lasted from 1931 to 1940. Following her exhibition at Julien Levy Gallery, Muray helped document Kahlo's paintings before they were sent to Paris. While she was abroad, Muray was her constant confidant, receiving long letters (see pp. 92–93, figs. 92–93) that vividly recounted her impressions of the Surrealists, her disappointment with preparations for the *Mexique* exhibition, her health struggles and hospitalization, and her fondness for Mary Reynolds. Muray's own letters from New York express his eagerness for Kahlo's return and

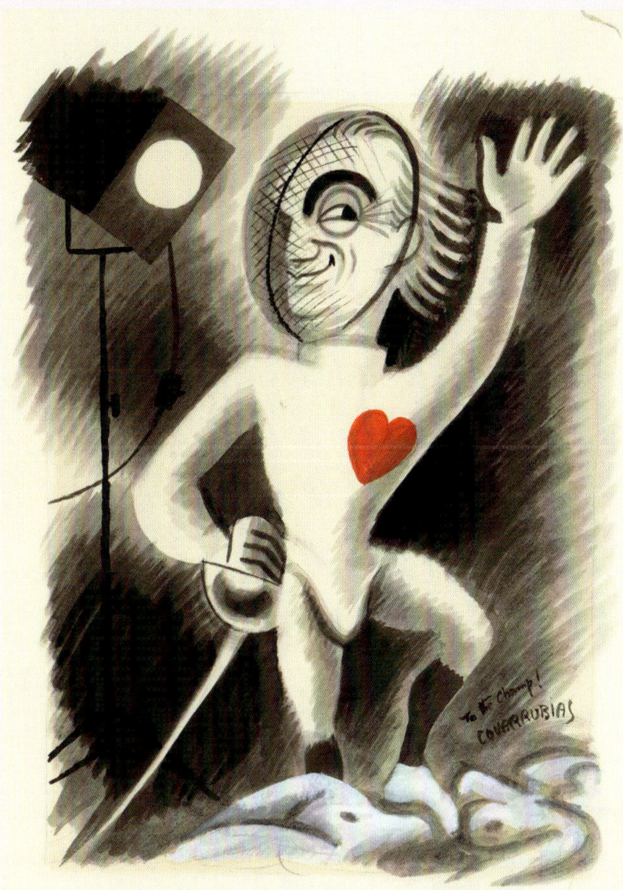

Fig. 24 Miguel Covarrubias (Mexican, 1904–1957). *Caricature of Nickolas Muray as "Lady Killer,"* about 1927. Graphite, gouache, and ink on paper; 35.9 × 27 cm (14⅛ × 10⅝ in.). National Portrait Gallery, Smithsonian Institution, Washington, DC, gift of Mimi and Nicholas C. Muray, NPG.91.132.

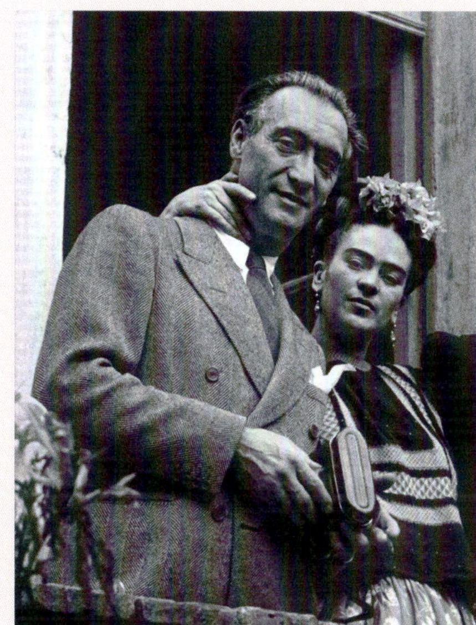

Fig. 23 Muray and Kahlo, Mexico City, 1939. Courtesy of the Nickolas Muray Photo Archives, Alta, Utah.

offer sympathy for her dealings with the Surrealists in Paris, whom he similarly viewed as indulgent and opportunistic.[25]

A man of many talents, Muray was a US national fencing champion as well as an acclaimed photographer working at the forefront of color photography. He was also a frequent traveler; his 1938 trip to Mexico City coincided with that of Jacqueline Lamba and André Breton.[26] During this visit, as the proposed Paris exhibition was being discussed, Breton asked Muray for a photograph of Kahlo, which Muray sent to Breton in January 1939.[27] This black-and-white image, known as *The Breton Portrait* (p. 12, fig. 4),

was taken in Muray's New York studio when Kahlo was about to depart for France.[28] Muray later produced these photos in color using the novel carbro print technique, creating the most iconic photographic portraits of the artist, wearing her signature magenta rebozo.—APS

"Get Europe out of your system and come back to me quick."

—Nickolas Muray to Frida Kahlo, 1939[24]

Pierre Colle
Born Dournenez, France, 1909
Died Paris, 1948

Maurice Renou
Born Saint-Germain-en-Laye, Yvelines, France, 1885
Died Neuilly-sur-Seine, France, 1974

The story of Pierre Colle's beginnings in art dealing is the stuff of legend. Armed with a phone book, he purportedly dialed numbers at random and proclaimed to anyone who answered, "I'm twenty years old, I'm a poet, and I'm selling gouaches." One day, fashion designer and art collector Jacques Doucet happened to respond and demanded every gouache he had, effectively launching Colle's career.[29]

After initially working for other gallerists, Colle opened Galerie Pierre Colle in Paris's Montmartre neighborhood in 1930 with the support of Jean Cocteau and artist and critic Max Jacob. Like Julien Levy in New York, Colle became especially known for exhibiting the Surrealists as well as many artists in Mary Reynolds's circle, such as Alexander Calder, Marcel Duchamp, and Man Ray.[30]

Colle partnered with the older and more experienced Maurice Renou in 1935, opening Galerie Renou et Colle at 164 rue du Faubourg Saint-Honoré, which presented the *Mexique* exhibition in 1939.[31] By all accounts, Renou's taste was more conservative than Colle's. As *Mexique* was coming together, Frida Kahlo lamented to Nickolas Muray that Renou thought only two of her paintings were suitable for showing, the rest being "too shocking for the public."[32] Renou's favorite work by Kahlo, *The Frame* (p. 68, fig. 67), became the artist's first work to enter a museum collection. Purchased for one thousand francs by the French government for the Jeu de Paume in Paris, it was also the only Kahlo painting that sold from *Mexique* as well as the last work to enter the museum's collection before the start of World War II.[33]—TK

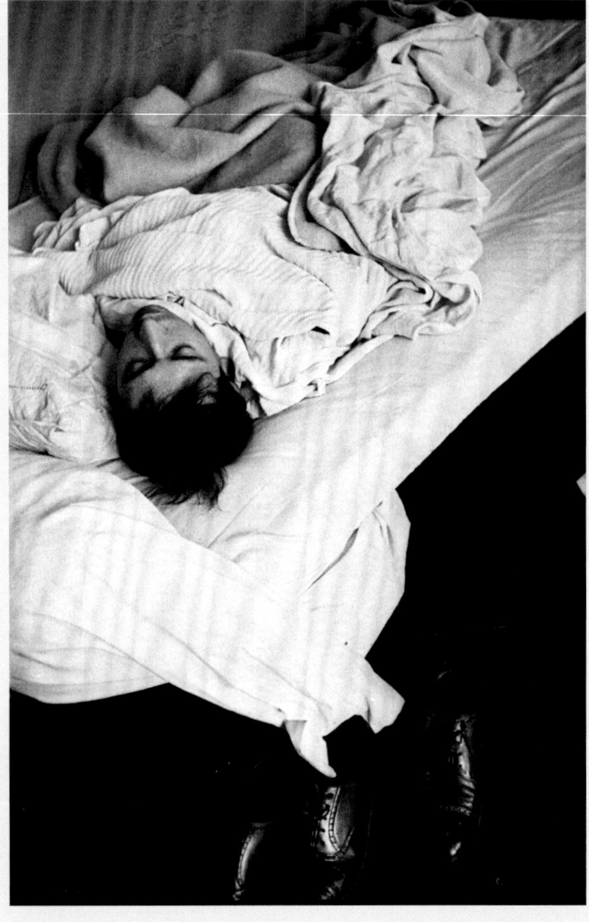

Fig. 25 Henri Cartier-Bresson (French, 1908–2004). *Pierre Colle*, 1932. Gelatin silver print; 8 × 12.3 cm (3⅛ × 4¹³/₁₆ in.). The Centre Pompidou, Paris, Cabinet de la photographie, AM 2014-678.

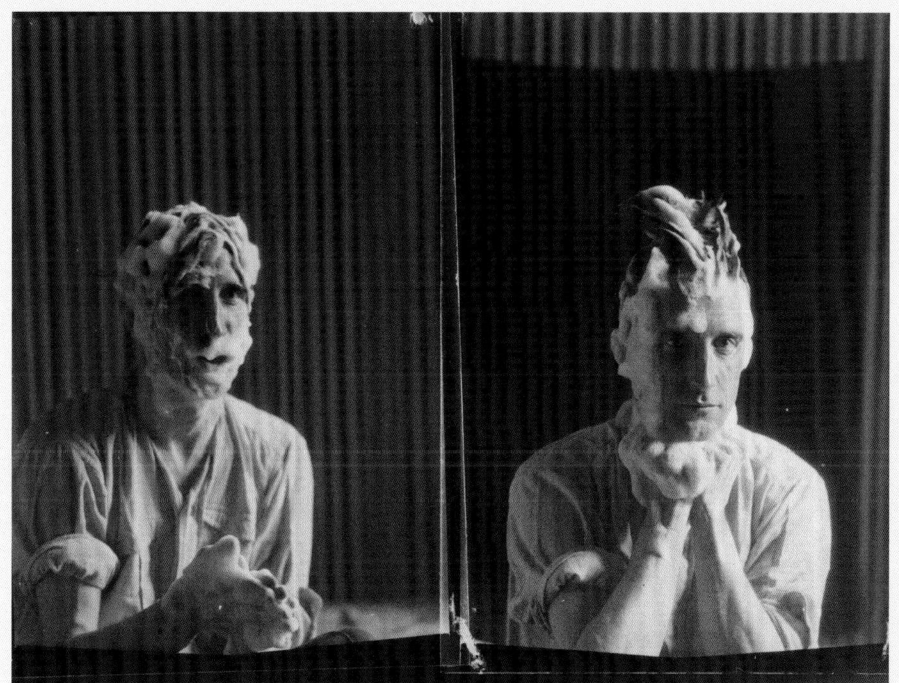

Fig. 26 Man Ray (American, 1890–1976), *Obligation pour la Roulette de Monte-Carlo*, 1924. Pigment inkjet proof; 8.9 × 11.9 cm (3½ × 4¹¹⁄₁₆ in.). The Centre Pompidou, Paris, Cabinet de la photographie, AM 1994-394 (2319).

> **"His finest work is his use of time."**
>
> —Henri-Pierre Roché, 1959[34]

Marcel Duchamp
Born Blainville-Crevon, France, 1887
Died Neuilly-sur-Seine, France, 1968

Mary Reynolds and Marcel Duchamp met in the 1910s when they were both living in New York's Greenwich Village. They renewed their acquaintance in Paris between late 1923 and early 1924, after Reynolds hired Duchamp to give her French language lessons.[35] It wasn't long before they became a couple, although they kept their relationship secret until 1927.

Reynolds and Duchamp were frequent collaborators, with both partners introducing ideas and helping each other bring them to fruition. Her expertise working with leather and bindings, for instance, likely influenced the housings for his *Boxes in a Valise* (see p. 85, fig. 85), boxed sets of miniature reproduc-tions of his life's work.[36] Duchamp's brilliant wordplay also made its way into book bindings the couple created, like those for Alfred Jarry's absurdist play *Ubu roi* (*King Ubu*; p. 21, fig. 14) and Giorgio de Chirico's dreamlike novel *Hebdomeros* (p. 56, fig. 54). Reynolds also bound Duchamp's compilation of puns, *Rrose Sélavy* (p. 48, fig. 44). This last volume was named after Duchamp's feminine alter ego, invented in the early 1920s, and was a play on the phrase *Eros, c'est la vie* (Eros, that's life).[37] Like Frida Kahlo, who depicted herself sporting men's clothes in her *Self-Portrait with Cropped Hair* (p. 86, fig. 86), Duchamp also at times adopted arch-femininity to challenge gender conventions in his work.

In his years with Reynolds, Duchamp organized exhibitions and worked as an advisor for artists, collectors, and gallerists such as Constantin Brancusi, Peggy Guggen-heim, and Julien Levy.[38] Duchamp's experience as an archivist and curator gained new significance after Reynolds's death in 1950, when he took on the responsibility of inven-torying her possessions and assisted Frank Brookes Hubachek in estab-lishing the Mary Reynolds Collec-tion at the Art Institute of Chicago. In the process, the famously private artist likely removed and destroyed many letters and other documents bearing his name, yet traces of his collaborations remain in the works themselves.[39] **—TK**

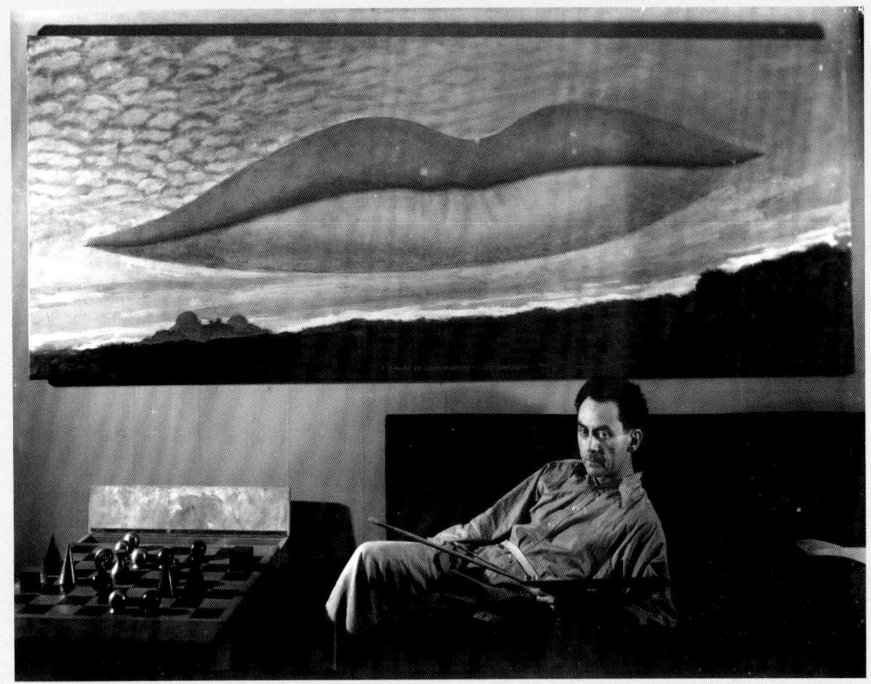

Fig. 27 Man Ray (American, 1890–1976). *Self-Portrait with "Observatory Time—The Lovers,"* about 1934. Gelatin silver negative on flexible support; 18 × 24 cm (7¹⁄₁₆ × 9⁷⁄₁₆ in.). The Centre Pompidou, Paris, Cabinet de la photographie, AM 1994-393 (5412).

Man Ray
Born Philadelphia, 1890
Died Paris, 1976

Man Ray (born Emmanuel Radnitzky) photographed Mary Reynolds numerous times throughout the 1920s. These elegant portraits reflect how he saw her: "Mary, tall, slender, and distinguished-looking," he wrote in his autobiography a few decades later.[41] They both arrived in Paris as American expatriates in 1921—Man Ray in summer, Reynolds in November.[42] Intimate friends with both Reynolds and Marcel Duchamp, Man Ray was one of the few people who knew about their complicated romantic involvement early on. He recounted that he and Reynolds "filled in the times" she could not spend with Duchamp exploring Montparnasse's nightlife together.[43]

Man Ray was a frequent guest at Reynolds's house on rue Hallé, and she made one of her most iconic and witty bindings for *Les mains libres* (Free hands; p. 58, fig. 56), a volume combining his drawings with Paul Éluard's poetry. The binding prominently features small, delicate kid gloves, split in half to embrace each cover; they not only reference the work's title but also suggest an unknown presence already holding the book, symbolically "freeing the hands" of the reader.[44]

In 1939, increasingly apprehensive about the escalating political tensions in Europe, Man Ray decided to depart France for America. He left numerous artworks and other belongings with Reynolds for safekeeping. Three years later, after settling in California, he was surprised to receive his painting *Observatory Time—The Lovers* (1932-36; private collection) in the mail: Reynolds, remembering that he had also stored some larger paintings with art-supply dealer Maurice Lefebvre-Foinet, made her own arduous escape through the Pyrenees in 1942 with few of her own belongings but ensured that these canvases were reunited with Man Ray.[45]—TK

Peggy Guggenheim
Born New York, 1898
Died Camposampiero, Italy, 1979

Peggy Guggenheim, who went on to become one of the world's most influential collectors of twentieth-century modern art, met Mary Reynolds in Paris in 1922 through Guggenheim's first husband, artist Laurence Vail. The two women connected as American expatriates, and their bond grew stronger as they attended parties within the Parisian artistic circle and traveled across Europe and North Africa together. They also shared an affinity for earrings, which, Guggenheim recalled, Reynolds "hung as decor instead of paintings."[47] Reynolds was present when Guggenheim's first son was born in London in 1923.[48] Guggenheim, for her part, witnessed the night Reynolds and Marcel Duchamp started their relationship, describing it as the beginning of "The Hundred Years War."[49]

Guggenheim was a frequent visitor at 14 rue Hallé, and in 1938 she spent twelve days living at Reynolds's house with writer Samuel Beckett.[50] Into the late 1930s she remained in regular conversation with Reynolds and Duchamp, benefitting from the latter's services as an advisor for her London gallery, Guggenheim Jeune.[51] In the first months of 1939, Guggenheim met Frida Kahlo through Reynolds and invited her to exhibit at Guggenheim Jeune. Kahlo declined the offer, believing that it was "not the best time for exhibtions" given the looming war.[52] As a sign of appreciation for the invitation, Kahlo gave Guggenheim a pair of Mexican earrings.[53] The two reconnected in 1943 when Guggenheim included one of Kahlo's drawings in *Exhibition by 31 Women* at her Art of this Century Gallery in New York. —APS

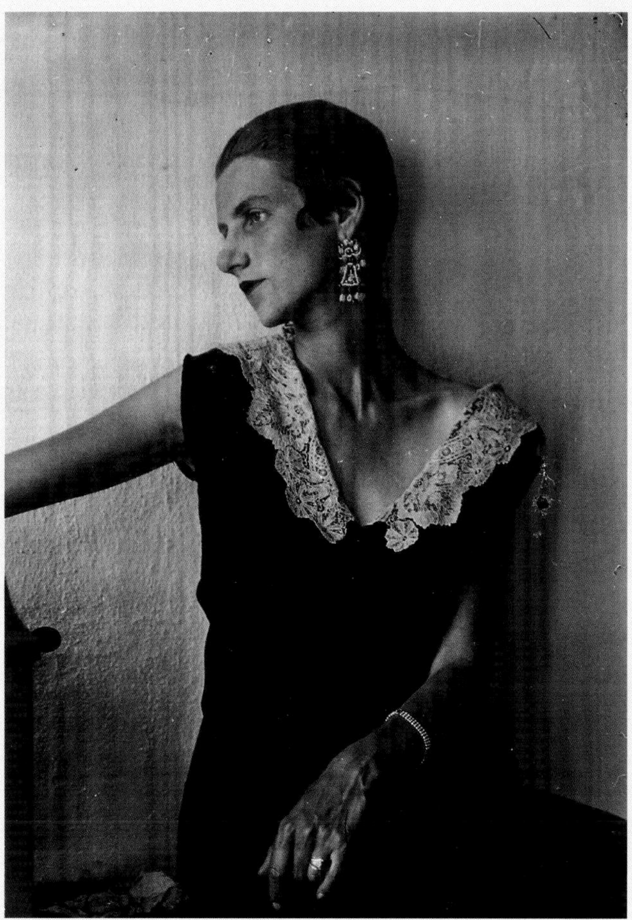

Fig. 28 Berenice Abbott (American, 1898–1991). *Peggy Guggenheim*, 1926 (printed 1978–79). Gelatin silver print; 8.1 × 5.9 cm (3³⁄₁₆ × 2⁵⁄₁₆ in.). Amon Carter Museum of American Art, Fort Worth, Texas, gift of P/K Associates, New York, P1984.35.388.

"Mary Reynolds was a wonderful friend, a real friend."

—Peggy Guggenheim, 1976[46]

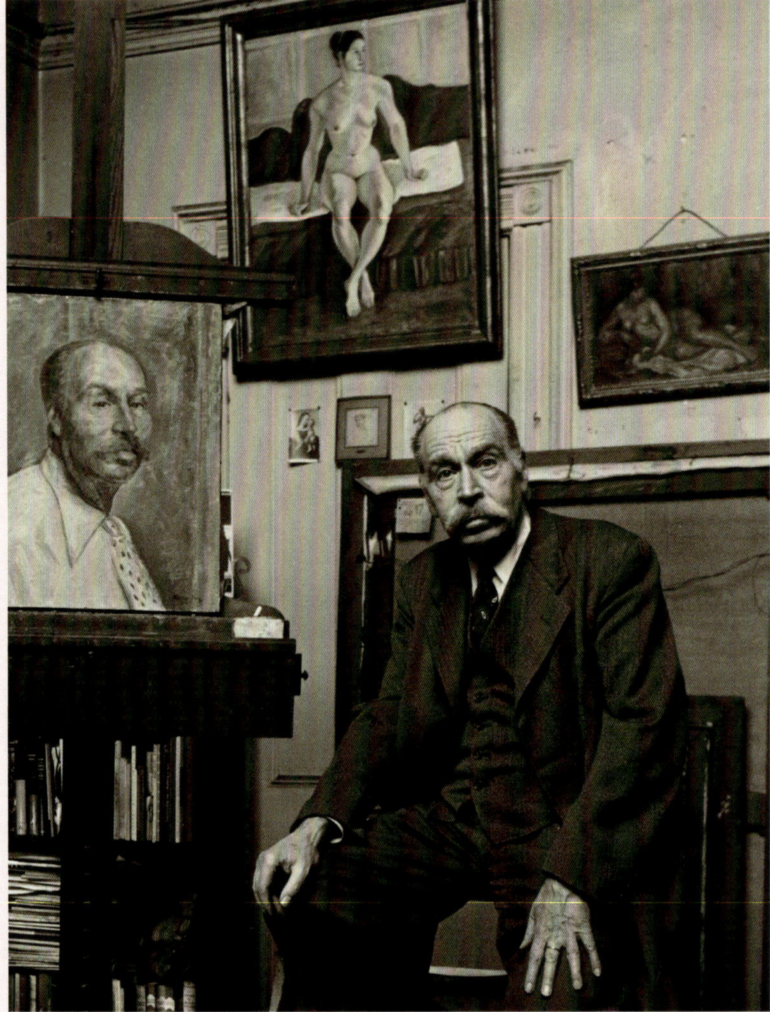

Fig. 29 Sidney J. Waintrob (American, 1902–2002) and Abraham L. Waintrob (American, 1908–2004). *Walter Pach*, 1957. Gelatin silver print; 24.3 × 19.5 cm (9⁹⁄₁₆ × 7¹¹⁄₁₆ in.). Buffalo AKG Art Museum, New York, gift of Samuel I. Hoffberg, 1981, P1981:25.46.

Walter Pach

Born New York, 1883
Died New York, 1958

Walter Pach first met Marcel Duchamp in Paris in 1907, and it was Pach who connected Duchamp, Frida Kahlo, and Mary Reynolds. In a letter he sent her before she left for Paris, Pach suggested that Kahlo befriend Duchamp and his brother Jacques Villon. "They are such good friends of mine," Pach wrote her, "that even without the letters I sent them, they will be your friends from the moment you mention my name."[55] It was also through Pach that Reynolds came to meet Kahlo in Paris. Approximately a month before Kahlo's exhibition opened at Julien Levy Gallery, Pach received a letter from Diego Rivera encouraging him to visit the show.[56] Pach was so impressed with her work that he purchased the painting *Survivor* (1938; now in the collection of Juan Antonio Pérez Simón, Mexico City). In December 1938, as she was preparing to leave New York, Kahlo gave Pach; his wife, Magdalene Frohberg; and their son, Raymond Pach, two recent photographs of her by Nickolas Muray (p. 12, fig. 4, and p. 95, fig. 95), which she carefully enclosed in a woven-fabric pouch that the Pachs retained.

As an artist, art historian, critic, and curator, Pach is most associated with the cultivation of international modern art, especially through his role in helping to organize the 1913 Armory Show. His research extended not only to Europe but also to Mexico. He taught at the National University in Mexico City, where he met Rivera in 1922. Together they organized the first exhibition of Mexican modern art in the United States as part of the Seventh Annual Exhibition of the Society of Independent Artists (City of Mexico) in New York in 1923. By 1939, when Kahlo returned from Paris, Pach was still working internationally, organizing the New York World's Fair and serving as its director general.[57] —APS

Henri-Pierre Roché

Born Paris, 1879
Died Sèvres, France, 1959

Henri-Pierre Roché and Marcel Duchamp were close friends for over forty years. They met in New York in 1916, when Roché was serving as an attaché to the French diplomatic mission there during World War I. Struck by Duchamp's charm, Roché started calling him "Victor" in homage to his victorious social interactions, particularly with women. The nickname soon turned reciprocal, and evolved to include various diminutive forms, like "Tor," "Toto," and, most commonly, "Totor."[58]

A prolific writer and lifelong diarist, Roché recorded his experience of the Parisian artistic and social scenes with remarkable candor. His volumes of private writing document his activities as an artist's agent and an advisor to collectors. They also recount Duchamp's relationship with Mary Reynolds as well as Roché's own budding friendship with her. "She is shy, delicate, melancholy," he wrote of Reynolds only a few days after meeting her in 1924.[59] Admiring her striking appearance, Roché immediately arranged to escort Reynolds to Sonia Delaunay-Terk's atelier for dresses and scarves, remarking that they suited her "perfectly."[60]

Roché's journals also offer enticing glimpses into the art in Reynolds's "funny, pretty, little home rue Hallé," as he described it.[61] In the mid-1930s Constantin Brancusi's *Two Penguins* (p. 19, fig. 12) was displayed in the garden, as Roché noted in his recollections of many meals there.[62] He also admired Reynolds's book bindings, and Reynolds enjoyed his books. She created a binding for one of Roché's novels on the subject of Don Juan (which he recalled viewing "not without emotion") as well as for an illustrated journal for Roché's young son, Jean-Claude.[63]—TK

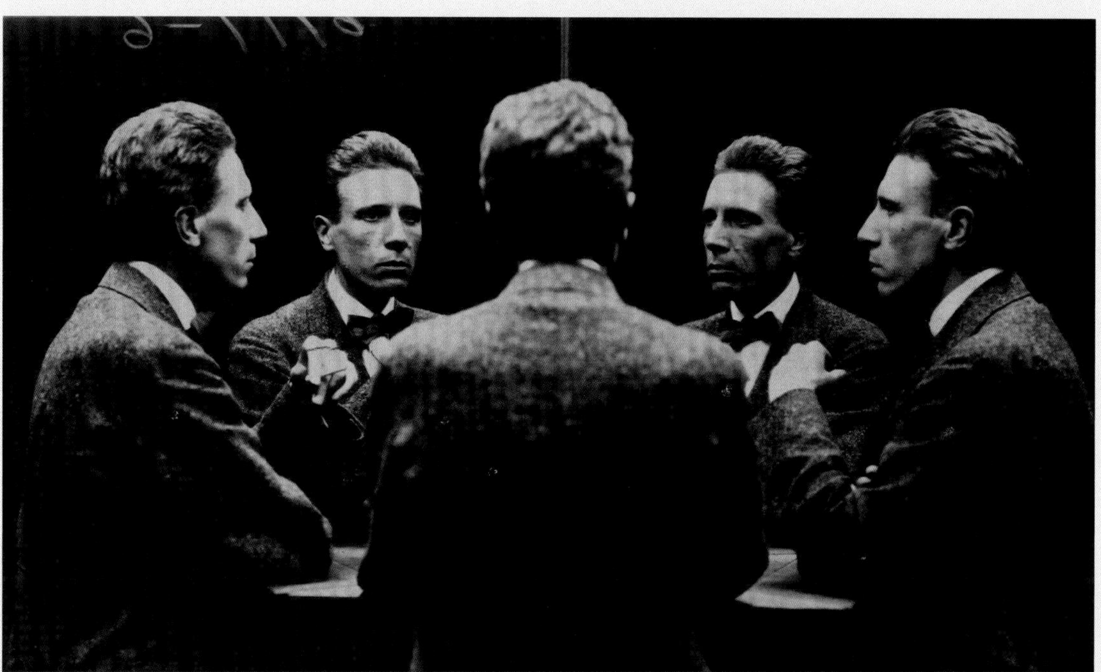

Fig. 30 Photographer unknown (Broadway Photo Shop, New York). *Multiple Portrait of Henri-Pierre Roché*, 1917. Gelatin silver print; 8.7 × 14 cm (3⁷⁄₁₆ × 5½ in.). The Centre Pompidou, Paris, Cabinet de la Photographie, AM 2004-178.

Alexander Calder

Born Lawnton, Pennsylvania, 1898
Died New York, 1976

As a fellow American living in Paris, Alexander Calder was very fond of Mary Reynolds. The two met when Reynolds brought guests to his performances of *Cirque Calder* (1926–32), a miniature set of circus animals and performers that he would animate through various means.[65] Calder's close friendship with both Reynolds and Marcel Duchamp proved important to his career. It was Duchamp who, on a visit with Reynolds to Calder's Paris studio in 1931, christened Calder's increasingly abstract and kinetic sculptures "mobiles." Duchamp often encouraged Calder to contact gallerists, leading him to show his work at Julien Levy Gallery in New York and Pierre Colle in Paris, in 1932 and 1933, respectively.

By the time *Mexique* opened in 1939, however, Calder had already left Europe for the United States. Reynolds acted as his agent once she returned to Paris after World War II. She played an instrumental role in preparations for his exhibition at the Galerie Louis Carré in 1946, assembling his collapsible sculptures, sent to her by mail, and verifying their correct orientations against drawings that Calder enclosed in the packages.[66]

Over the course of their friendship, Calder gave Reynolds numerous mobiles and pieces of jewelry of his own design; the latter may have included the silver earrings fashioned into her initials that Duchamp rendered in his 1951 bookplate for

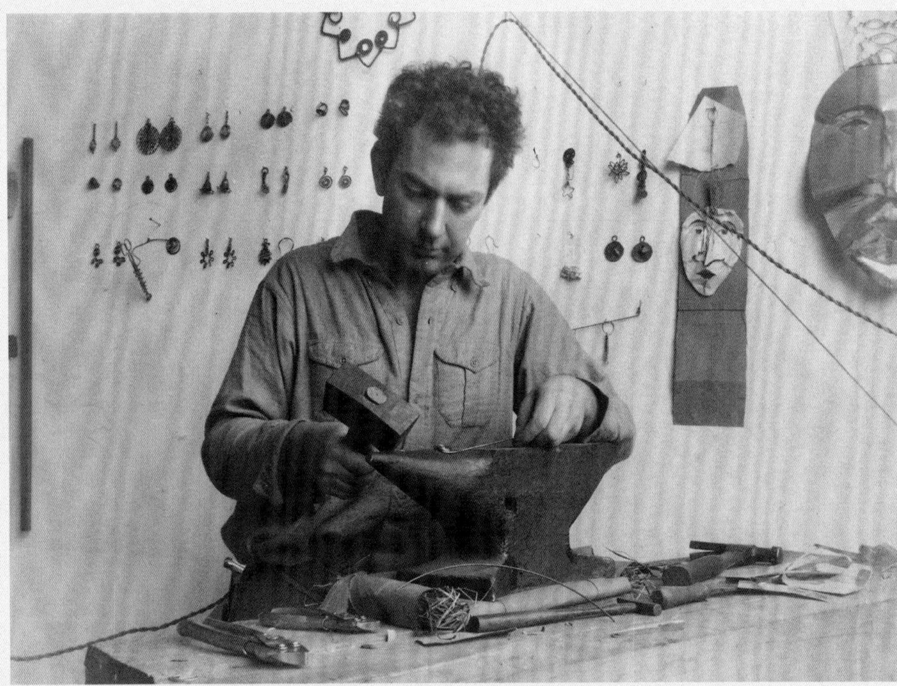

Fig. 31 Calder working jewelry at his anvil at 7 Villa Brune, Paris, 1930. Courtesy of the the New York Public Library, Miriam and Ira D. Wallach Division of Art, Prints and Photographs: Photography Collection.

the Mary Reynolds Collection (p. 8, fig. 2). In the mid-1950s Calder also produced a posthumous tribute to Reynolds commissioned by Frank Brookes Hubachek. His drawing (p. 18, fig. 10), as he explained in a letter to Hubachek, was inspired by Reynolds's love of cats and her reluctance to stay with Duchamp in New York during the war: "a moulting cat adopted her on 11th St., and Marcel thought that might well be the means to keep her in America."[67]
—TK

> **"In fact have done nothing but become Carré's sec[retary] who sends love to all Calders animal and mineral."**
>
> —Mary Reynolds to Alexander Calder, 1945[64]

Constantin Brancusi

Born Hobița, Romania, 1876
Died Paris, 1957

Although Marcel Duchamp had known Constantin Brancusi for over a decade, it was Henri-Pierre Roché who introduced the Romanian expatriate sculptor to Mary Reynolds on a visit to Brancusi's studio in June 1924.[69] Reynolds was shy at their initial meeting, but they soon became close friends.[70] Brancusi's relationship with Duchamp and Reynolds served him well professionally. In 1926 Duchamp and Roché jointly purchased Brancusi's works from the estate of American collector John Quinn, preventing their probable devaluation on the art market.[71] Reynolds later ensured the safety of several of these works during the Nazi occupation of Paris in the vaulted basement of her residence at 14 rue Hallé.[72]

Duchamp and Brancusi referred to each other as "Maurice" or "Morice," an honorific that Brancusi bestowed on a privileged few in his inner circle.[73] The sculptor's special nickname for Mary was "Gallina" (likely derived from the Romanian *găină*, meaning "hen" or "chicken").[74] "We need your studio or our garden," Reynolds wrote Brancusi from Barcelona in 1933, a note suggesting that they shared the duty of hosting their circle, with his place at the Impasse Ronsin serving as a second venue for gatherings.[75] Indeed, Reynolds and Duchamp were frequent guests at the famous dinner parties Brancusi hosted in his studio. They even invited the sculptor to vacation with them in Villefranche-sur-Mer outside Nice in September 1931 (see fig. 32), when Reynolds rented the famed Villa Marguerite.

An avid photographer, Brancusi brought his camera to document their leisurely breakfasts on the villa's ample terrace (see p. 4, fig. 1). The following year, he used a movie camera to film a party celebrating his new limestone fireplace, likely the only surviving video footage of Reynolds.[76] —**TK**

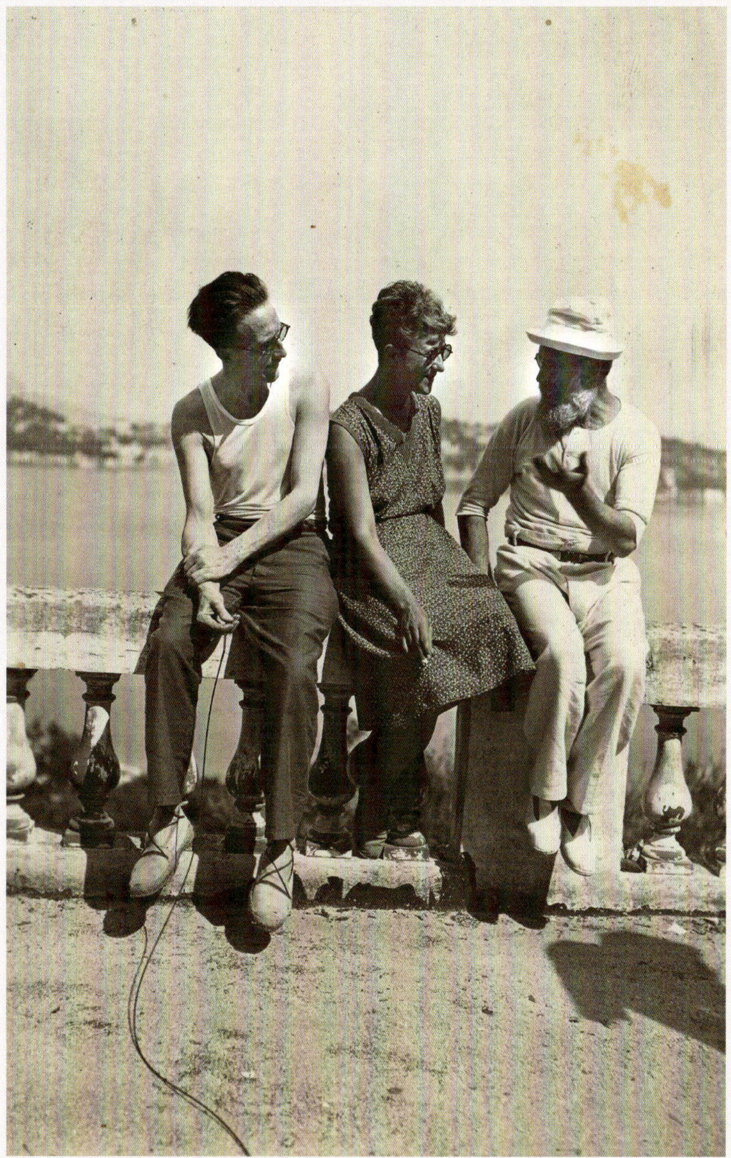

Fig. 32 Marcel Duchamp (American, born France, 1887–1968), *Constantin Brancusi, Marcel Duchamp, and Mary Reynolds at Villefranche*, 1931. Gelatin silver print, 15 x 10 cm (6 x 4 in.). The Art Institute of Chicago Archives, purchased by the Ryerson and Burnham Libraries, Mary Reynolds Collection, 2004.

"This is no country of Maurices but we're doing our best and the quantity of vineyards is helping."

—Mary Reynolds and Marcel Duchamp to Constantin Brancusi, 1946[68]

Jean Cocteau
Born Maisons-Laffitte, France, 1889
Died Milly-la-Forêt, France, 1963

Artist and avant-garde visionary Jean Cocteau contributed to Paris's artistic community as a filmmaker, novelist, painter, playwright, and poet. His friendship with Mary Reynolds was the catalyst for twenty-five of her bookbindings, constituting nearly a quarter of her total production. These books—distinguished by Cocteau's signature star on the spines, covers, or end-papers—demonstrate the full range of Reynolds's approach to *reliure* (bookbinding), utilizing paper, vellum, and board to creating increasingly intricate designs, as seen, for example, in her application of decorative threads on the cover for *Maison de santé* (The clinic; p. 57, fig. 55). Cocteau often added autographs, inscriptions, and profile drawings dedicated to Reynolds to the title pages of her bindings (see pp. 62–63, figs. 60–62), transforming them into intimate testaments to their friendship and collaboration. Like others in Reynolds's circle, Cocteau exhibited his work at Peggy Guggenheim's London gallery, Guggenheim Jeune. That relationship was facilitated by his close friendship with Marcel Duchamp and Reynolds, who recommended him for its inaugural show in 1938.[78]

As World War II loomed, Cocteau notably abstained from political critique. This was in great contrast to Reynolds, who actively fought for the French Resistance during the German occupation of France. Cocteau infuriated his artist friends when he published "Salut à Breker," a short text on the front page of artistic journal *Comœdia* commending Arno Breker, an artist acclaimed by the Nazi regime.[79] This tribute was seen by some as a measure of self-protection, yet Cocteau maintained his admiration for Breker even after the occupation ended. Cocteau created a final drawing of Reynolds for the Mary Reynolds Collection at the Art Institute of Chicago.—**APS**

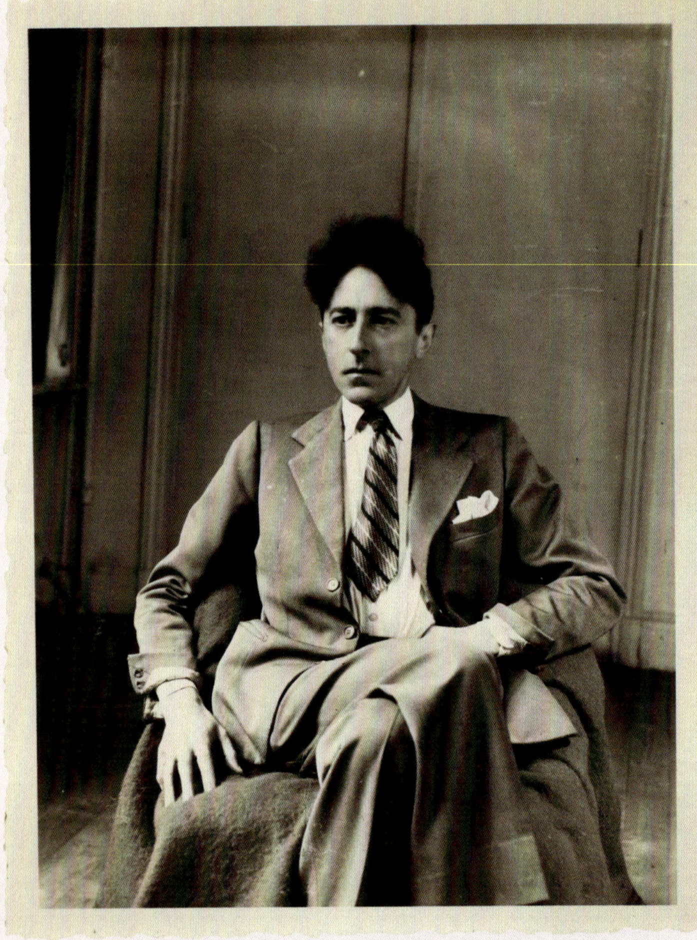

Fig. 33 Dora Maar (French, 1907–1997). *Portrait of Jean Cocteau*, about 1935. Gelatin silver print; 11.6 × 8.9 cm (4⁹⁄₁₆ × 3½ in.). The Centre Pompidou, Paris, Cabinet de la photographie, AM 2004-0164.

"It is rare that death leaves warm ashes. Thanks to you that is what is happening for Mary."

—Jean Cocteau to Marcel Duchamp, 1957[77]

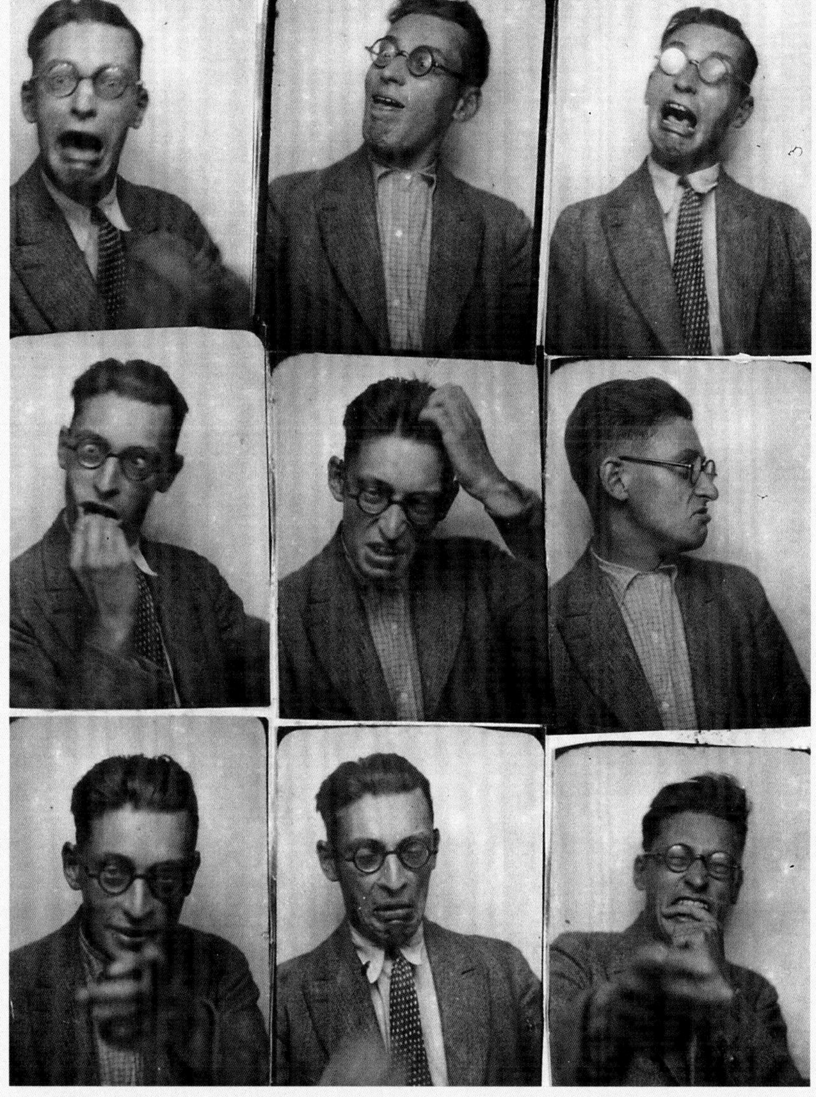

Fig. 34 Photobooth images of Queneau (detail from a larger sheet), 1928.

Raymond Queneau
Born Le Havre, France, 1903
Died Paris, 1976

Raymond Queneau was an experimental novelist and one of Mary Reynolds's close friends. Except for Jean Cocteau, no other author received as much attention in her bindings: over the years, she bound twelve of Queneau's works, many of which feature tender dedications from the author.

Queneau had met André Breton in 1924 and had close ties to the Surrealists in the 1920s.[81] By 1939 he was an editor at the Gallimard publishing company and had begun to devise an idiosyncratic writing style informed by mathematical structures and formal, often playful constraints on the French language.[82] The mathematical symbols Reynolds used in the binding for his semi-autobiographical novel *Odile* (p. 74, fig. 74) emphasize these self-imposed rules, which departed from the Surrealists' love of chance and automatism.[83]

For *Chêne et chien* (p. 55, fig. 53), Reynolds rendered the title in tiny, applied dots of leather, an additive approach inversing Marcel Duchamp's use of punctures in his *Green Box* (p. 54, fig. 52). In other bindings, Reynolds incorporated three-dimensional elements that refer to Queneau's stories. Along the spine of *Un rude hiver* (*A Hard Winter*; p. 77, fig. 77), for instance, she placed a broken thermometer displaying 0 degrees Celsius. For *Saint Glinglin* (p. 82, fig. 82), she included a broken porcelain handle, alluding to a key scene in the novel in which hundreds of dishes are smashed at the titular festival.

Like Man Ray and Duchamp, Queneau was a member of the Collège de 'Pataphysique (see p. 40), holding the title of Transcendent Satrap. With mathematician François Le Lionnais, Queneau founded the Ouvroir de Littérature Potentielle (Workshop for Potential Literature), known as Oulipo, as a subset of the society in 1960.[84]—TK

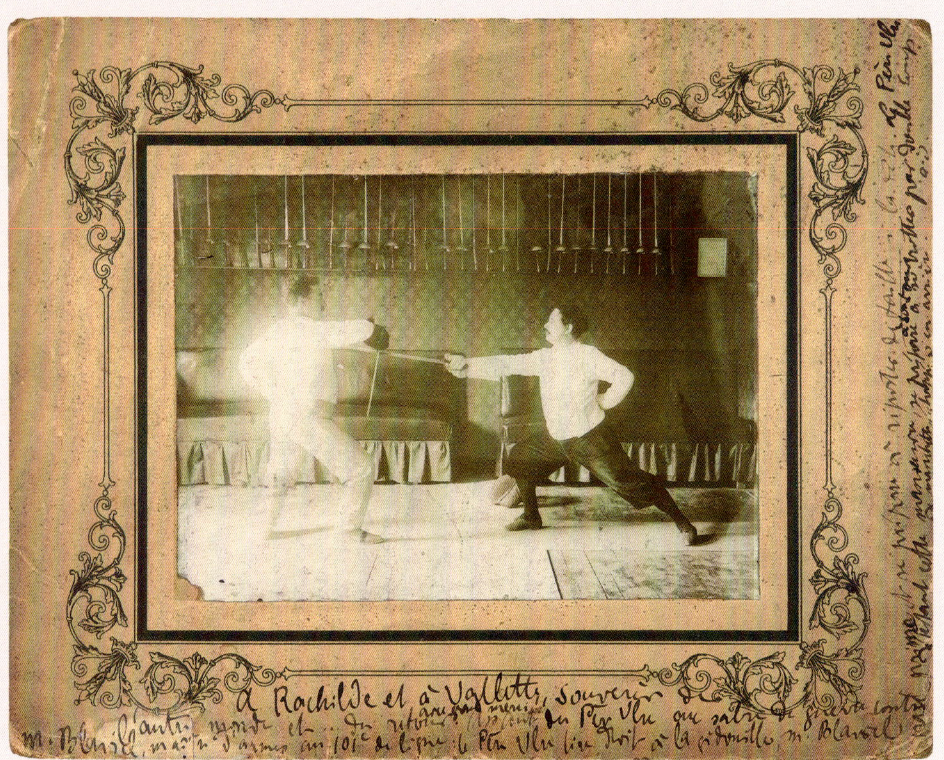

"Merdre."

—**Opening line of Alfred Jarry's *Ubu roi,* 1896**[85]

Alfred Jarry

**Born Laval, Mayenne, France, 1873
Died Paris, 1907**

Alfred Jarry cultivated the ridiculous and absurd in all its guises. His daily uniform included all-black cyclists' clothes, a silver skeleton tiepin, and a British Bull Dog revolver.[86] He kept an owl as a pet, drank far too much absinthe, and lived in one half of an apartment split height-wise.[87] Although he was deceased by the time Mary Reynolds and Frida Kahlo met, the fin-de-siècle playwright, novelist, and puppeteer had an outsized influence on their Parisian cultural milieu. His scandalous 1896 play *Ubu roi* (*King Ubu*) captured the imagination of many Surrealists. The violent and farcical play is known for its opening line—"*Merdre!*" (French for "Shit!" with an extra, absurdist *r*)—bellowed by King Ubu, a grotesque character based on Jarry's hapless high school physics teacher.[88]

Reynolds bound seven works by Jarry, among them *Ubu roi* (p. 21, fig. 14) and its two sequels, *Ubu cocu* (*Ubu Cuckolded*; p. 80, fig. 80) and *Ubu enchaîné* (*Ubu in Chains*; p. 81, fig. 81). Her binding for Jarry's darkly humorous science-fiction novel *Le Surmâle* (*The Supermale*; p. 75, fig. 75) is particularly clever: the metal corset stay emerging from a butterfly on the book's spine alludes to the narrative's interest in the limits of mechanical and human sexual prowess.

Jarry's *Gestes et opinions du docteur Faustroll, pataphysicien* (*Exploits and Opinions of Doctor Faustroll, Pataphysician*; p. 50, fig. 47) described pataphysics, the author's invented "science of imaginary solutions," which was also foundational to *Ubu roi*. Pataphysics used actual scientific and mathematical theories to parody science and situate it within the absurd.[89] Marcel Duchamp and Man Ray were both members of the Collège de 'Pataphysique, founded in 1948 to mark the fiftieth anniversary of *Faustroll*'s publication.—**TK**

Manuel Álvarez Bravo
Born Mexico City, 1902
Died Mexico City, 2002

Like Frida Kahlo, Manuel Álvarez Bravo was associated with the Surrealist movement because of the promotional activities of André Breton. Although the photographer never formally affiliated with the movement, his images appeared in *Mexique*, Surrealist journal *Minotaure*, and the 1940 *International Exhibition of Surrealism* at the Galería de Arte Mexicano in Mexico City, for which Breton commissioned him to design the catalogue cover.[91] In the May 1939 issue of *Minotaure*, Breton recounted his travels to Mexico the previous year, illustrating his essay "Souvenir du Mexique" with eleven of Álvarez Bravo's photographs. Looking through the lens of Surrealism, Breton viewed Mexico as a place where the polarity of life and death permeated aspects of culture and found in Álvarez Bravo's work a visual document of that perspective.[92] For the artist himself, the association with Surrealism was overstated: "I believe that when a person is attentive to reality he finds all that is fantastic. People don't realize the fantasy that life itself contains."[93]

Breton may have first noticed Álvarez Bravo's work in April 1935, when Julien Levy exhibited it at his New York gallery in the show *Documentary and Anti-Graphic Photographs*, a three-artist exhibition that also included works by Henri Cartier-Bresson and Walker Evans.[94] But the two did not meet until three years later, when Álvarez Bravo documented the meeting between Breton, Diego Rivera, and exiled Soviet leader Leon Trotsky at the Kahlo family home in Coyoacán, Mexico City. After that pivotal encounter, Breton selected more than thirty of the photographer's works for *Mexique*, giving Álvarez Bravo's *Muchacha Viendo Pájaros* (*Girl Watching Birds*; 1931) pride of place on the exhibition catalogue's cover (p. 22, fig. 15).[95] —APS

> "All the pathos of Mexico is placed within our reach, where Álvarez Bravo stopped, where he took the time to capture a ray of light, a sign, a silence, there the heart of Mexico beats."
>
> —André Breton, 1939[90]

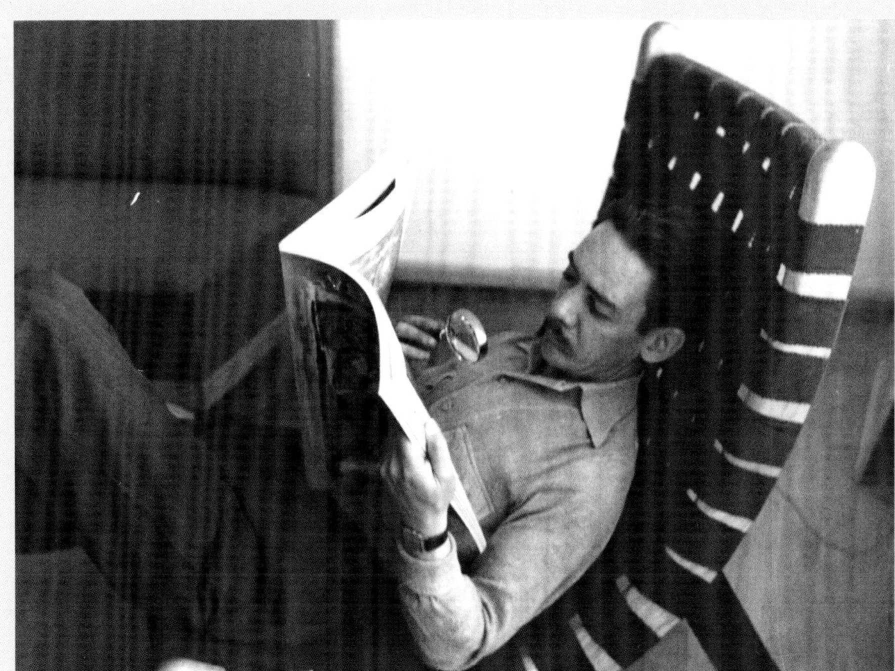

Fig. 36 Lola Álvarez Bravo (Mexican, 1903–1993). *Manuel Álvarez Bravo*, about 1934. Gelatin silver print; 15.4 × 20.2 cm (6⅛ × 7¹⁵⁄₁₆ in.). University of Arizona, Tucson, Center for Creative Photography, Lola Álvarez Bravo Archive, 93.6.1.

Wolfgang Paalen
Born Vienna, 1905
Died Taxco, Mexico, 1959

Alice Rahon
Born Chenecey-Buillon, France, 1904
Died Mexico City, 1987

Artists Alice Rahon and Wolfgang Paalen joined the Surrealist ranks in 1935, one year after their wedding. During Frida Kahlo's time in Paris, Rahon was known best as a poet while Paalen was a painter whose work would soon be shown at Guggenheim Jeune in London.[97] In letters to Diego Rivera, Kahlo recounted her meetings with Rahon, whom she described as "a poet on fire," and it pleased her that Paalen, one of the "'big shots' of Surrealism," had attended the opening of *Mexique*.[98]

Later in 1939 Rahon and Paalen traveled to Mexico via British Columbia and California, arriving in Mexico City in September.[99] With Breton guiding his efforts from afar, Paalen, along with Peruvian writer César Moro, began organizing the 1940 *International Exhibition of Surrealism* in the city.[100] The show included many artists featured in *Mexique* and in the May 1939 issue of Surrealist magazine *Minotaure*, which Breton edited. Rahon, inspired by her time in Mexico, presented her own visual art for the first time at the exhibition. Mexico had such a profound effect on Rahon and Paalen that even after their 1947 divorce they both maintained residences in the country for the rest of their lives.[101]

Rahon and Kahlo were drawn to each other as artists whose identities were shaped by their health issues, both having suffered severe injuries in childhood accidents. These physical impairments became subjects of their work and led them to challenge social convention. After Paalen and Rahon moved to Mexico, he was increasingly active as a writer and as publisher of art magazine *Dyn*, becoming an especially influential art theorist during World War II. His ties to Breton and to Surrealism grew strained, and in 1943 he authored an essay titled "Farewell to Surrealism."[102] **—APS**

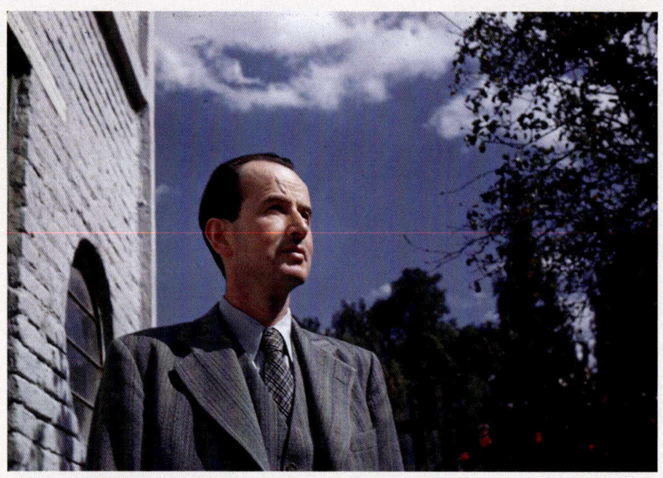

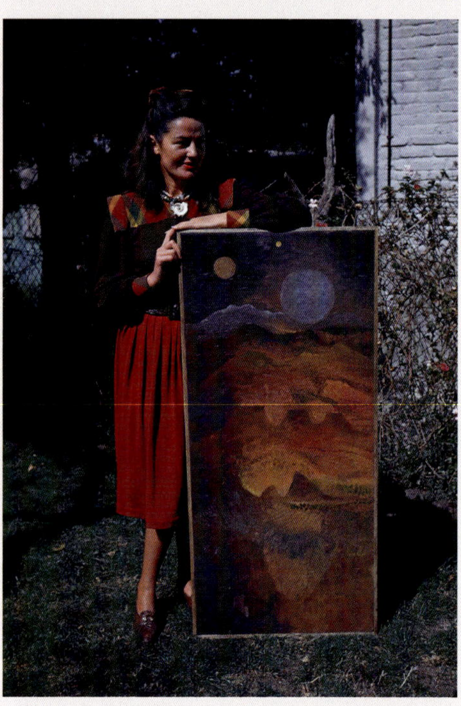

Figs. 37 and 38 Florence Arquin (American, 1900–1974). *Wolfgang Paalen in Mexico City* and *Alice Rahon in Mexico City*, about 1948. Kodachrome transparencies; 2.3 × 3.4 cm (⅞ × 1⁵⁄₁₆ in.). Florida Atlantic University, Boca Raton, The Arquin Slide Collection.

"I love and admire Frida even more than in Paris."

—Wolfgang Paalen, 1939[96]

Frank Brookes Hubachek

Born Minneapolis, 1894
Died Highland Park, Illinois, 1986

Frank Brookes Hubachek, known as "Brookes," was Mary Reynolds's younger brother and the guiding hand behind the establishment of the Mary Reynolds Collection at the Art Institute of Chicago. A lawyer by profession and a trustee of the Art Institute from 1947 to 1970, he worked closely with Marcel Duchamp in the 1950s to have the contents of Reynolds's library and art collection transferred to Chicago and catalogued by curator Hugh Edwards.[104]

Even after Reynolds expatriated to Paris, she and Hubachek maintained a close relationship, with her brother serving as the primary link to her family in the United States. Hubachek provided financial and emotional support to his sister when their parents objected to her "bohemian ways."[105] He also facilitated her return to the United States after her involvement in the French Resistance, which continued through 1942, well after most in Reynolds's circle had departed Paris. When Reynolds became ill, Hubachek assisted with her medical care, sending a nurse from Chicago to attend to her shortly before her death. This nurse, Louise Elizabeth Bailey, took the few extant photographs made of 14 rue Hallé while Reynolds was alive, creating some of the only remaining views of the home that welcomed so many artists.[106] After Reynolds's death, Hubachek worked with Duchamp over several months to create the bookplate for the Mary Reynolds Collection (p. 8, fig. 2), as a tribute to his sister. Additionally, he arranged for Duchamp to receive part of Reynolds's inheritance, creating a trust fund for the artist from which he drew income until his death in 1968.[107]—APS

> "[Mary] was an extraordinary woman, a supreme individualist and one who loved not only to participate but to sit beside the road and watch the procession of humanity go by."
>
> —Frank Brookes Hubacheck, 1963[103]

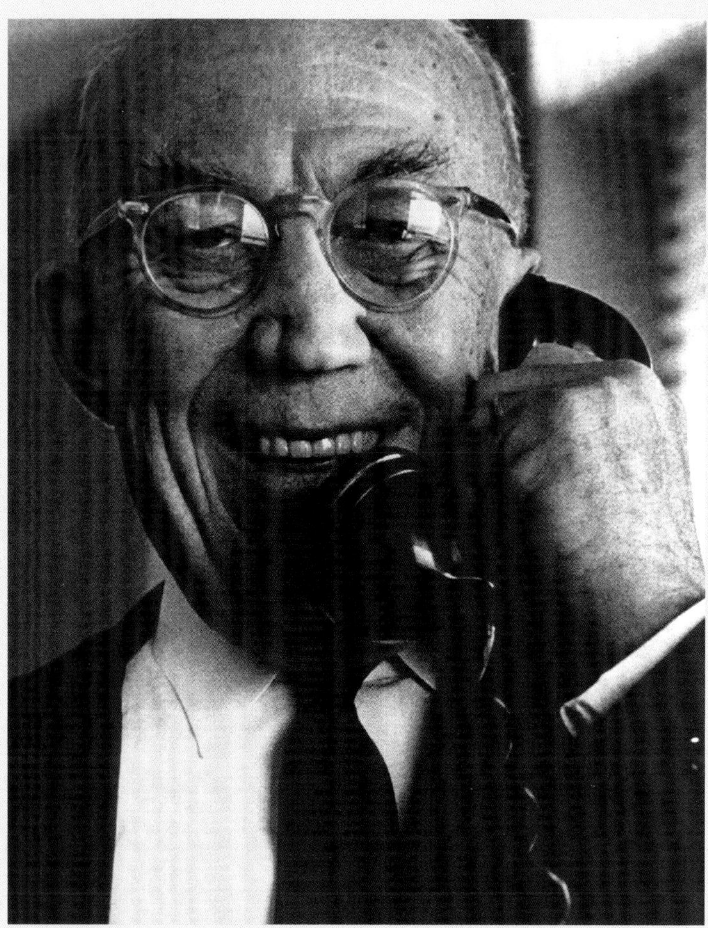

Fig. 39 Hubachek, about 1960s.

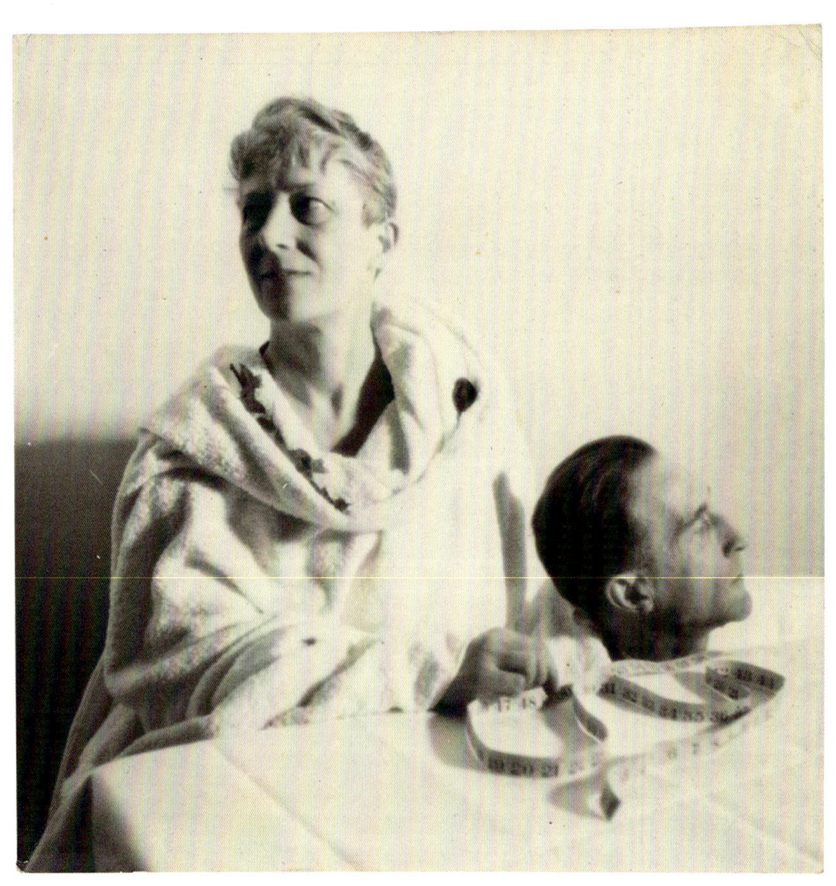

Fig. 40 Constantin Achillopoulos (Greek, born France, 1908–1995).
Mary Reynolds and Marcel Duchamp, **1937.**

Gelatin silver print; 15 × 14.9 cm (5¹⁵⁄₁₆ × 5⅞ in.). The Art Institute of Chicago,
gift of Frank B. Hubachek, 1970.796.

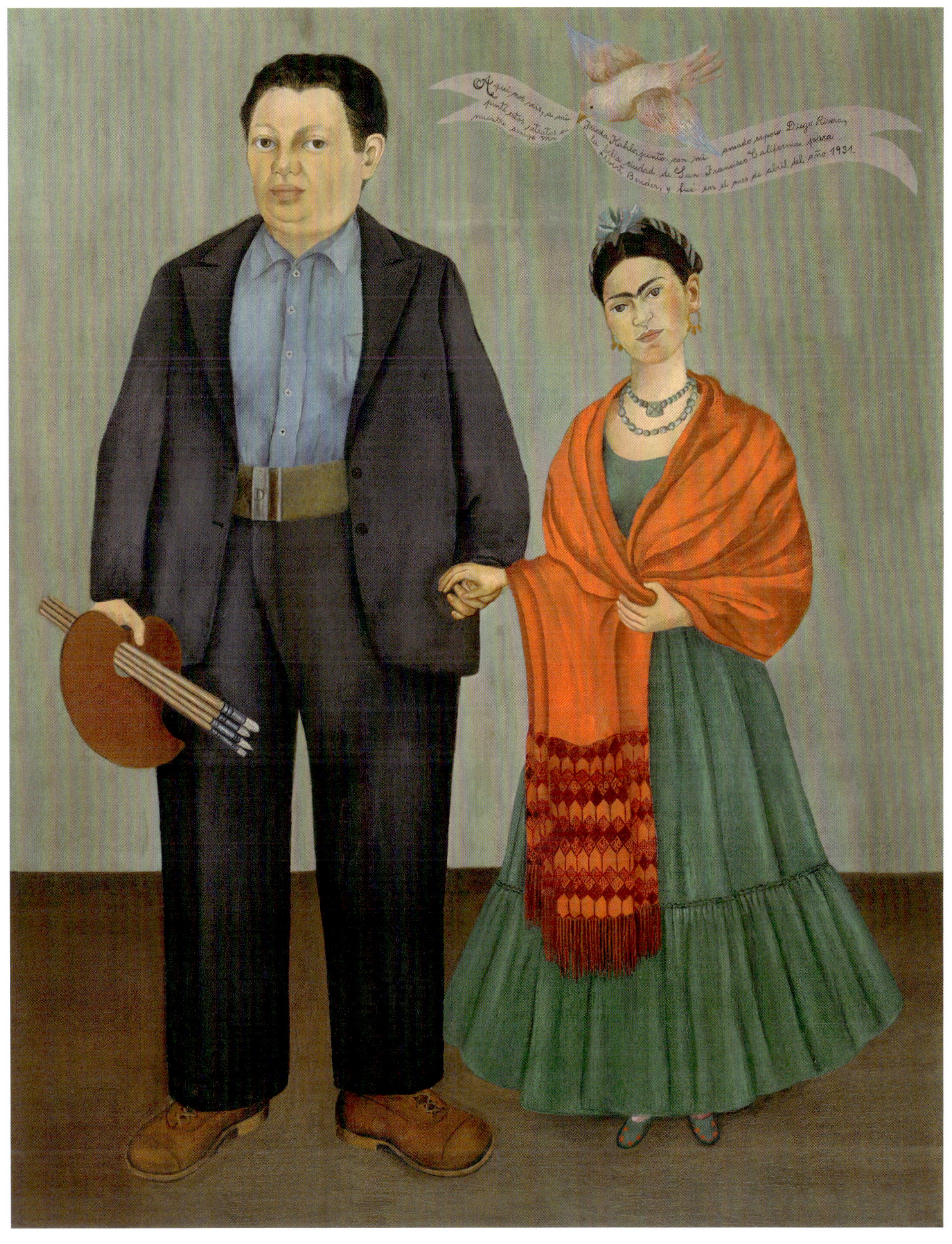

Fig. 41 Frida Kahlo (Mexican, 1907–1954). *Frieda and Diego Rivera*, **1931.**

Oil on canvas; 100 × 78.74 cm (39⅜ × 31 in.). San Francisco Museum of Modern Art,
Albert M. Bender Collection, gift of Albert M. Bender.

Fig. 42 Constantin Brancusi (Romanian, active France, 1876–1957). *Untitled (Clockwise from Lower Right: Constantin Brancusi, Marcel Duchamp, Ezra Pound, Vera Moore, and Mary Reynolds)*, 1932.

Gelatin silver print; 8 × 24 cm (7 × 9⁷⁄₁₆ in.). The Art Institute of Chicago Archives, Mary Reynolds Collection.

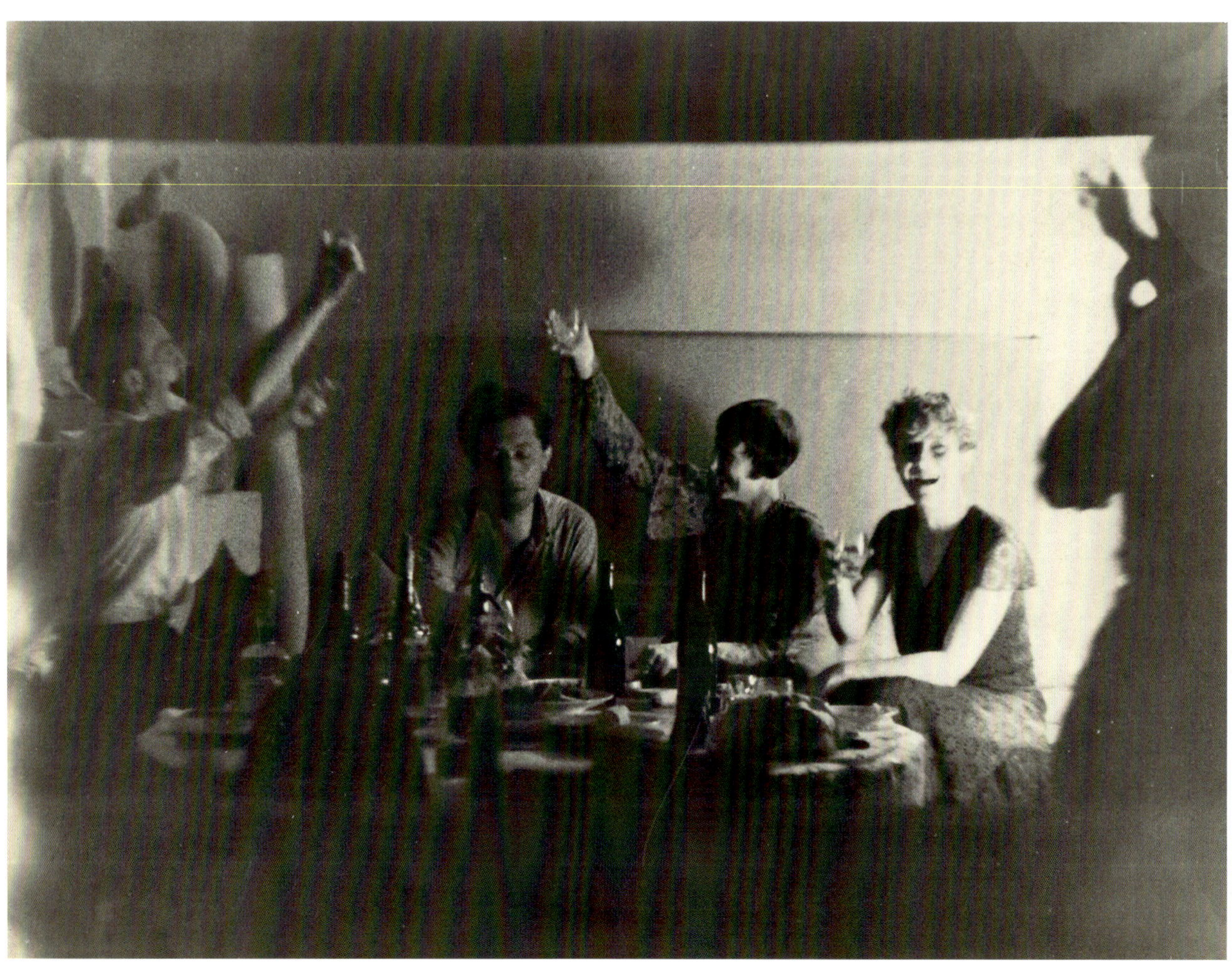

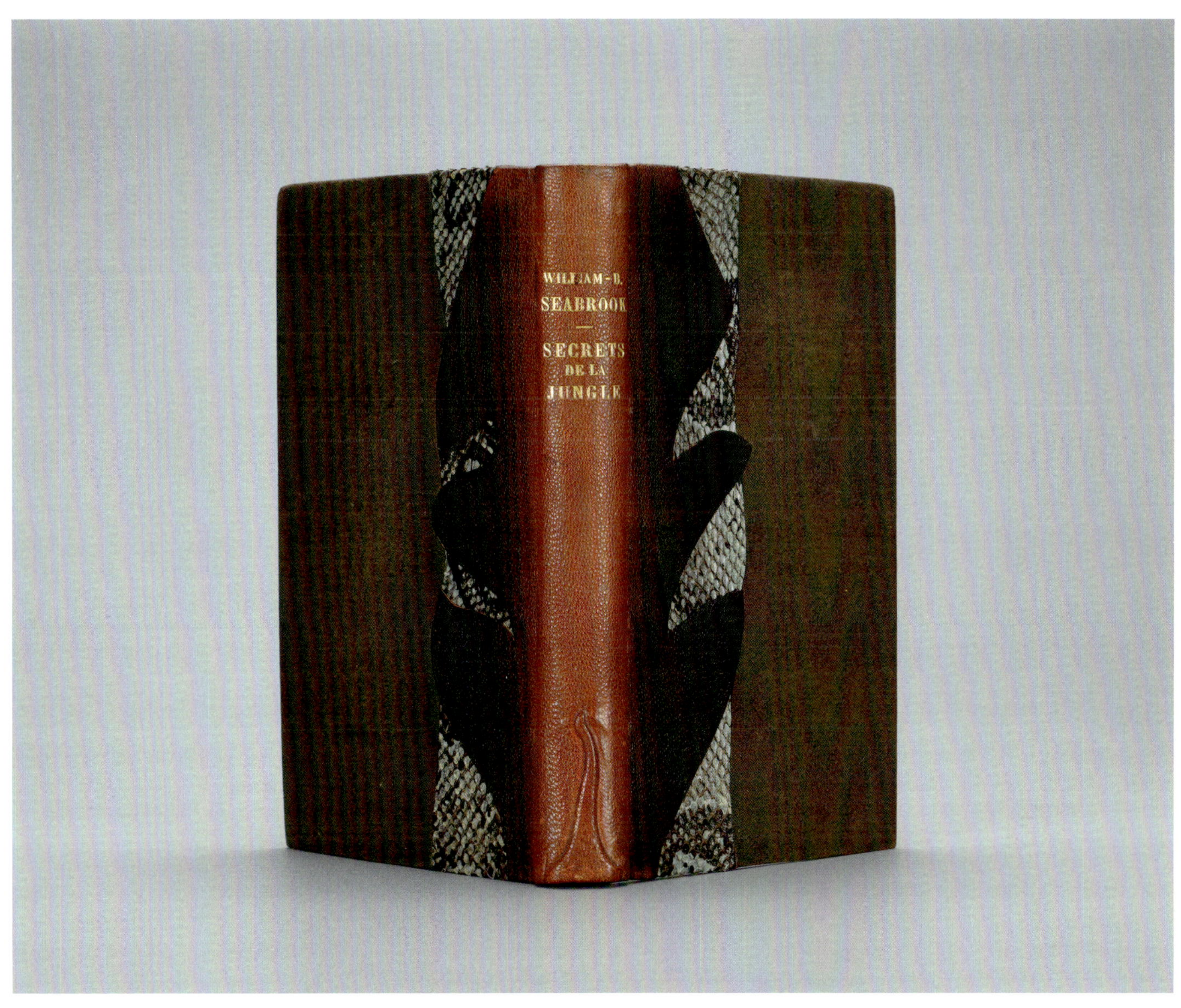

Fig. 43 Mary Reynolds (American, 1891–1950). *Secrets de la jungle* (originally published in English as *Jungle Ways*) by William B. Seabrook, trans. Suzanne Flour (Paris: Éditions Jacques Hemont, 1931), 1931–42.

Quarter goatskin with brown paper, reptile-skin inlays, and gold stamping. Brown endpapers; 19 × 13 × 2.5 cm (7½ × 5⅛ × 1 in.). The Art Institute of Chicago, Ryerson and Burnham Libraries, Mary Reynolds Collection, 2019.934.

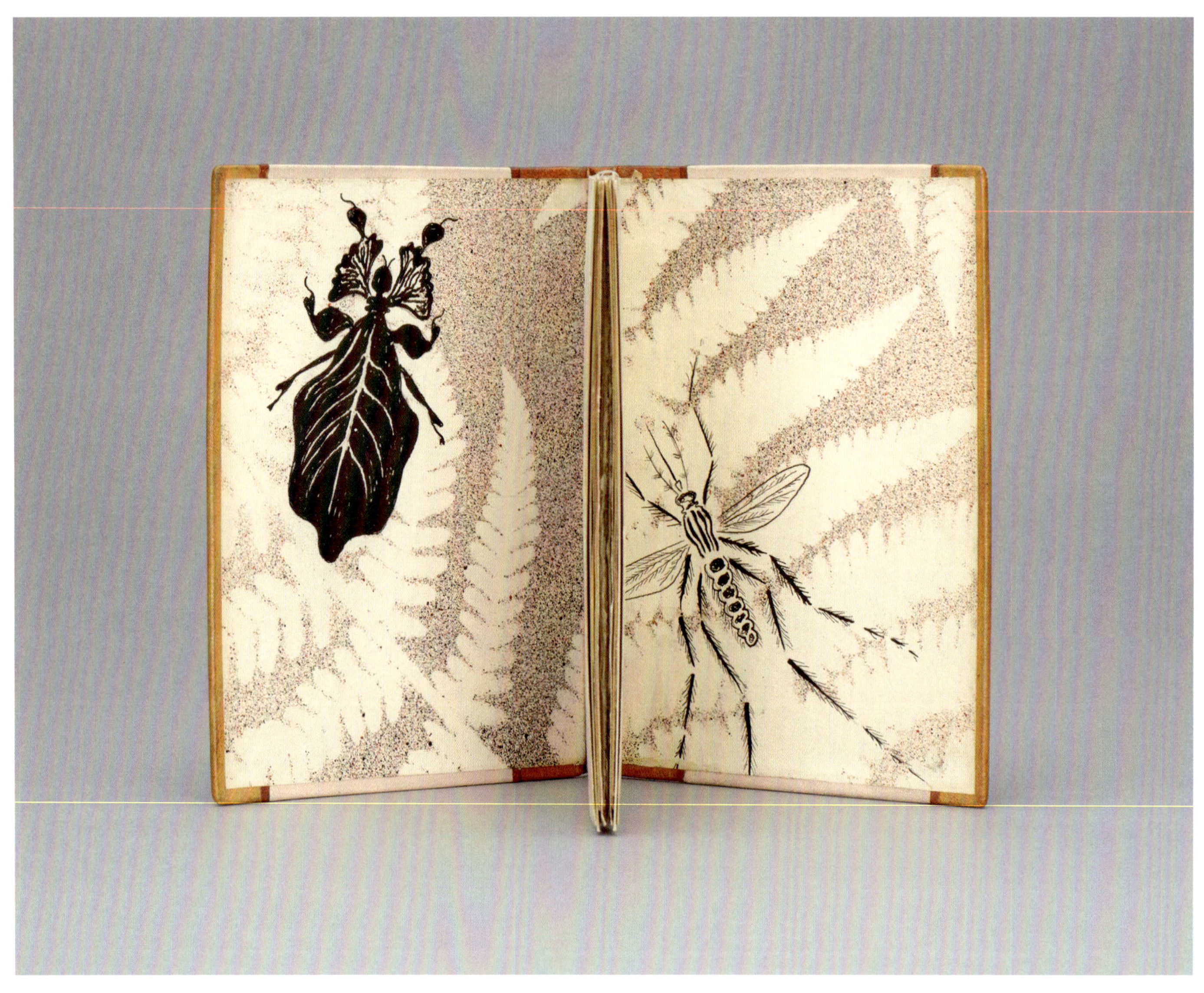

Fig. 44 Mary Reynolds (American, 1891–1950). *Rrose Sélavy* by Marcel Duchamp (Paris: Éditions GLM, 1939), 1940–41.

Full sienna, pink, and beige goatskin with cotton cord, grey-card onlays with trial stamps of a typographic plate made for Duchamp's *Box in a Valise* (p. 85, fig. 85). Endpapers printed in pochoir with fern-leaf pattern and hand-drawn insects in black ink; 17.1 × 12.2 × 1.1 cm (6¾ × 4¹³⁄₁₆ × ⁷⁄₁₆ in.). The Art Institute of Chicago, Ryerson and Burnham Libraries, Mary Reynolds Collection, 2019.172.

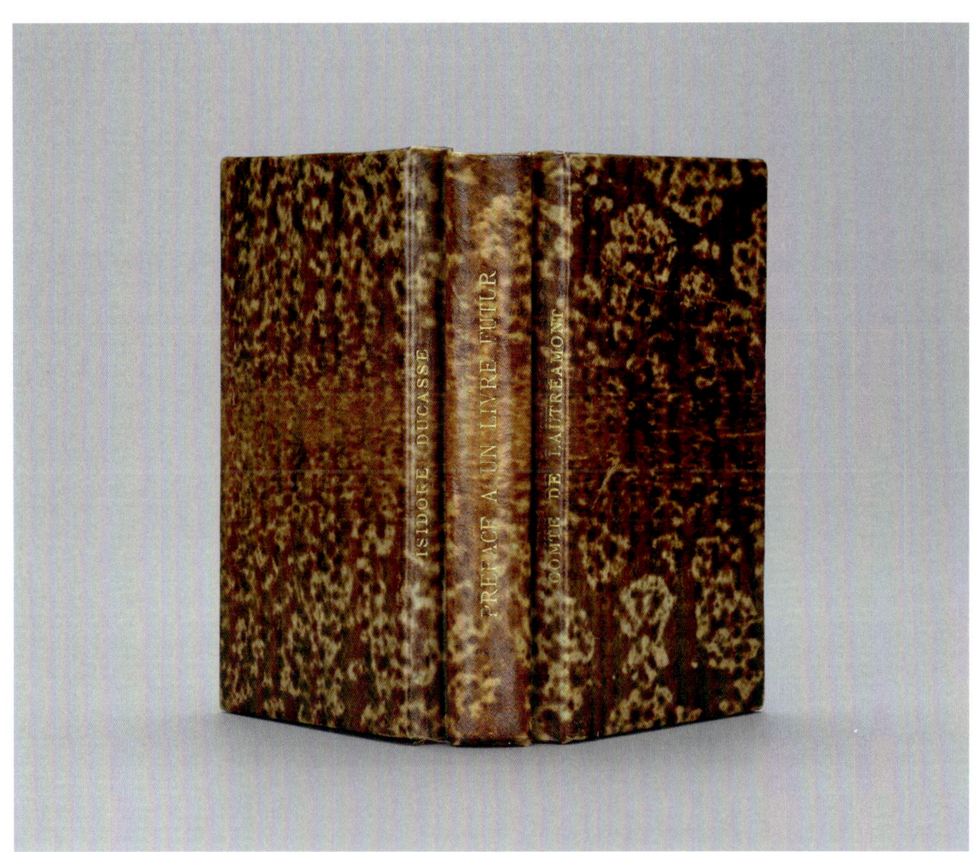

Fig. 45 Mary Reynolds (American, 1891–1950). *Préface à un livre future* (Preface to a future book) **by Comte de Lautréamont [Isidore Ducasse] (Paris: Éditions de la Sirène, 1922), 1930–42.**

Full vellum with thick boards and gold stamping. Orange endpapers and gilt edges; 16.5 × 9.8 × 1.3 cm (6½ × 3⅞ × 9/16 in.). The Art Institute of Chicago, Ryerson and Burnham Libraries, Mary Reynolds Collection, 2019.185.

Fig. 46 Mary Reynolds (American, 1891–1950). *Les yeux fertiles* (Fertile eyes) **by Paul Éluard (Paris: Éditions GLM, 1936), 1940.**

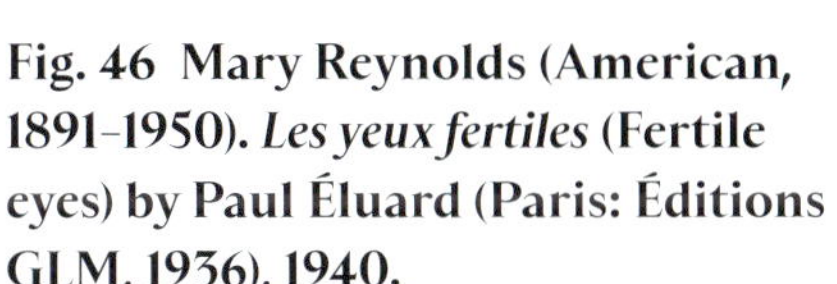

Full ostrich with gold stamping on black calfskin. Gold-speckled, lilac endpapers; 19.3 × 12.5 × 2.5 cm (7⅝ × 4¹⁵/₁₆ × 1 in.). The Art Institute of Chicago, Ryerson and Burnham Libraries, Mary Reynolds Collection, 2019.933.

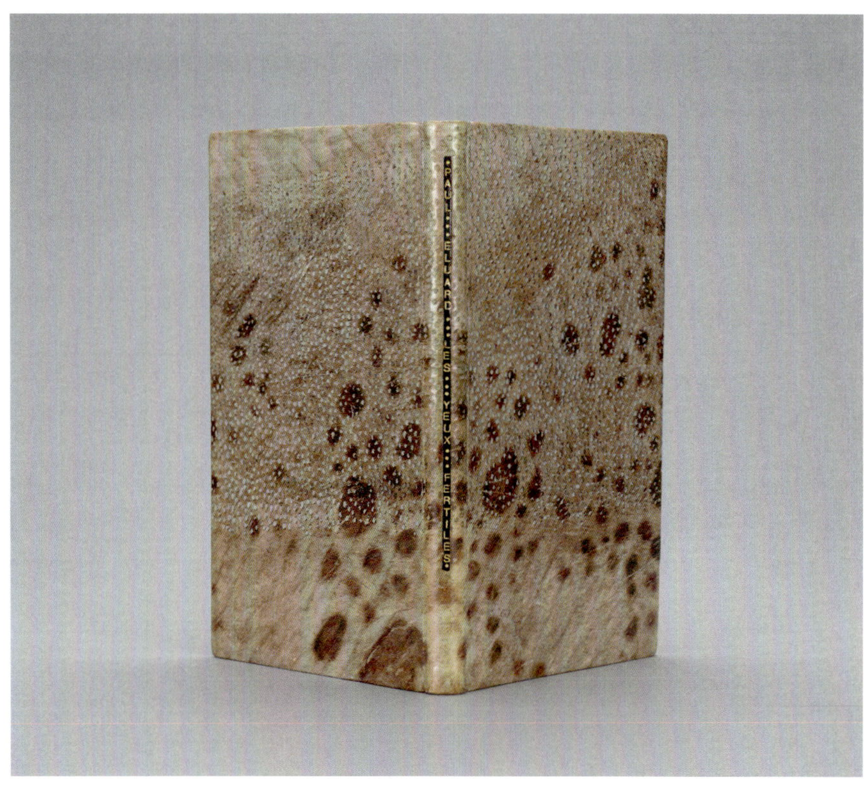

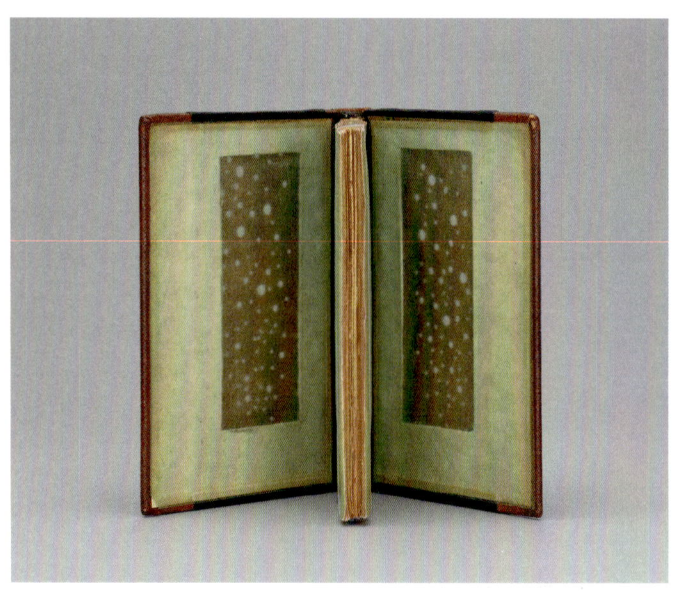

Fig. 47 Mary Reynolds (American, 1891–1950). *Gestes et opinions du docteur Faustroll, pataphysicien (Exploits and Opinions of Doctor Faustroll, Pataphysician)* **by Alfred Jarry (Paris: Librairie Stock, 1923), 1930–42 or 1945–50.**

Full brown leather embossed in a herringbone pattern, with black-calfskin-covered, die-cut panels; gold stamping; and inlaid perforated copper sheets. Green glassine endpapers and gilt edges; 14.5 × 10.5 × 1.7 cm (5¾ × 4³⁄₁₆ × ¹¹⁄₁₆ in.). The Art Institute of Chicago, Ryerson and Burnham Libraries, Mary Reynolds Collection, 2019.178.

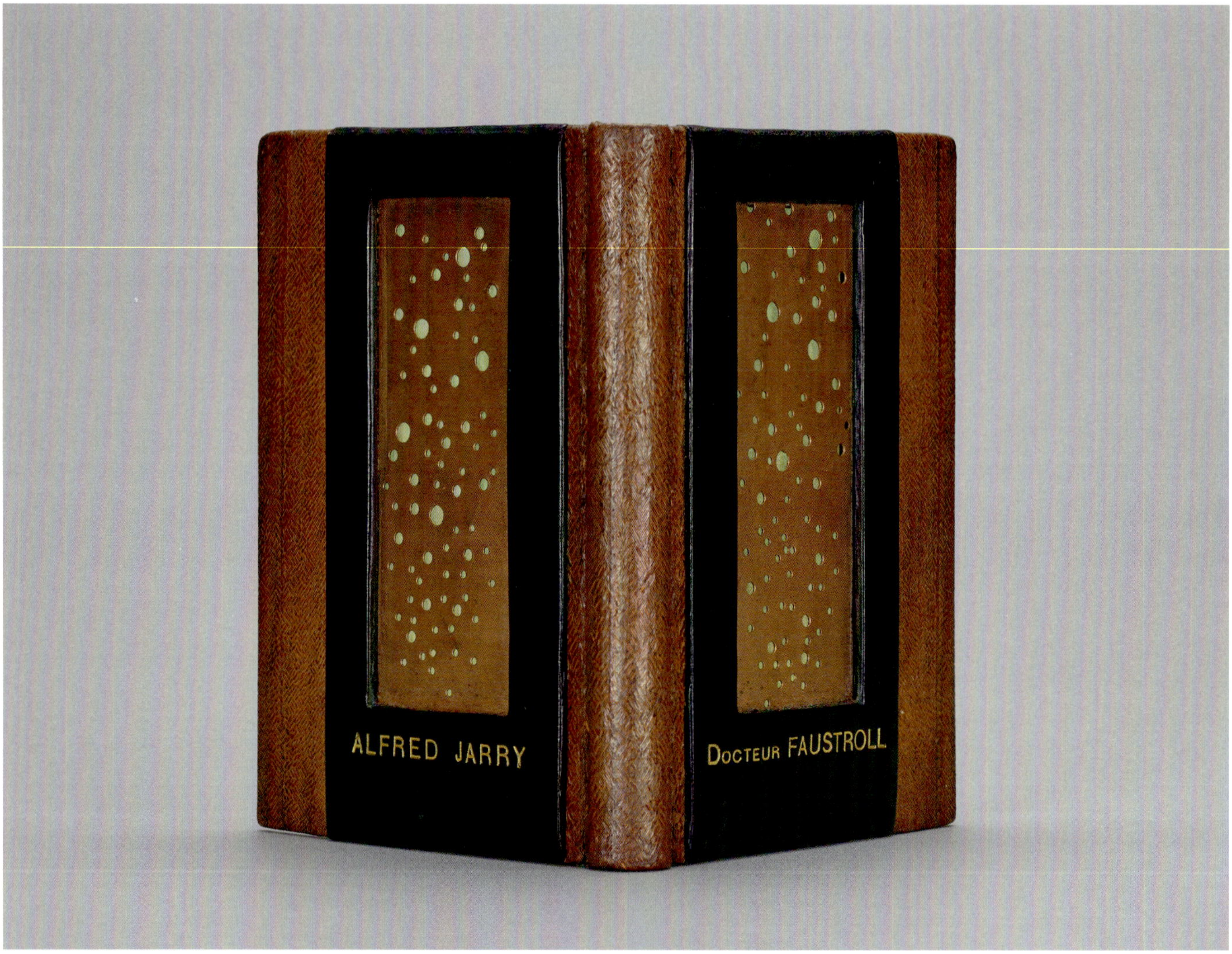

Fig. 48 Mary Reynolds (American, 1891–1950).
La science de Dieu, ou La création de l'homme
(*The Science of God, or The Creation of Man*) **by
Jean-Pierre Brisset (Paris: Chamuet, Éditeur,
1900), 1930–42.**

Black and green calfskin over triple boards with toadskin
onlays. Green calfskin doublures with gold stamping.
Paper-covered slipcase with calfskin trim and felt lining
(not illustrated); 20.7 × 18.5 × 4.6 cm (8⅛ × 7¼ × 1¹³⁄₁₆ in.).
The Art Institute of Chicago, gift of Mr. Frank B. Hubachek,
1963.757.

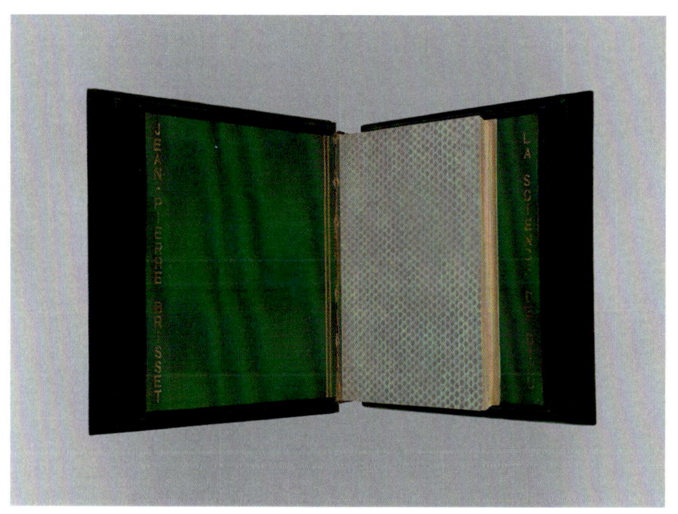

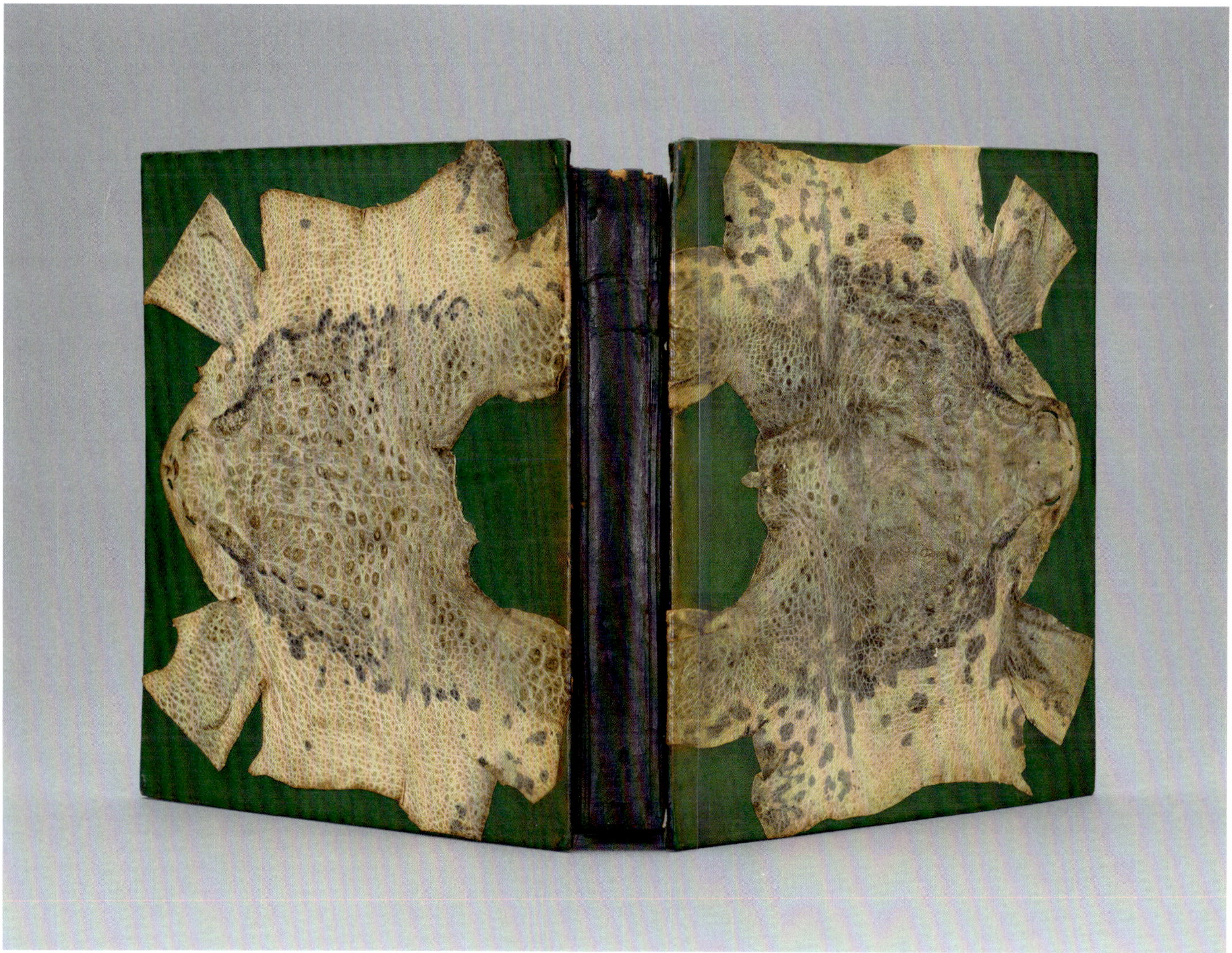

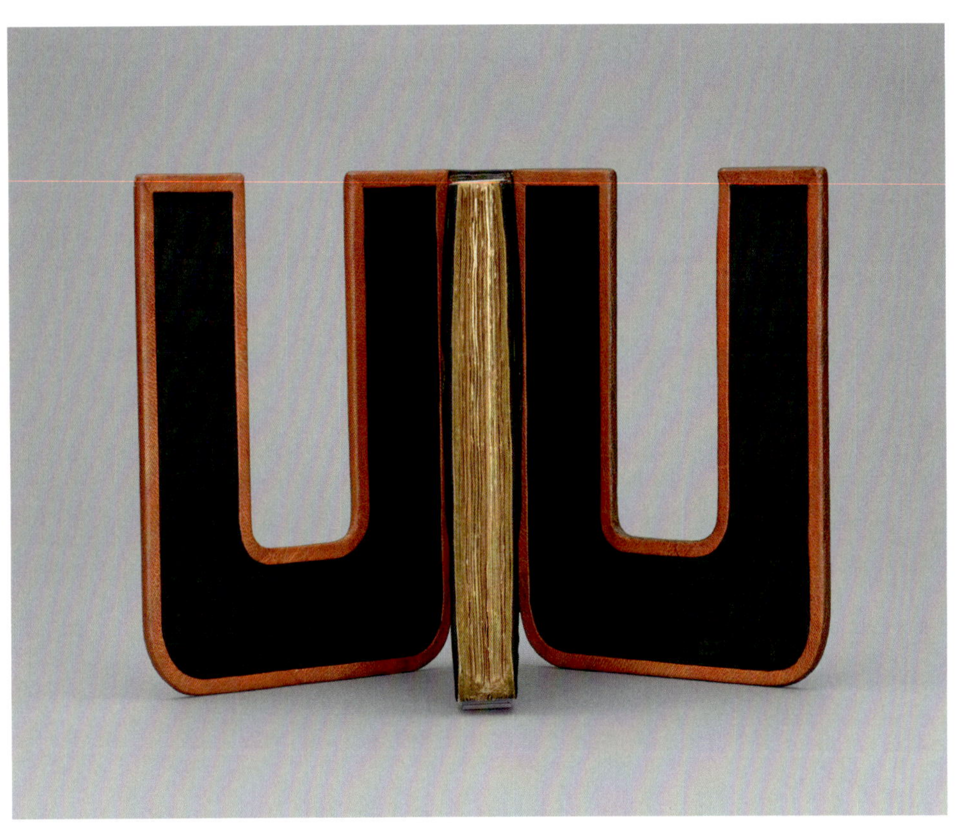

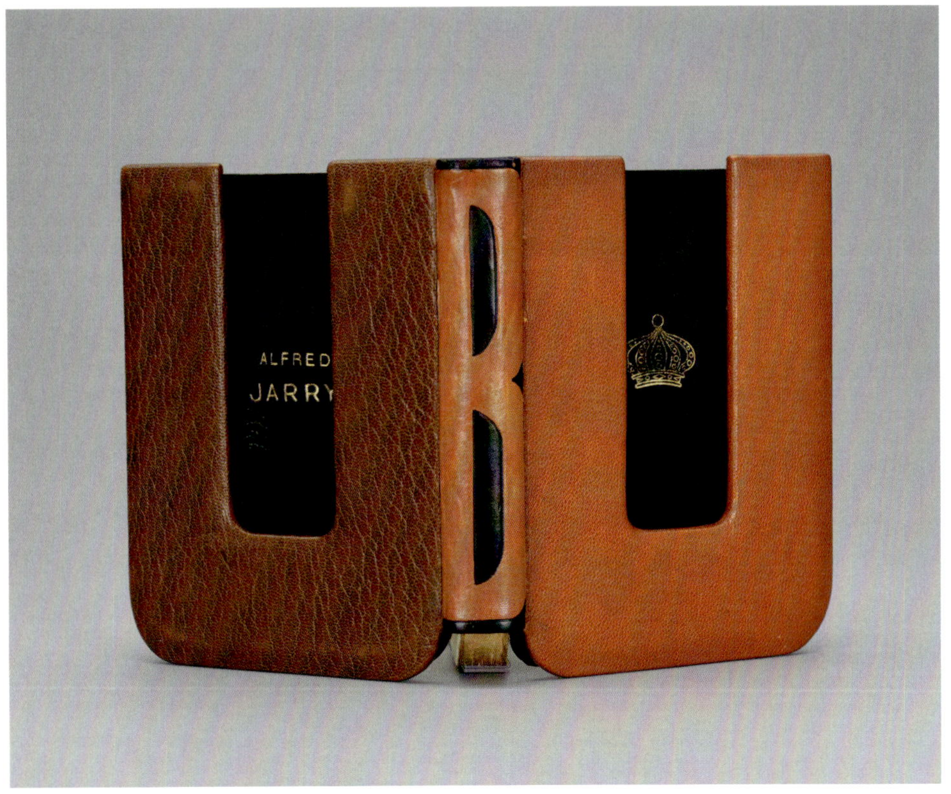

Fig. 49 Mary Reynolds (American, 1891–1950) and Marcel Duchamp (American, born France, 1887–1968). *Ubu roi (King Ubu)* by Alfred Jarry (Paris: Librairie Charpentier et Fasquelle, 1921), 1935.

Full goatskin with onlay in the shape of a *B* and die-cut boards in the shape of a *U*. Black-silk endleaves with gold stamping and gilt edges; 16.8 × 13.5 × 2.8 cm (6⅝ × 5⅜ × 1⅛ in.). The Art Institute of Chicago, Ryerson and Burnham Libraries, Mary Reynolds Collection, 2019.180. See additional view on p. 21.

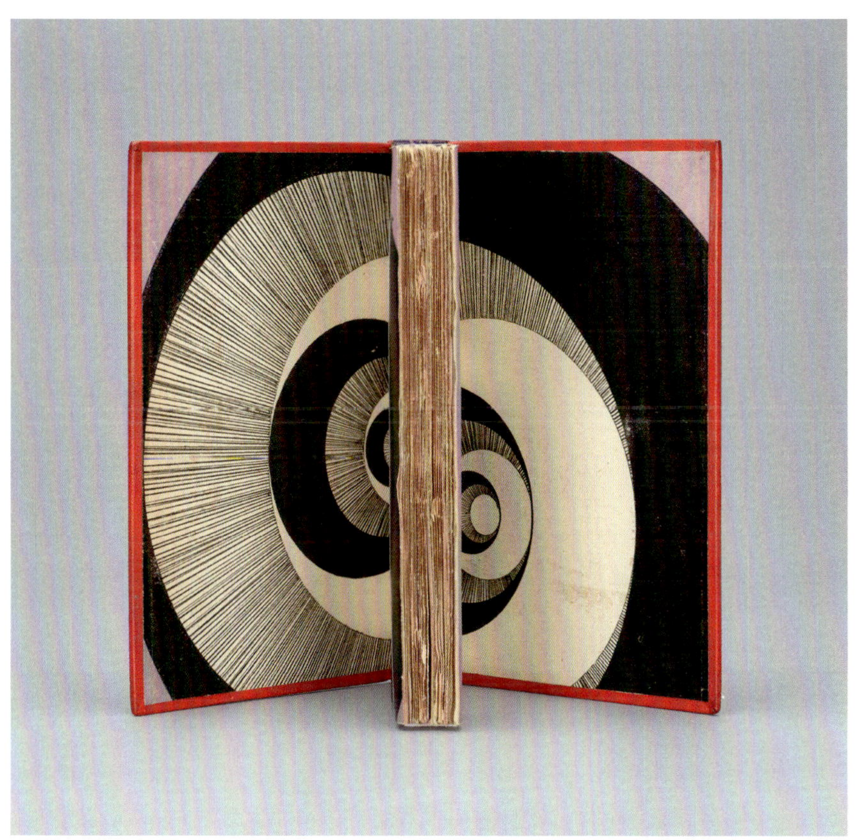

Fig. 50 Mary Reynolds (American, 1891–1950). *Loin de Rueil* (published in English as *The Skin of Dreams*) by Raymond Queneau (Paris: Gallimard, 1944), 1945–50.

Full red goatskin with raised bands and gold stamping. Endpapers of trial proofs for Marcel Duchamp's 1935 cover of *Minotaure*; 19 × 12 × 3.2 cm (7½ × 4¾ × 1¼ in.). The Art Institute of Chicago, Ryerson and Burnham Libraries, Mary Reynolds Collection, 2024.858.

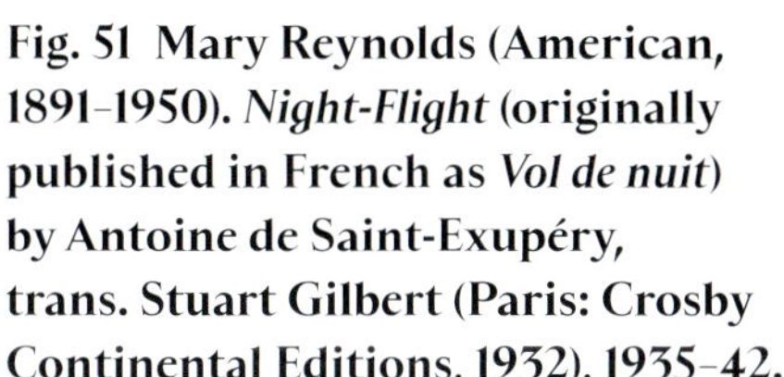

Fig. 51 Mary Reynolds (American, 1891–1950). *Night-Flight* (originally published in French as *Vol de nuit*) by Antoine de Saint-Exupéry, trans. Stuart Gilbert (Paris: Crosby Continental Editions, 1932), 1935–42.

Full navy, vegetable-tanned sheepskin. Endpapers of trial proofs for Marcel Duchamp's 1935 cover of *Minotaure*; 16.7 × 12.7 × 2.3 cm (6⁹⁄₁₆ × 5 × ⅞ in.). The Art Institute of Chicago, Ryerson and Burnham Libraries, Mary Reynolds Collection, 2024.860.

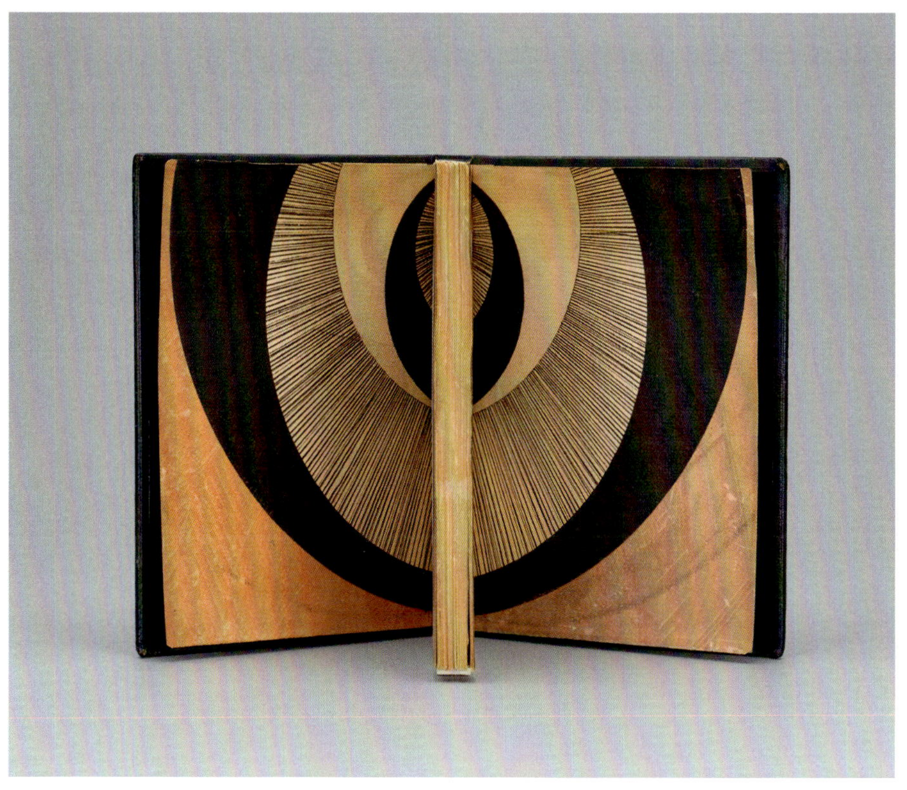

Cardboard box with punched holes forming the title; a green, flocked interior; and copper strips forming an *M* on the front cover and a *D* on the back cover. Facsimiles of manuscript notes, drawings, and photographs; one color print of *Nine Malic Molds* under glass in the back cover; and one manuscript item. Dedication to Mary Reynolds formed by punched holes; 33.2 × 28 × 2 cm (13⅛ × 11¹¹⁄₁₆ × ¹³⁄₁₆ in.). The Art Institute of Chicago, Ryerson and Burnham Libraries, Mary Reynolds Collection, 2019.155.

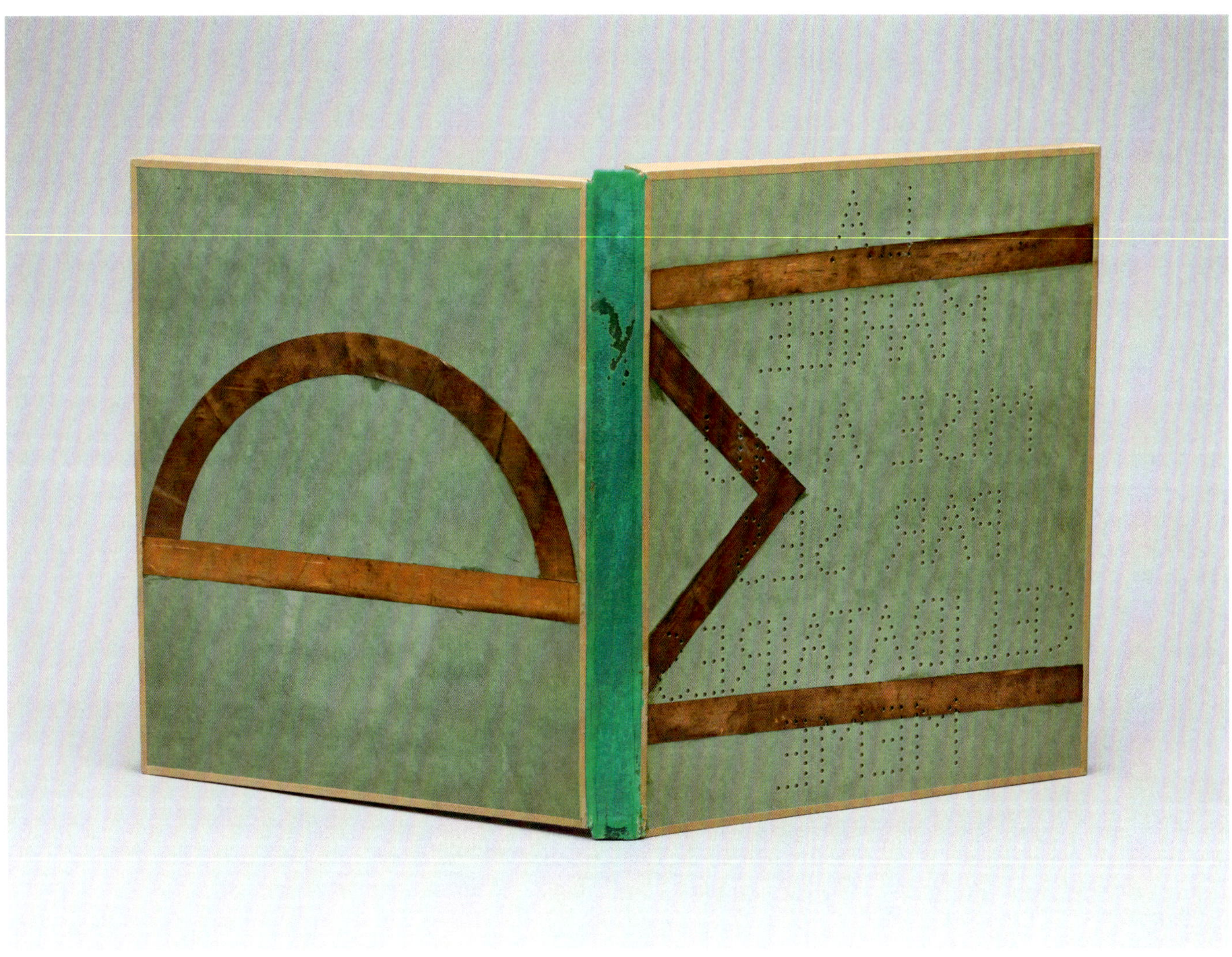

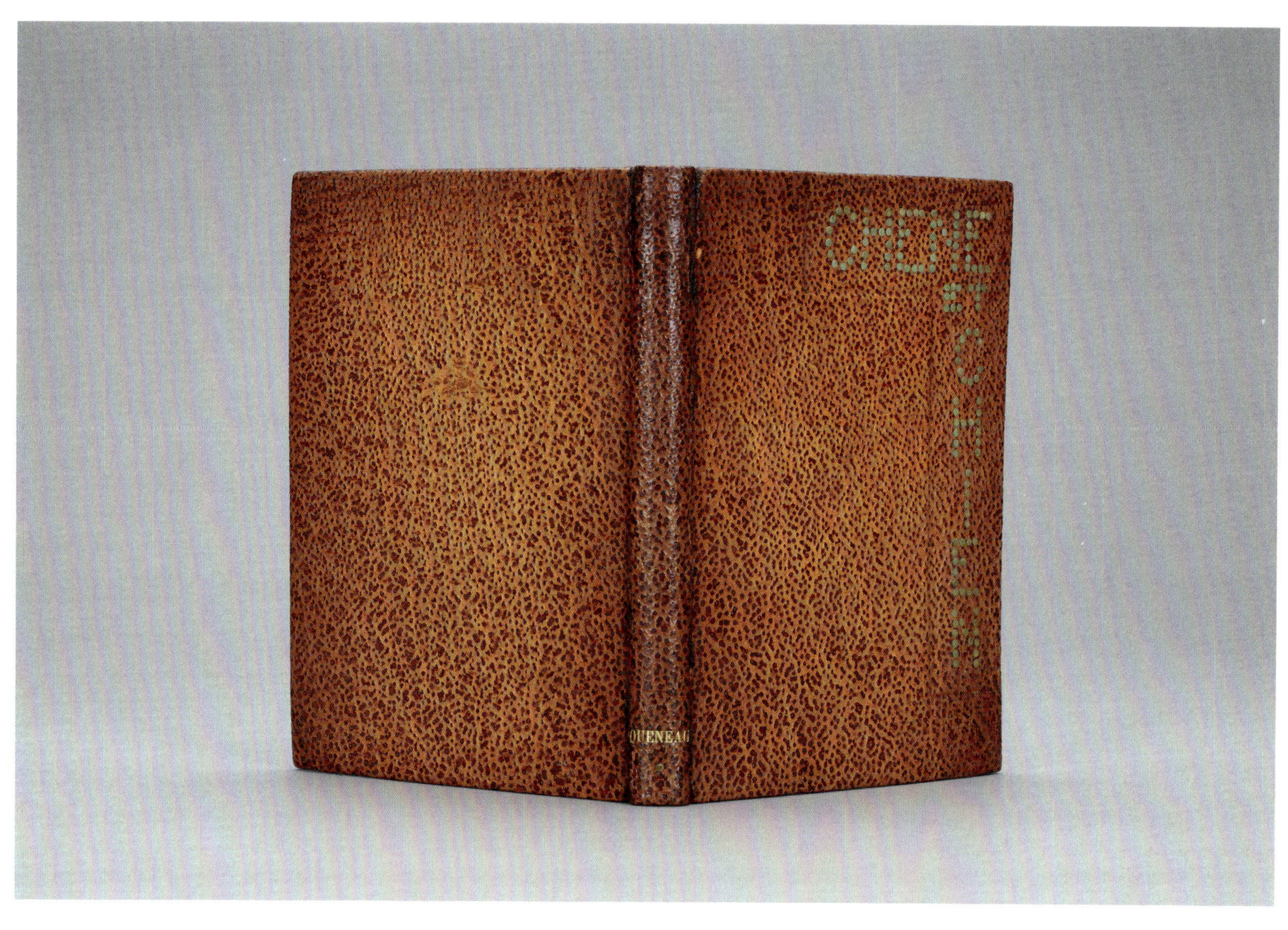

Fig. 53 Mary Reynolds (American, 1891–1950). *Chêne et chien* **(published in English as** *Chêne et chien***) by Raymond Queneau (Paris: Les Éditions Denoël, 1937), 1937–42.**

Full goatskin with dotted-blue-calfskin onlays and gold stamping. Tan wove endpapers speckled with gold leaf; 20 × 14.5 × 2.5 cm (7⅞ × 5¹¹⁄₁₆ × 1 in.). The Art Institute of Chicago, Ryerson and Burnham Libraries, Mary Reynolds Collection, 2024.844.

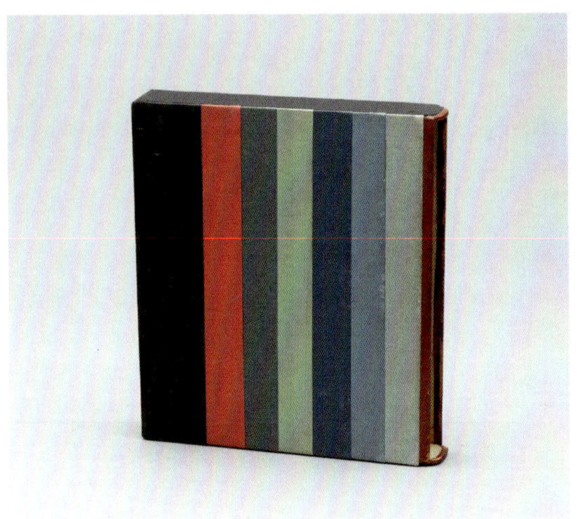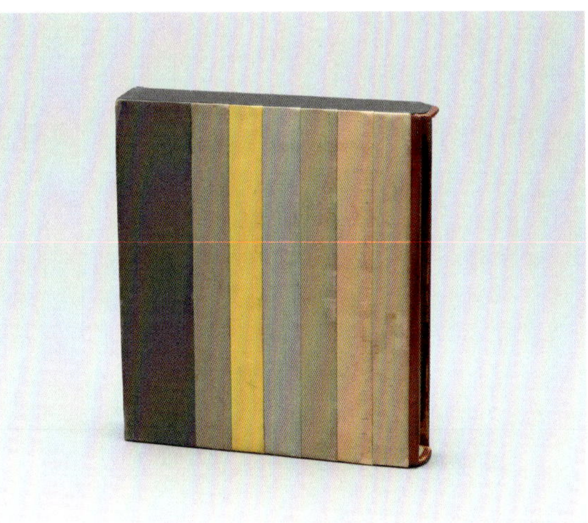

Fig. 54 Mary Reynolds (American, 1891–1950) and Marcel Duchamp (American, born France, 1887–1968).
Hebdomeros **by Giorgio de Chirico (Paris: Éditions du Carrefour, 1929), about 1936–39.**

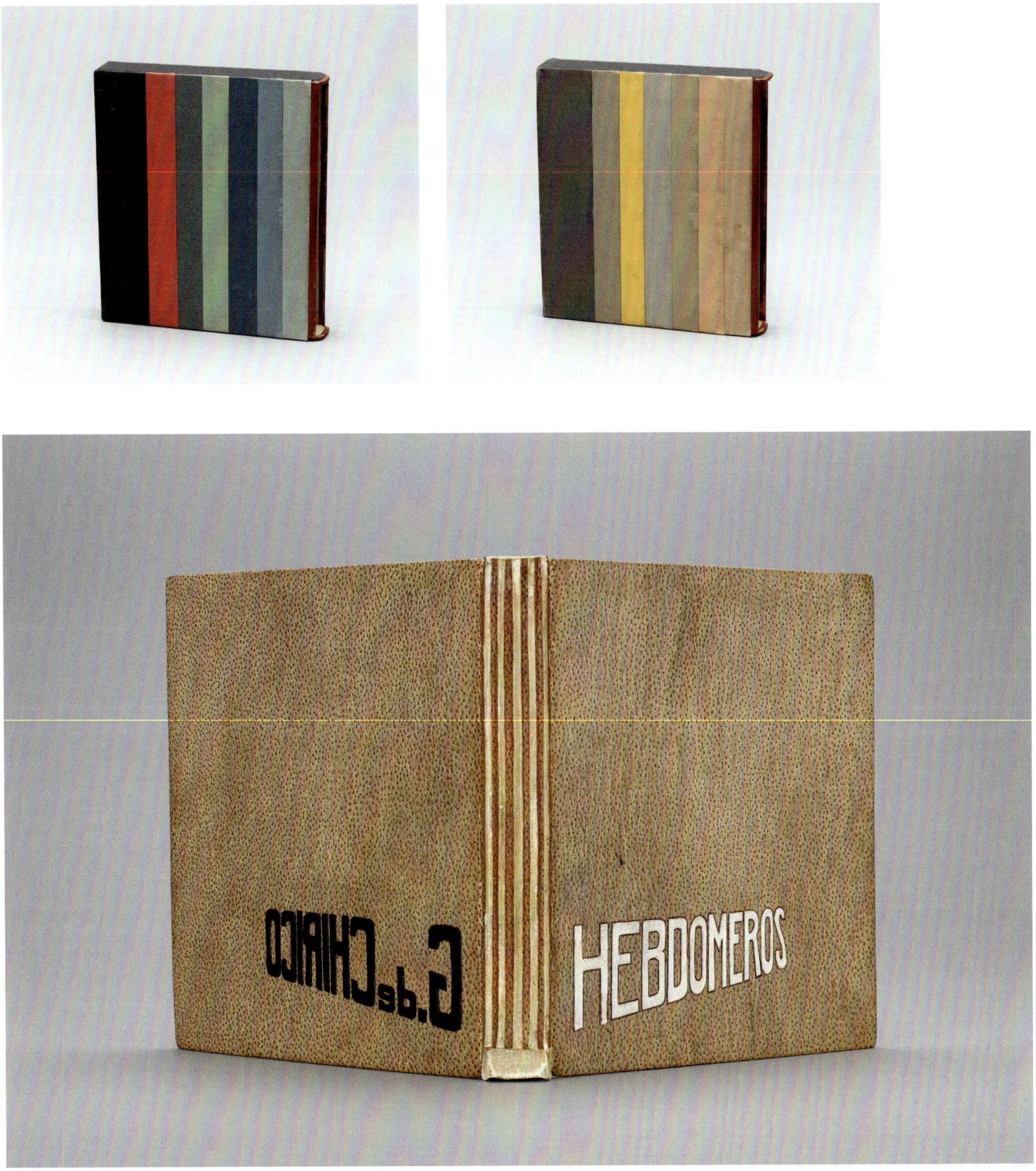

Full leather with fluted spine and white- and black-goatskin onlays. Orange-silk endpapers, emerald- and terracotta-goatskin doublures, top edge gilt. Paper-covered slipcase with goatskin trim and felt lining; 20.2 × 18.5 × 3.7 cm (8 × 7⁵⁄₁₆ × 1½ in.). The Art Institute of Chicago, Ryerson and Burnham Libraries, Mary Reynolds Collection, 2019.173.

"Opium balances the nerves. It hooks cork into some and sinks others."

—Jean Cocteau

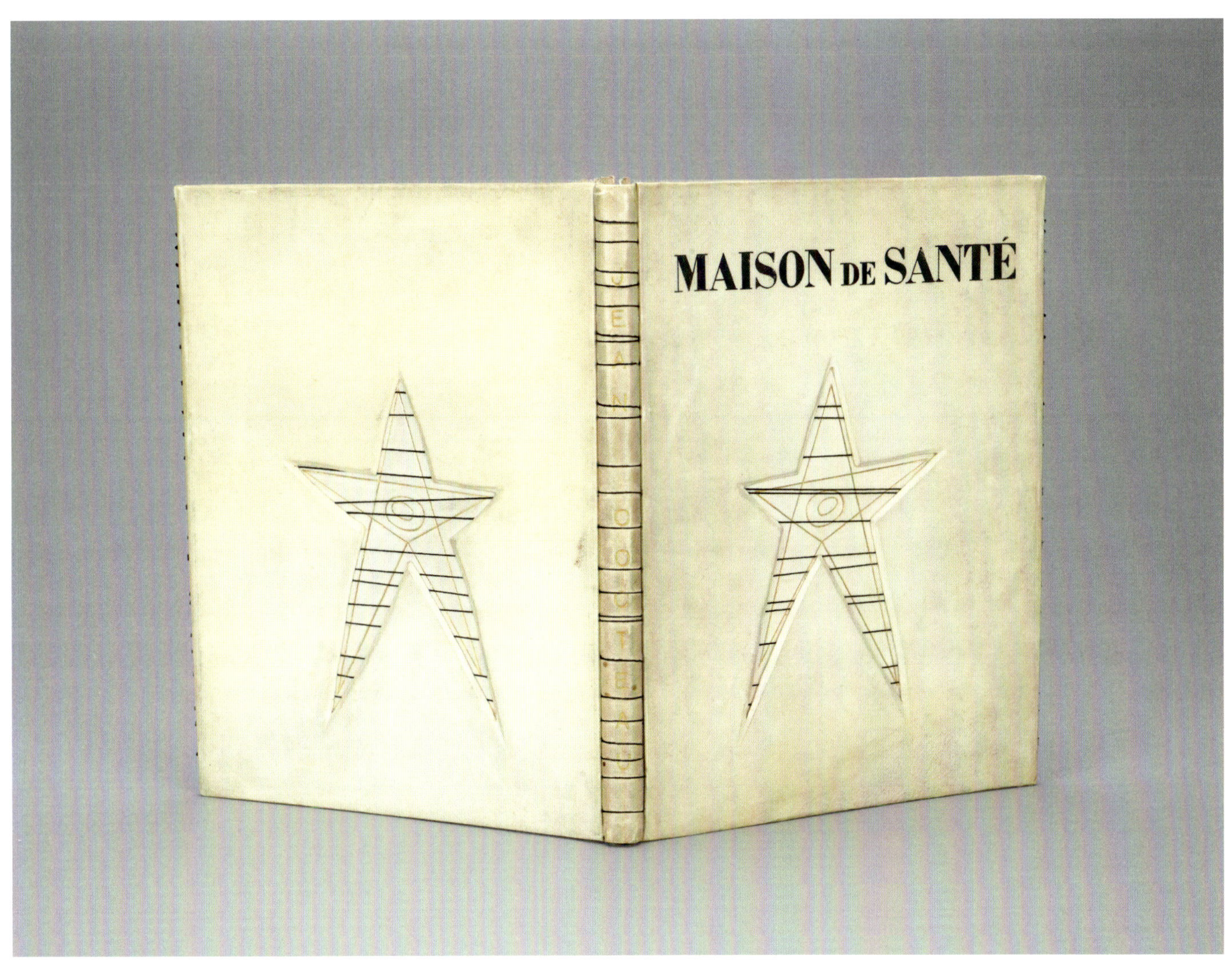

Fig. 55 Mary Reynolds (American, 1891–1950). *Maison de santé* **(The clinic) by Jean Cocteau (Paris: Éditions Briant-Robert, 1926), 1930–42.**

Full vellum with star cutouts, threads, and gold stamping. Maroon endpapers; 28.8 × 22.1 × 1.5 cm (11⅜ × 8¾ × ⅝ in.). The Art Institute of Chicago, Ryerson and Burnham Libraries, Mary Reynolds Collection, 2019.174.

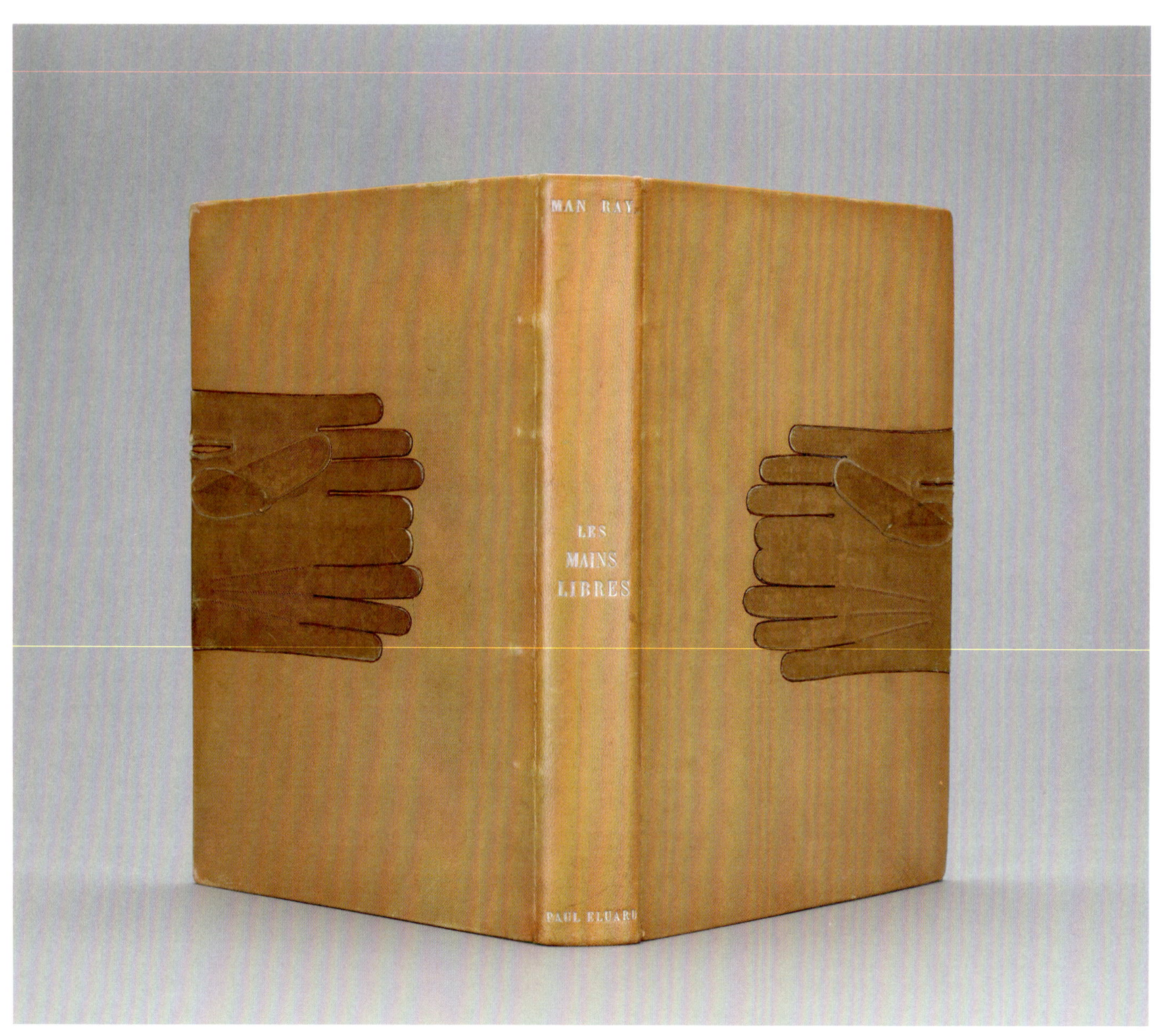

Fig. 56 Mary Reynolds (American, 1891–1950). *Les mains libres* (Free hands) by Man Ray, with poetry by Paul Éluard (Paris: Éditions Jeanne Bucher, 1937), 1937–42.

Full goatskin with onlaid leather gloves and palladium stamping. Silk endpapers, top edge gilt; 28.8 × 23 × 4.3 cm (11⅜ × 9¹⁄₁₆ × 1¾ in.). The Art Institute of Chicago, Ryerson and Burnham Libraries, Mary Reynolds Collection, 2019.171.

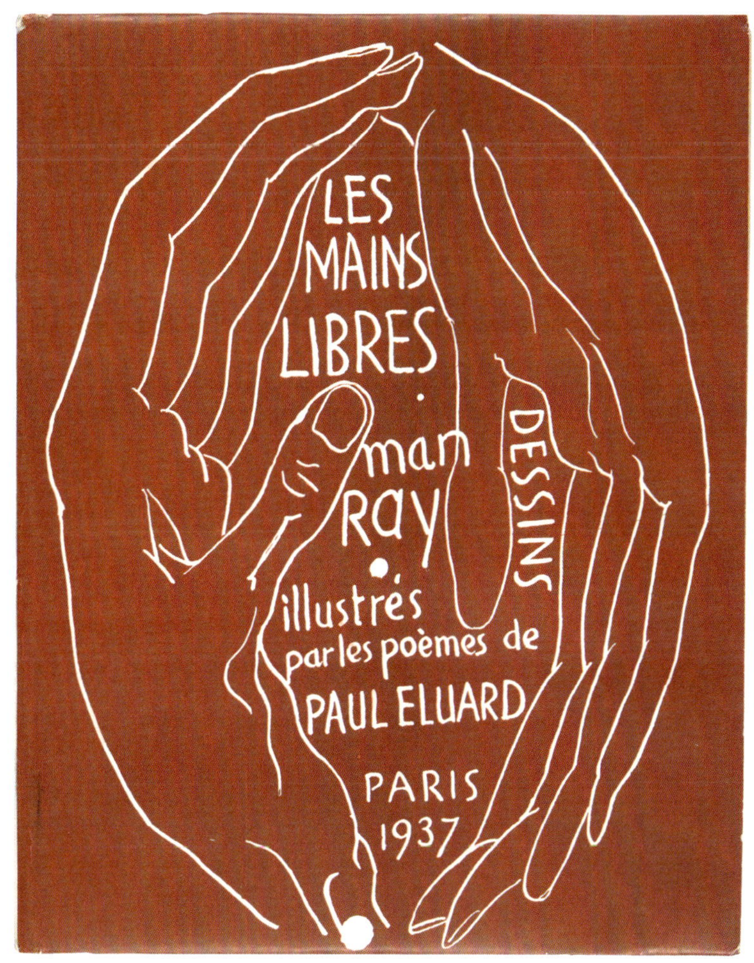

Fig. 57 Man Ray (American, 1890–1976). *Les mains libres* (Free hands), **with poetry by Paul Éluard (Paris: Aux Éditions Jeanne Bucher, 1937), 1937.**

Illustrated book with 54 plates. Inscribed by Man Ray to Marcel Duchamp; 29 × 23 × 3 cm (11⁷⁄₁₆ × 9⁵⁄₁₆ × 1³⁄₁₆ in.). The Art Institute of Chicago, Ryerson and Burnham Libraries, Mary Reynolds Collection, 2019.948.1.

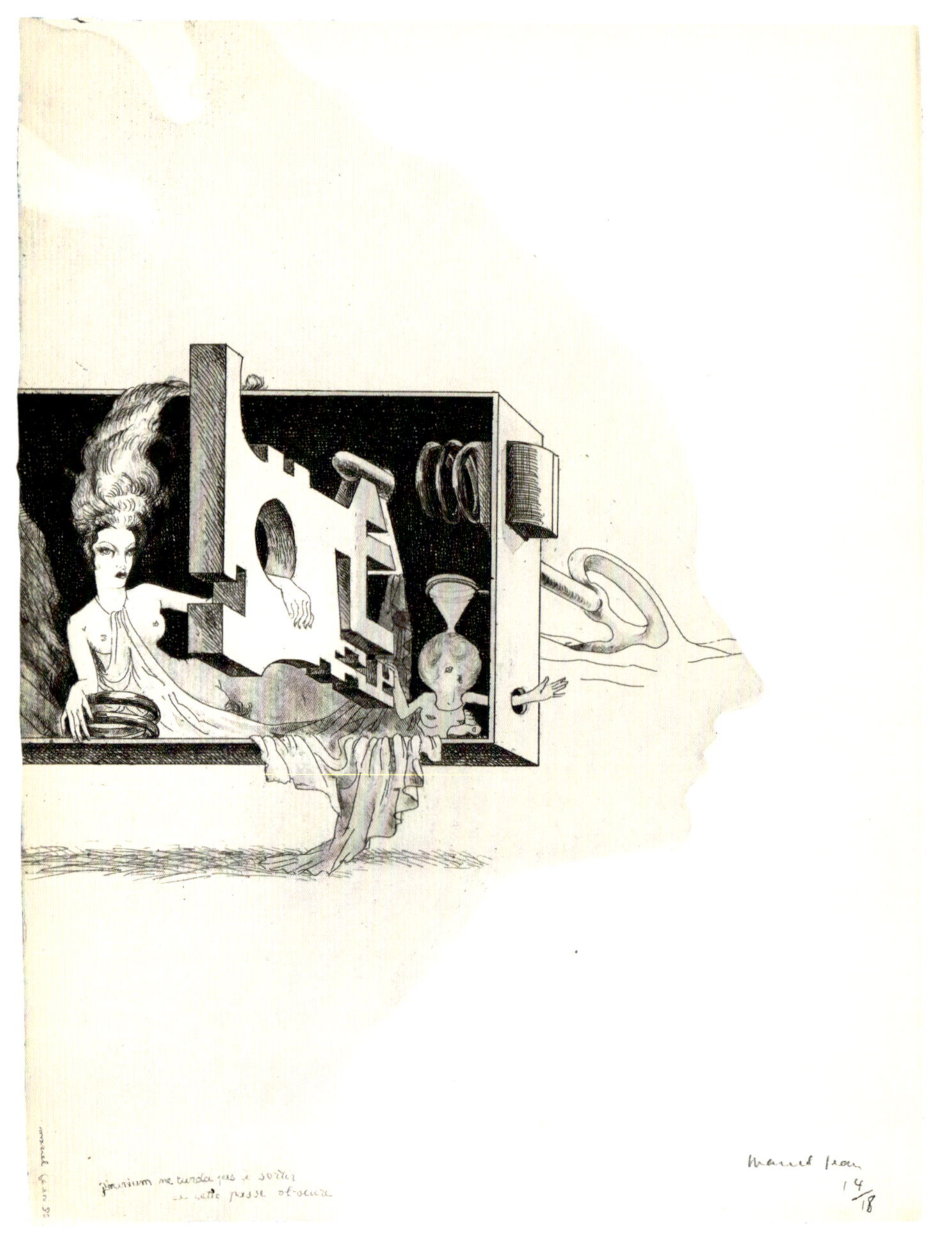

Fig. 58 Marcel Jean (French, 1900–1993). Etching from *Mourir pour la patrie* (To die for the fatherland) by André Jean and Marcel Jean (Paris: Éditions Cahiers d'Art, 1935), 1935.

Etching in black ink on cream laid paper; 34 x 25 cm (13⅞₆ x 9⅞ in.). The Art Institute of Chicago, Ryerson and Burham Libraries, Mary Reynolds Collection, 2020.41.

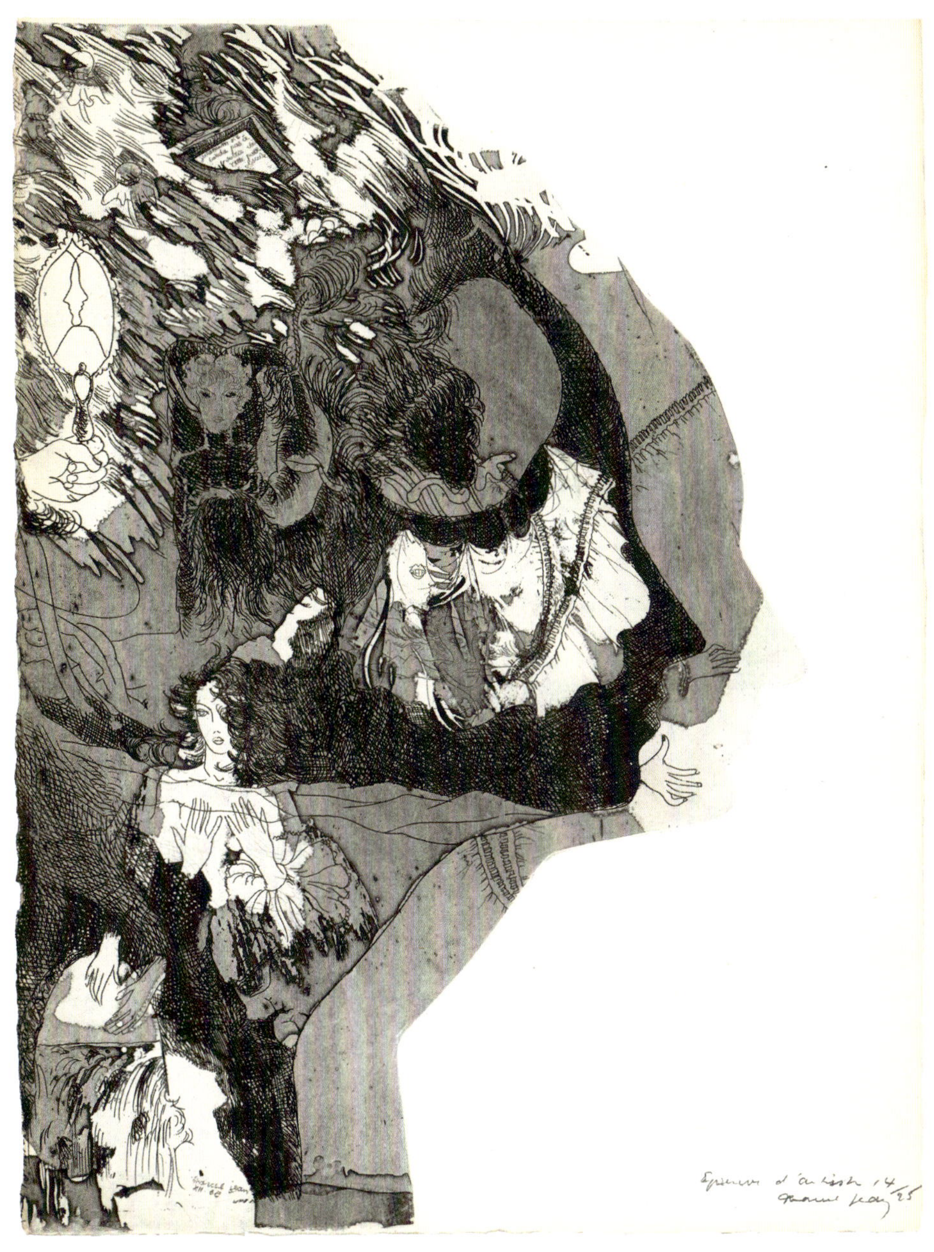

Fig. 59 Marcel Jean (French, 1900–1993). Etching from *Mourir pour la patrie* (To die for the fatherland) by André Jean and Marcel Jean (Paris: Éditions Cahiers d'Art, 1935), 1935.

Etching in black ink on cream laid paper; 34 × 25 cm (13⁷⁄₁₆ × 9⁷⁄₈ in.). The Art Institute of Chicago, Ryerson and Burnham Libraries, Mary Reynolds Collection, 2020.41.

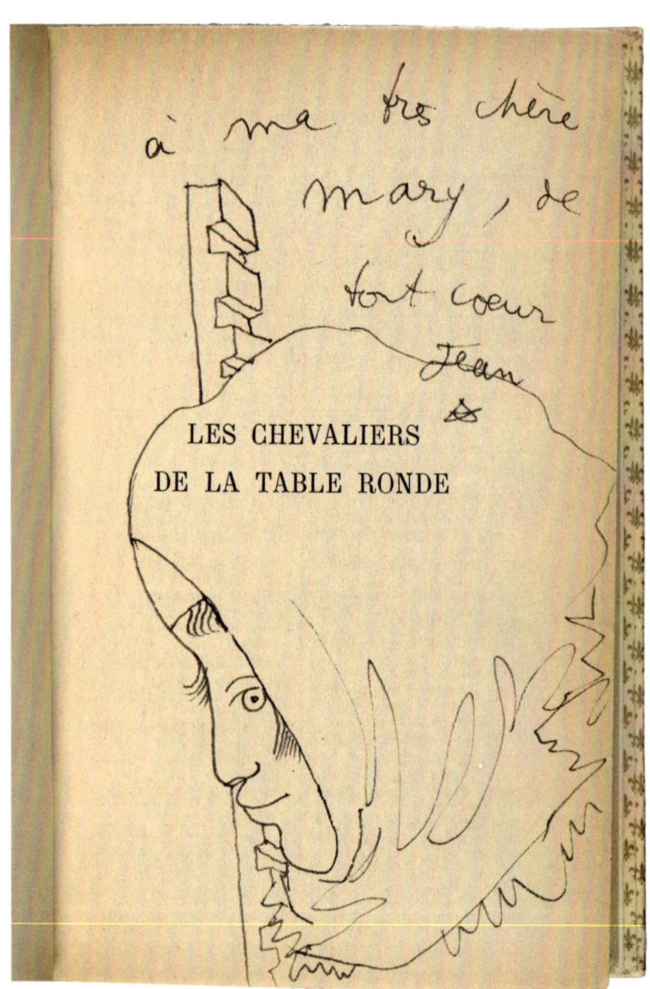

Fig. 61 **Mary Reynolds (American, 1891–1950).** *Les parents terribles* **(published in English as** *Indiscretions***) by Jean Cocteau (Paris: Gallimard, 1938), 1938–42.**

Quarter vellum with marbled paper. Marbled endpapers. Inscribed, with signed drawing, by Jean Cocteau to Mary Reynolds on half-title; 19.2 × 12.3 × 2.7 cm (7½ × 4¹³⁄₁₆ × 1¹⁄₁₆ in). The Art Institute of Chicago, Ryerson and Burnham Libraries, Mary Reynolds Collection, 2024.856.

Fig. 60 **Mary Reynolds (American, 1891–1950).** *Les chevaliers de la table ronde* (*The Knights of the Round Table*) **by Jean Cocteau (Paris: Gallimard, 1937), 1937–42.**

Quarter vellum with white paper decorated with fleurs-de-lis. Endpapers decorated with gold fleurs-de-lis. Inscribed, with signed drawing, by Jean Cocteau to Mary Reynolds on half-title; 19.5 × 12.2 × 2.5 cm (7¹¹⁄₁₆ × 4¹³⁄₁₆ × 1 in.). The Art Institute of Chicago, Ryerson and Burnham Libraries, Mary Reynolds Collection, 2024.853.

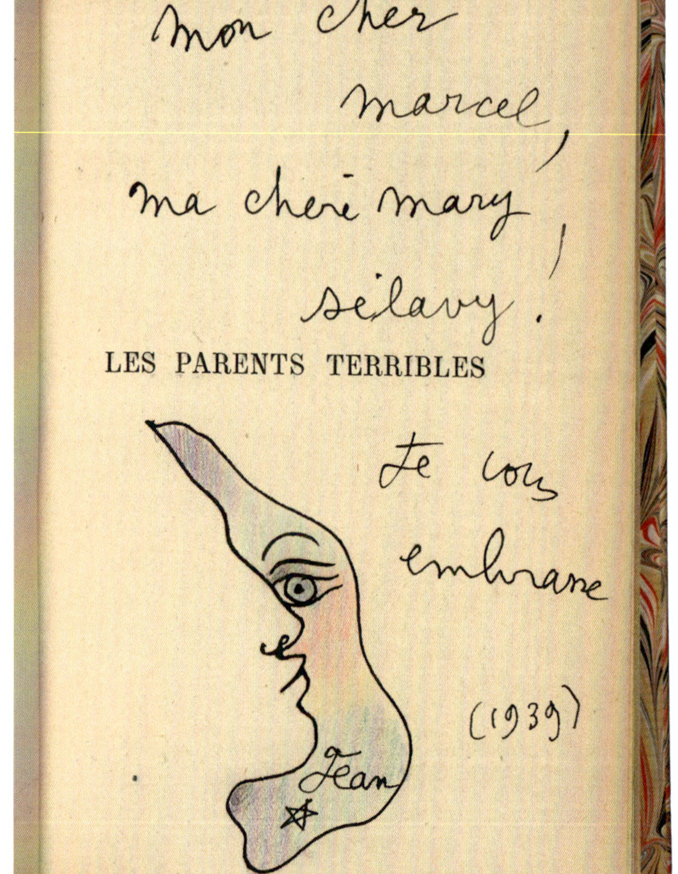

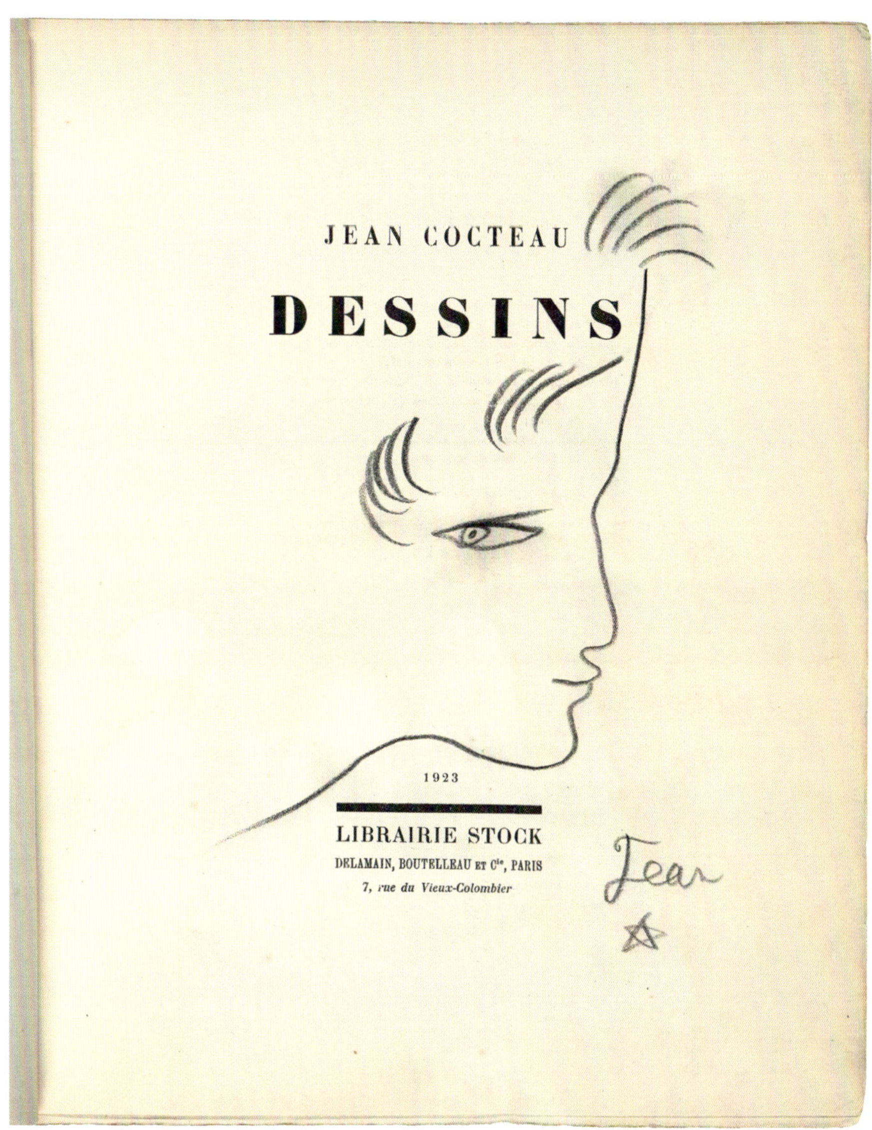

Fig. 62 Mary Reynolds (American, 1891–1950). *Dessins* **(Drawings) by Jean Cocteau (Paris: Librairie Stock, Delamain, Boutelleau et Cie., 1924), 1930–42.**

Full vellum with gold stamping on black-calfskin label. Wine-colored, glazed-paper endpapers. Inscribed, with signed drawing, by Jean Cocteau to Mary Reynolds; 28.8 × 22.6 × 3.8 cm (11⁵⁄₁₆ × 8⅞ × 1½ in.). The Art Institute of Chicago, Ryerson and Burnham Libraries, Mary Reynolds Collection.

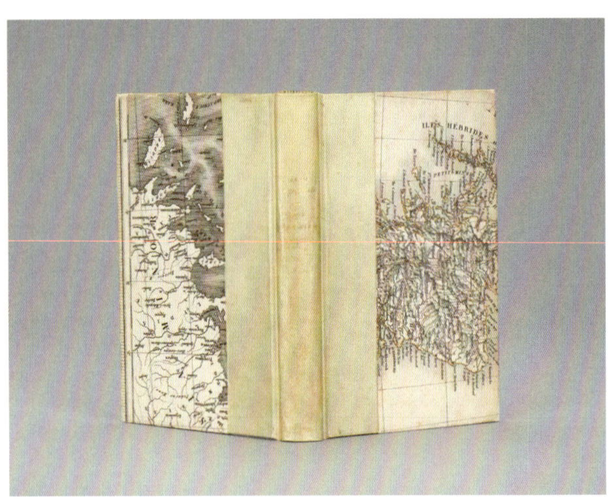

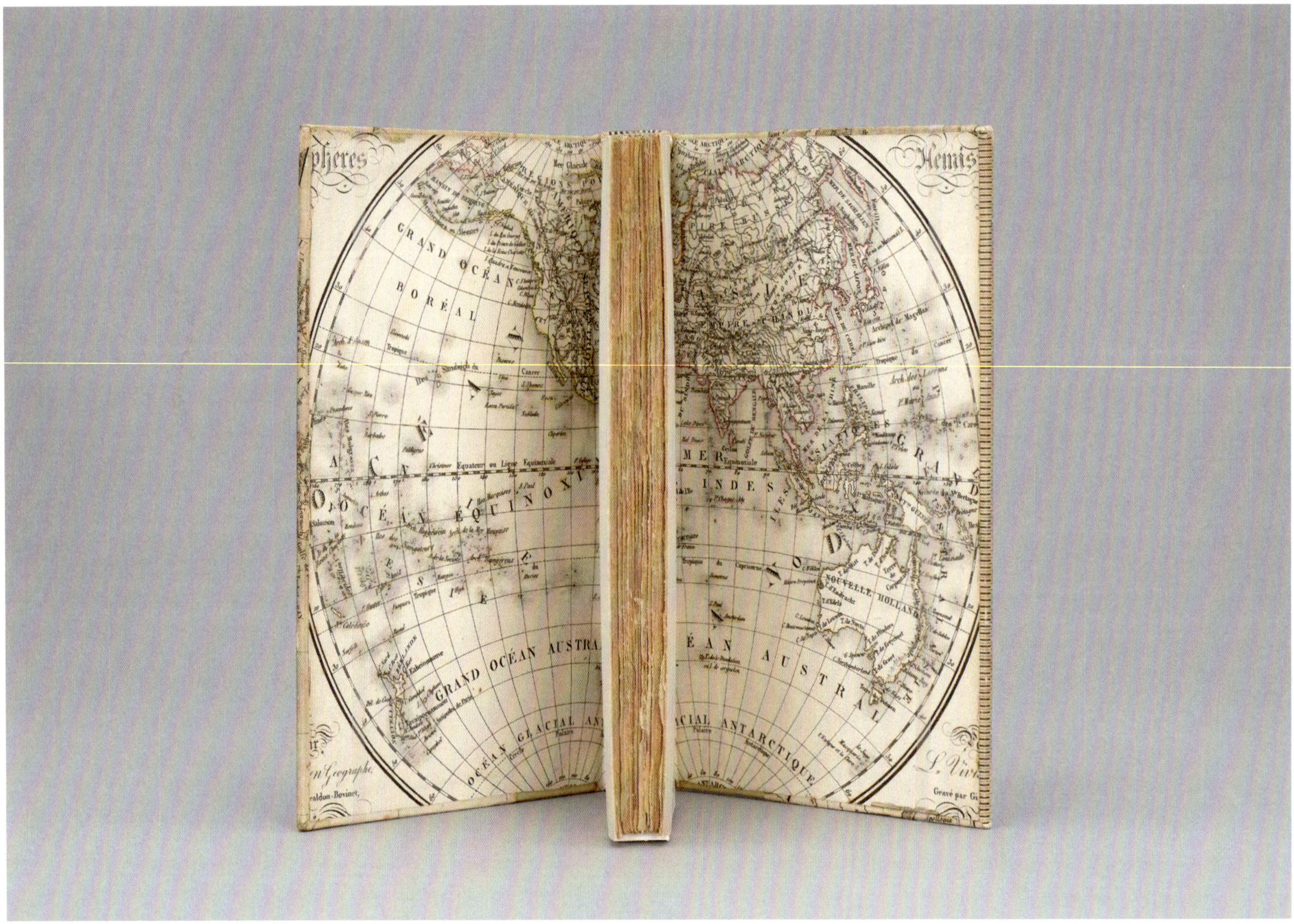

Fig. 63 Mary Reynolds (American, 1891–1950). *Mon premier voyage: Tour du monde en 80 Jours* **(published in English as** *Round the World Again in 80 Days***) by Jean Cocteau (Paris: Gallimard, 1936), 1936–42.**

Quarter vellum with gold stamping. Paper-map sides and endpapers; 19.3 × 12.5 × 2.7 cm (7½ × 5 × ⅛ in.).
The Art Institute of Chicago, Ryerson and Burnham Libraries, Mary Reynolds Collection, 2024.859.

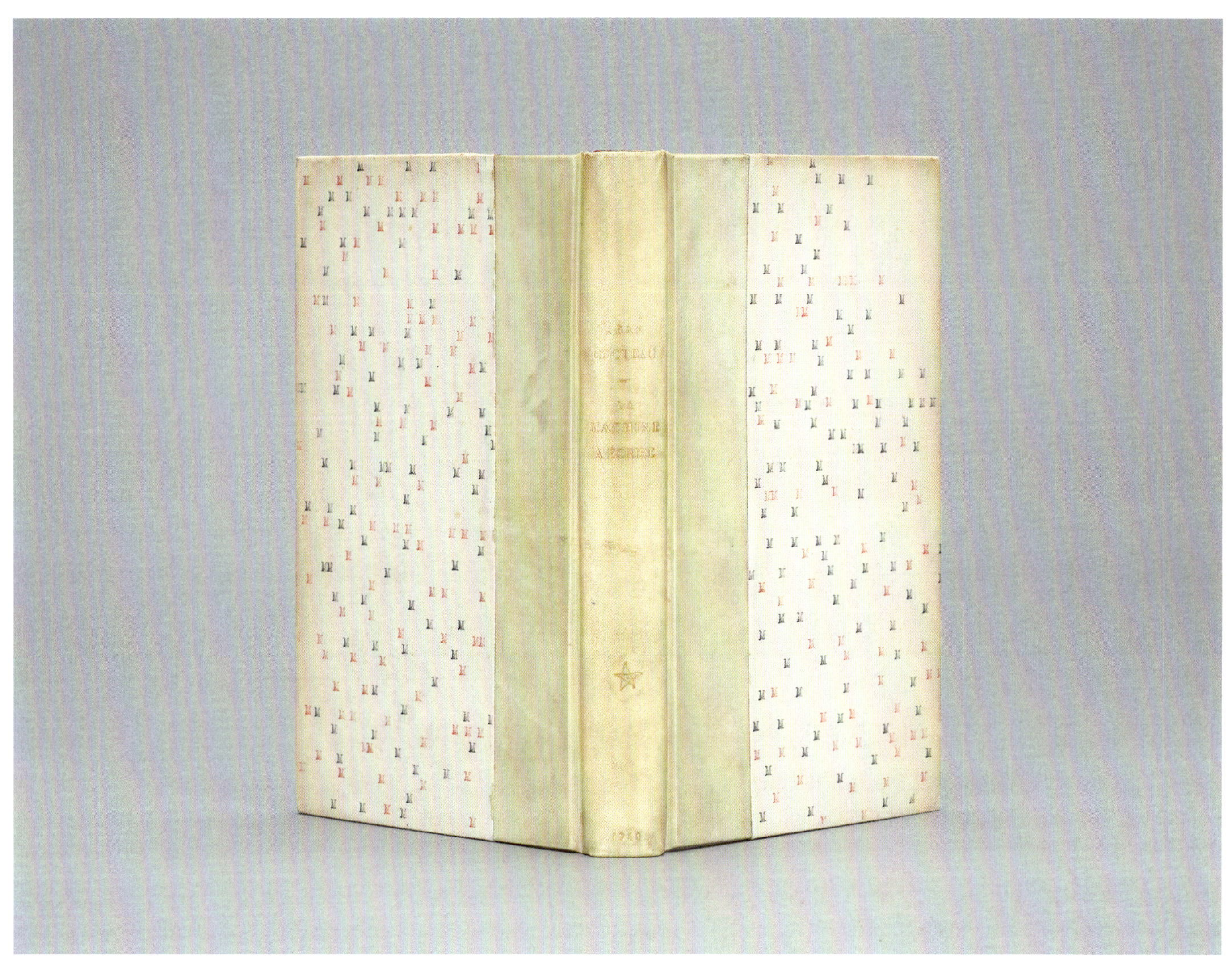

Fig. 64 Mary Reynolds (American, 1891–1950). *La machine à écrire (The Typewriter)* **by Jean Cocteau (Paris: Gallimard, 1941), 1941–42.**

Quarter vellum with gold stamping and white paper repeatedly stamped with an uppercase *M* in red and black. Plain ivory endpapers; 19.1 × 12.8 × 2.9 cm (7⁹⁄₁₆ × 5¹⁄₁₆ × 1³⁄₁₆ in.). The Art Institute of Chicago, Ryerson and Burnham Libraries, Mary Reynolds Collection, 2019.175.

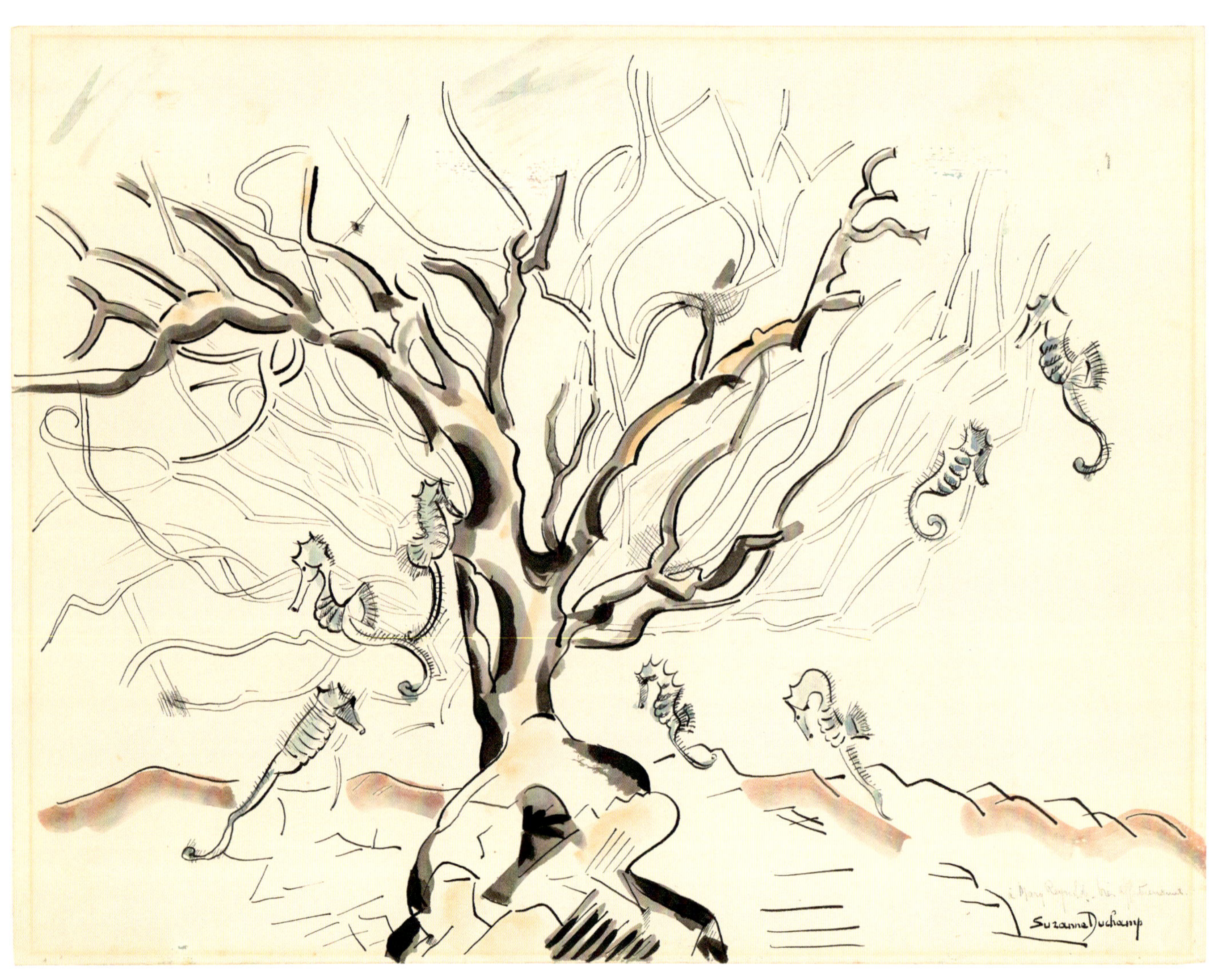

Fig. 65 Suzanne Duchamp (French, 1889–1963). *Sea Horses,* **about 1929–32.**

Watercolor, pen, and brush and black ink on cream wove paper, laid down onto buff wove paper.
Inscribed by Suzanne Duchamp to Mary Reynolds; 40.4 × 53 cm (15$\frac{15}{16}$ × 20$\frac{7}{8}$ in.). The Art Institute
of Chicago, gift of Mr. Frank B. Hubachek, 1957.88.

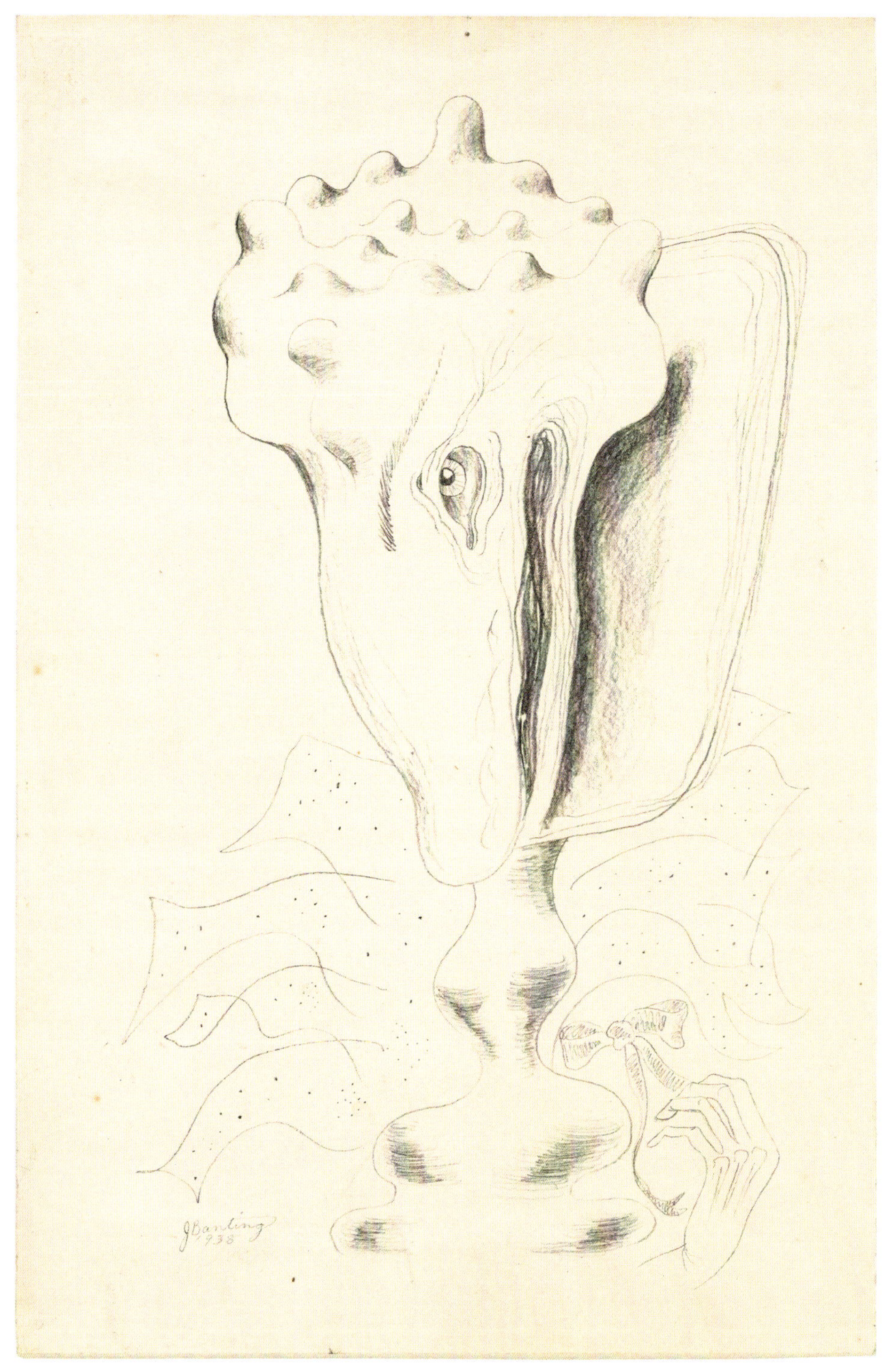

Fig. 66 John F. Banting (English, 1902–1971). *Untitled,* 1938.

Graphite on ivory wove paper; 34.2 × 23.8 cm (13½ × 9⅜ in.). The Art Institute of Chicago, gift of Frank B. Hubachek, 1957.80.

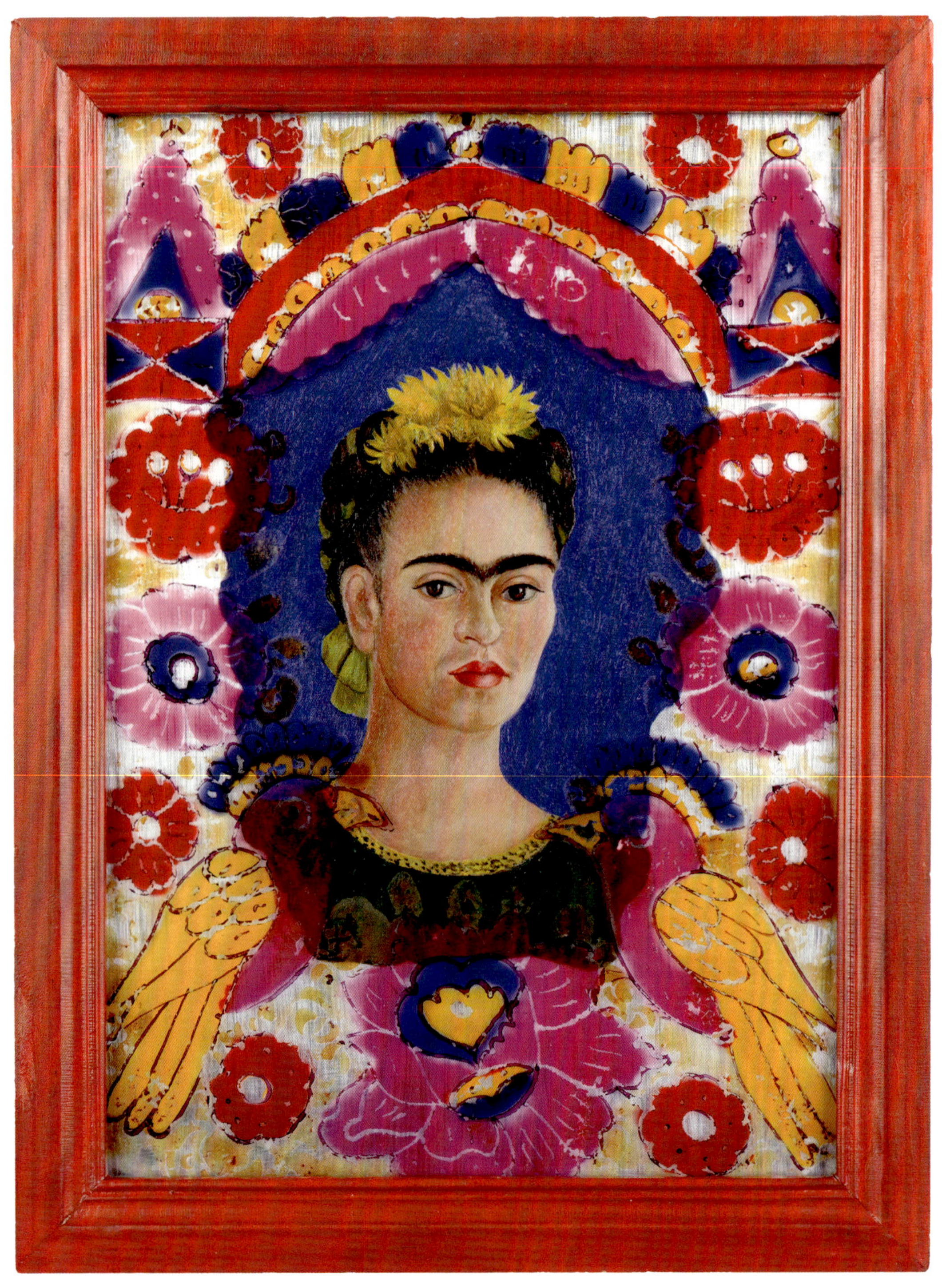

Fig. 67 Frida Kahlo (Mexican, 1907–1954). *The Frame,* **1938.**

Oil on aluminum in artisanal frame with painted glass; 29.5 × 20.7 cm (11¼ × 8⅛ in.).
The Centre Pompidou, Paris, state purchase, 1939, JP 929 P (1).

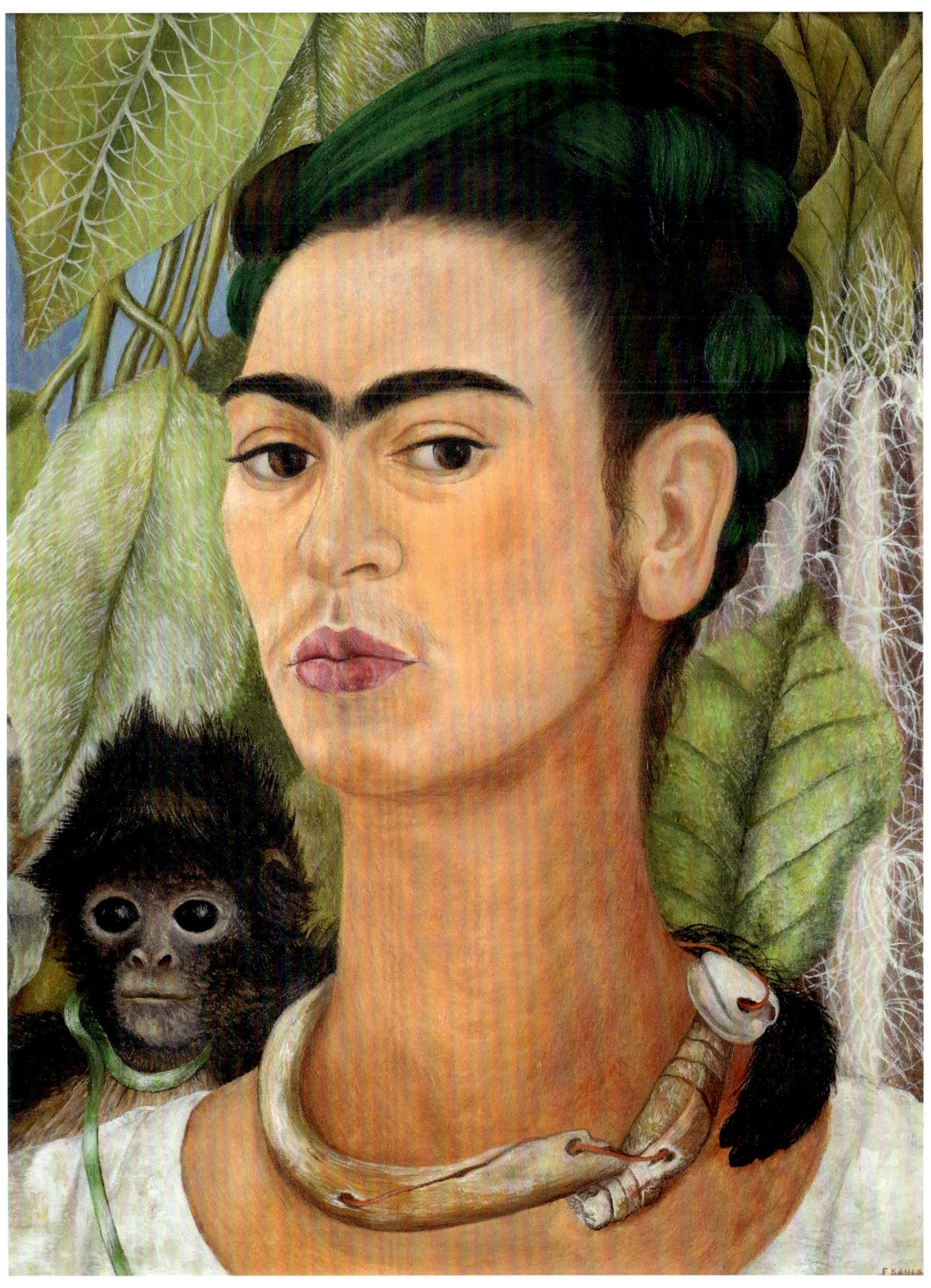

Fig. 68 Frida Kahlo (Mexican, 1907–1954). *Self-Portrait with Monkey*, 1938.

Oil on hardboard; 40.6 × 30.5 cm (16 × 12 in.). Buffalo AKG Art Museum, New York, bequest of A. Conger Goodyear, 1966.

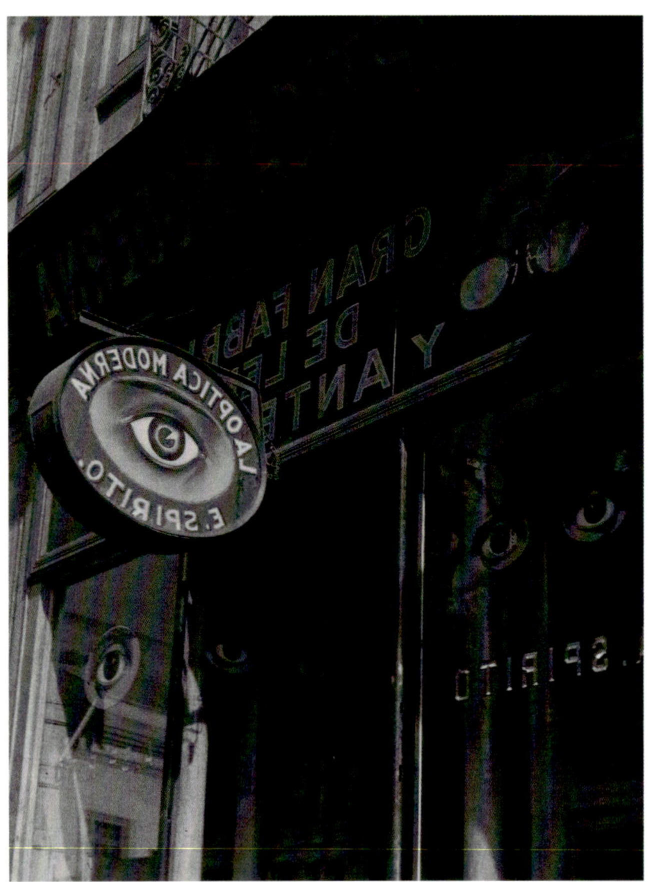

Fig. 69 Manuel Álvarez Bravo (Mexican, 1902–2002). *Optical Parable,* **1931.**

Gelatin silver print; 23.8 × 18.1 cm (9⅜ × 7³⁄₁₆ in.). The Art Institute of Chicago, purchased with funds provided by Exchange National Bank, 1975.315.

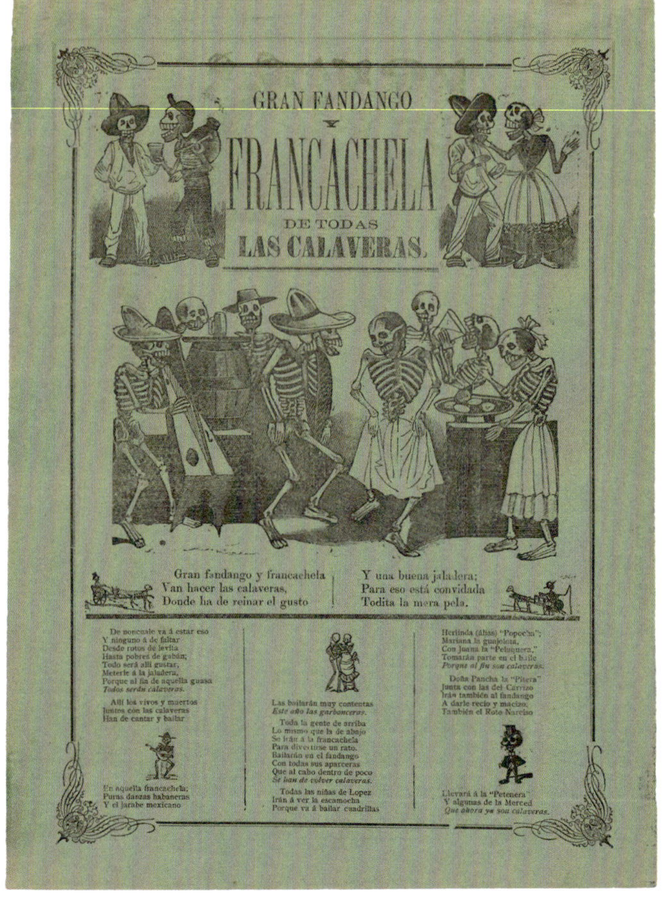

Fig. 70 José Guadalupe Posada (Mexican, 1852–1913). *Grand Dance and Wild Party of All the Calaveras,* **about 1900.**

Relief engraving or photo-relief etching on green wove paper; 36.3 × 25.9 cm (14⁵⁄₁₆ × 10¼ in.). The Art Institute of Chicago, William McCallin McKee Memorial Endowment, 1943.1339.

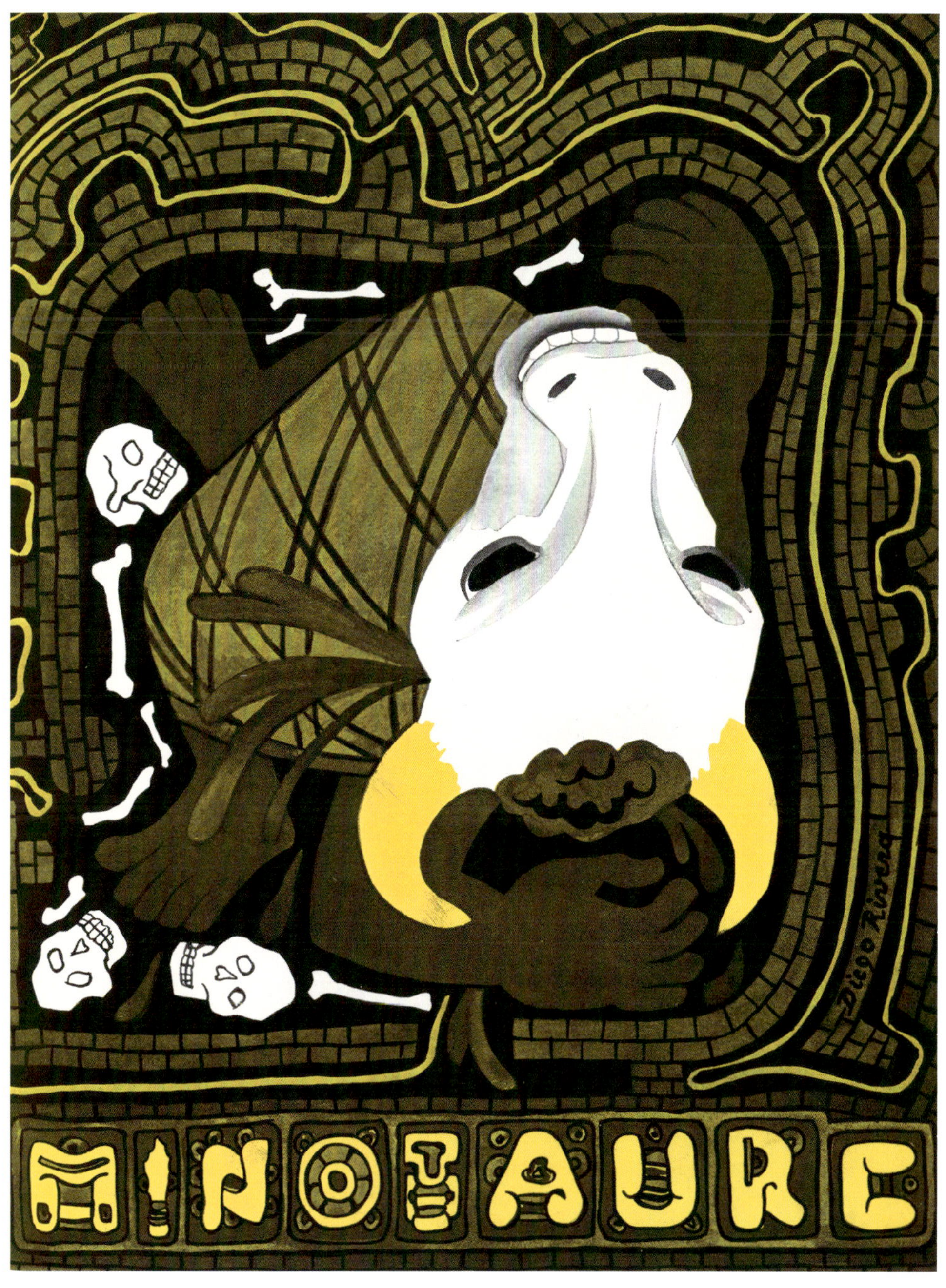

Fig. 71 Diego Rivera (Mexican, 1886–1957). Insert for *Minotaure* No. 12/13, 1939.

Letterpress halftone in yellow and black ink on ivory coated paper; 30.5 × 22.9 cm (12⅜ × 9½ in.).
The Art Institute of Chicago, Ryerson and Burnham Libraries.

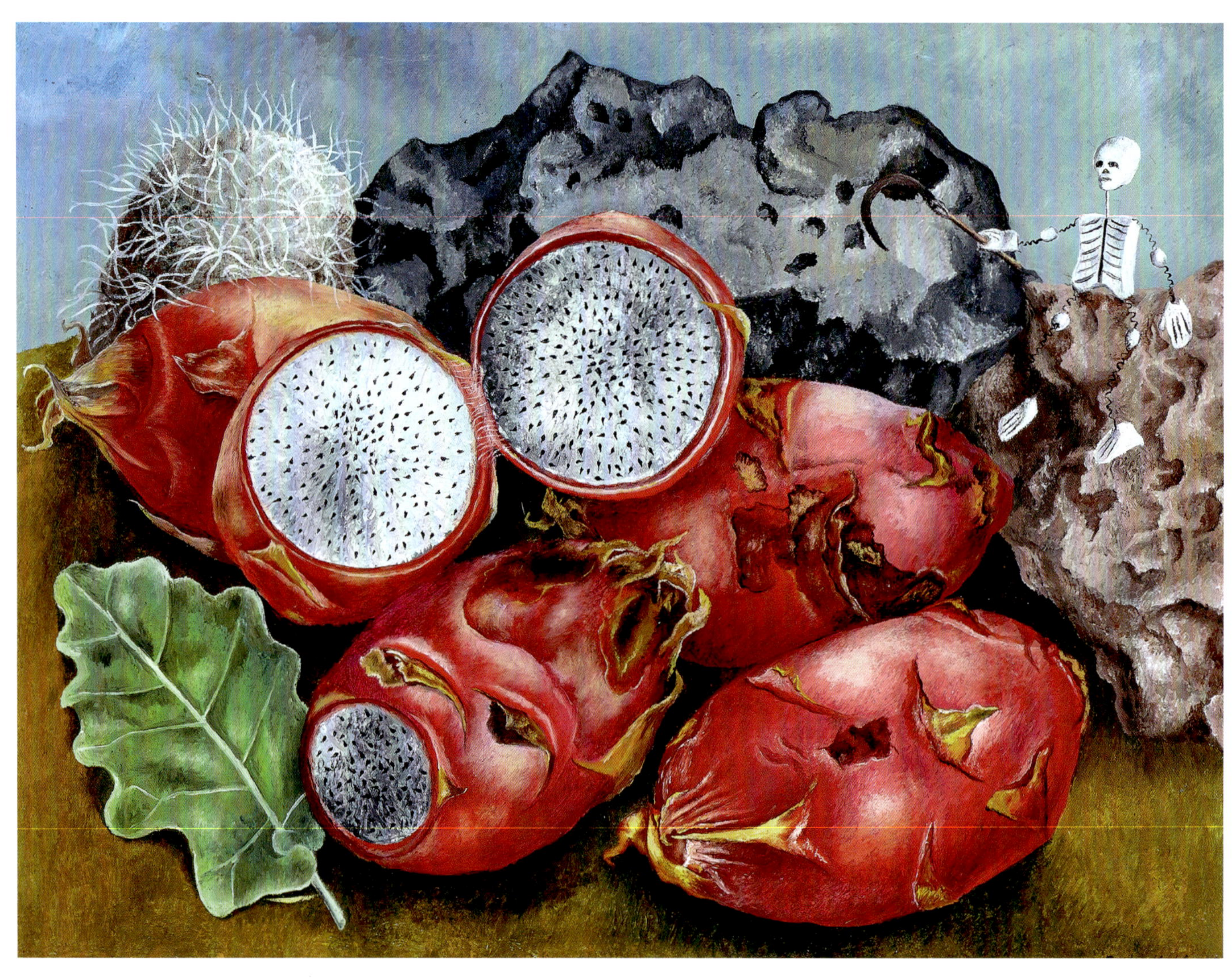

Fig. 72 Frida Kahlo (Mexican, 1907–1954). *Pitahayas,* **1938.**

Oil on aluminum; 25.4 × 35.5 cm (10 × 14 in.). Madison Museum of Contemporary Art,
bequest of Rudolph and Louise Langer.

Fig. 73 Frida Kahlo (Mexican, 1907–1954). *Food from the Earth,* 1938.

Oil on hardboard; 40.6 × 60 cm (16 × 23⅝ in.). Banco Nacional de México Collection, Mexico City.

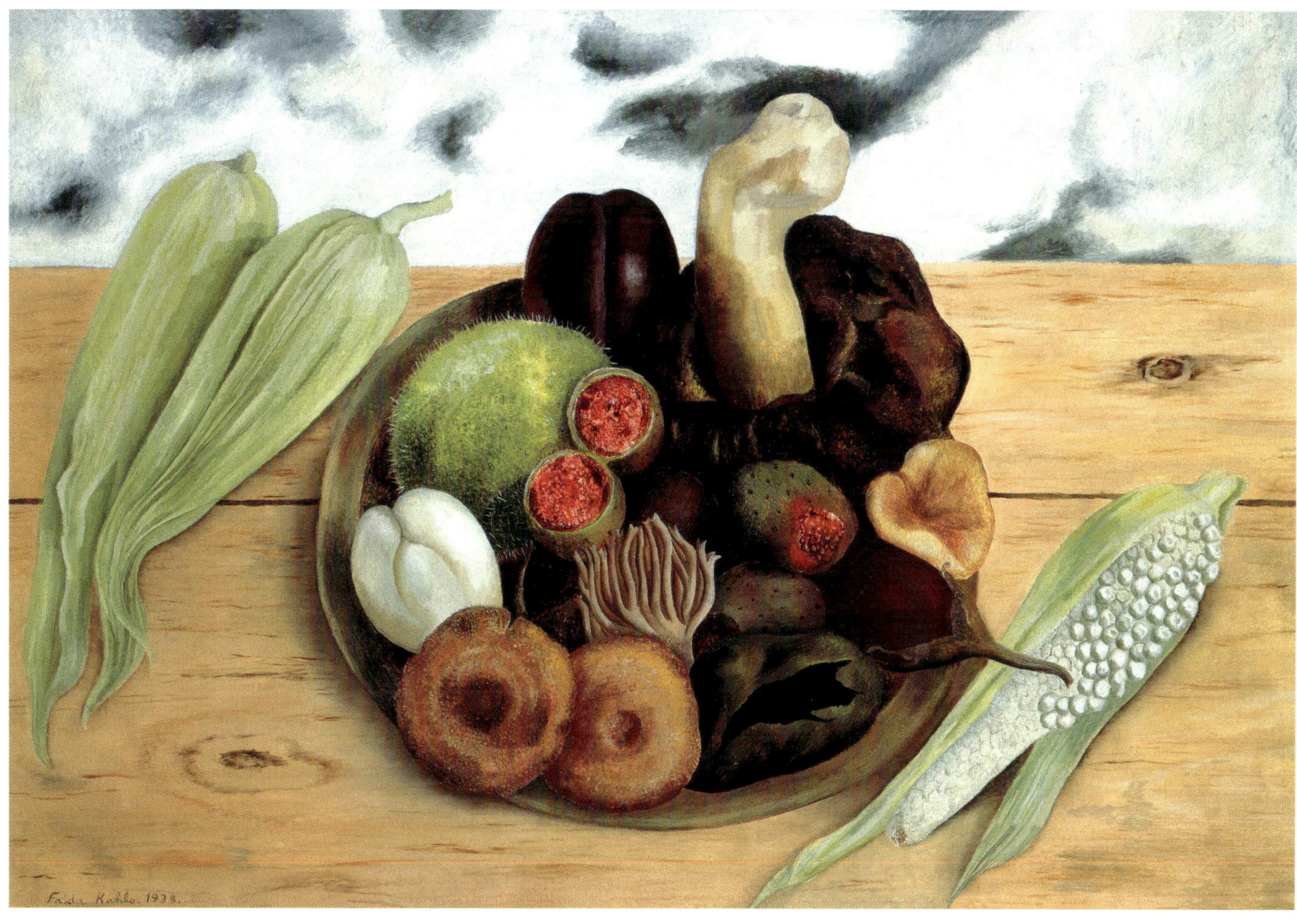

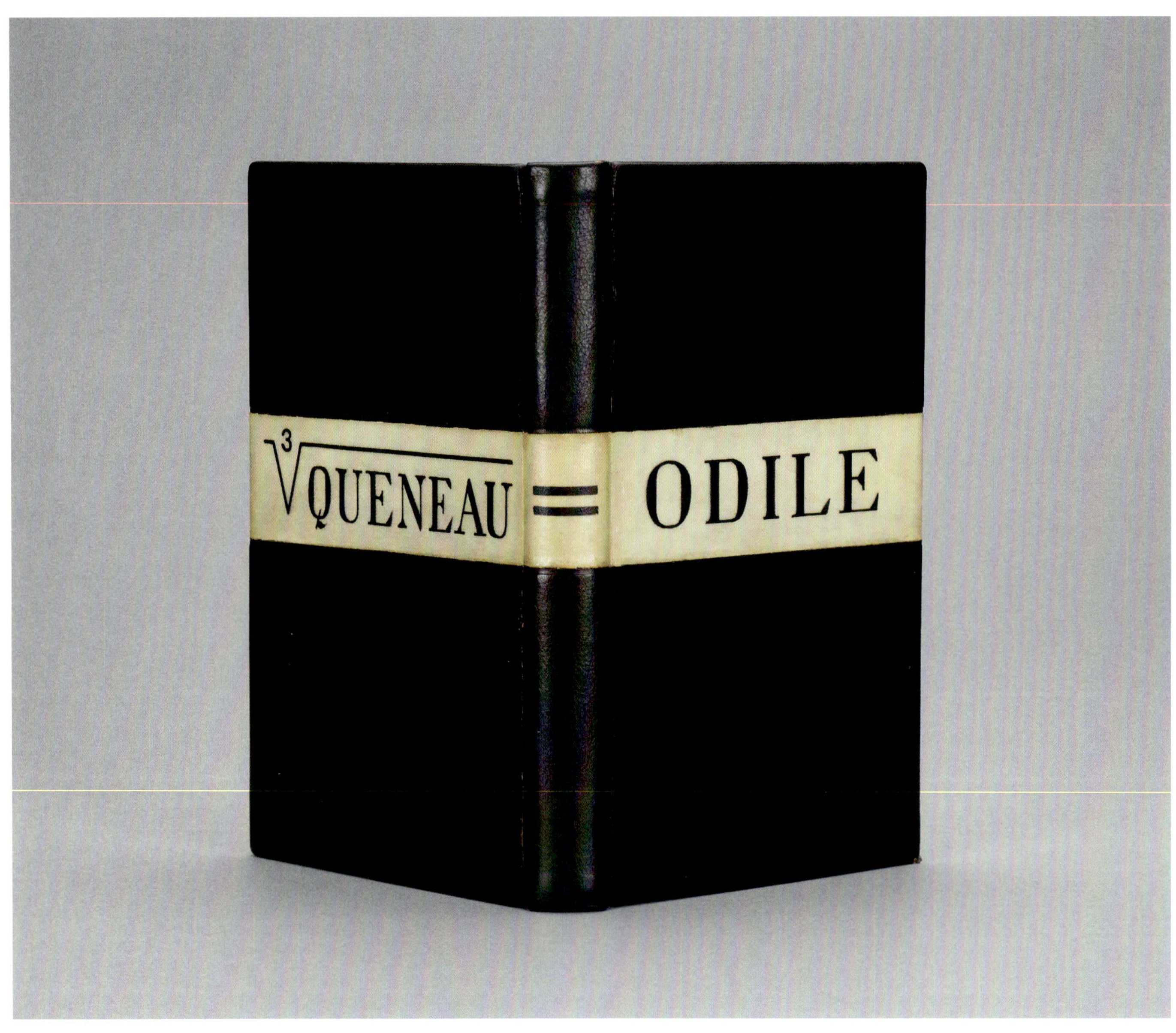

"So there must be a mathematical unconscious . . . "

—Raymond Queneau

Fig. 74 Mary Reynolds (American, 1891–1950). *Odile* by Raymond Queneau (Paris: Gallimard, 1937), 1937–42.

Full calfskin with horizontal vellum onlay and black ink. Ivory Japanese endpapers. Inscribed by Raymond Queneau to Mary Reynolds; 19.5 × 12.5 × 2.5 cm (7¹¹⁄₁₆ × 4¹⁵⁄₁₆ × 1 in.). The Art Institute of Chicago, Ryerson and Burnham Libraries, Mary Reynolds Collection, 2019.929.

Fig. 75 Mary Reynolds (American, 1891–1950). *Le surmâle* (*The Supermale*) **by Alfred Jarry (Paris: Fasquelle, Éditeurs, 1945), 1945–50.**

Full black goatskin with onlay, gold stamping, and metal corset stay. Mauve endpapers printed with wire-mesh pattern; 22.3 × 13.7 × 2.2 cm (8¹³⁄₁₆ × 5⁷⁄₁₆ × ⅞ in.). The Art Institute of Chicago, Ryerson and Burnham Libraries, Mary Reynolds Collection, 2019.179.

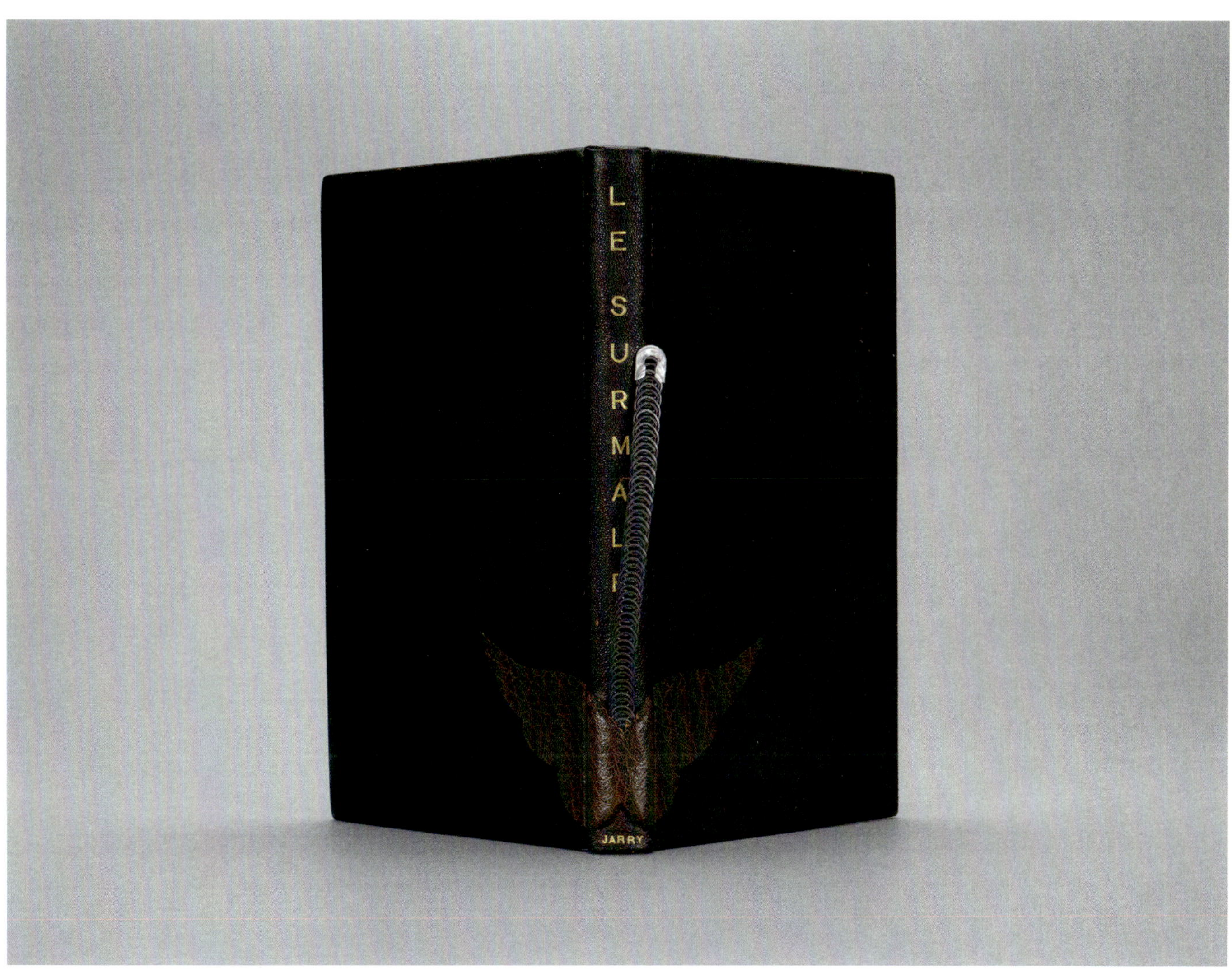

Fig. 76 Mary Reynolds (American, 1891–1950). *Le vrai visage du Marquis de Sade* **(The true face of the Marquis de Sade) by Jean Desbordes (Paris: Éditions de la Nouvelle Revue Critique, 1939), 1939–42 or 1945–50.**

Full goatskin with calfskin inlays, diagonal false bands on spine, and gold stamping. Black endpapers and black-painted top edge; 21.1 × 13.1 × 3 cm (8⁵⁄₁₆ × 5³⁄₁₆ × 1³⁄₁₆ in.). The Art Institute of Chicago, Ryerson and Burnham Libraries, Mary Reynolds Collection, 2019.177.

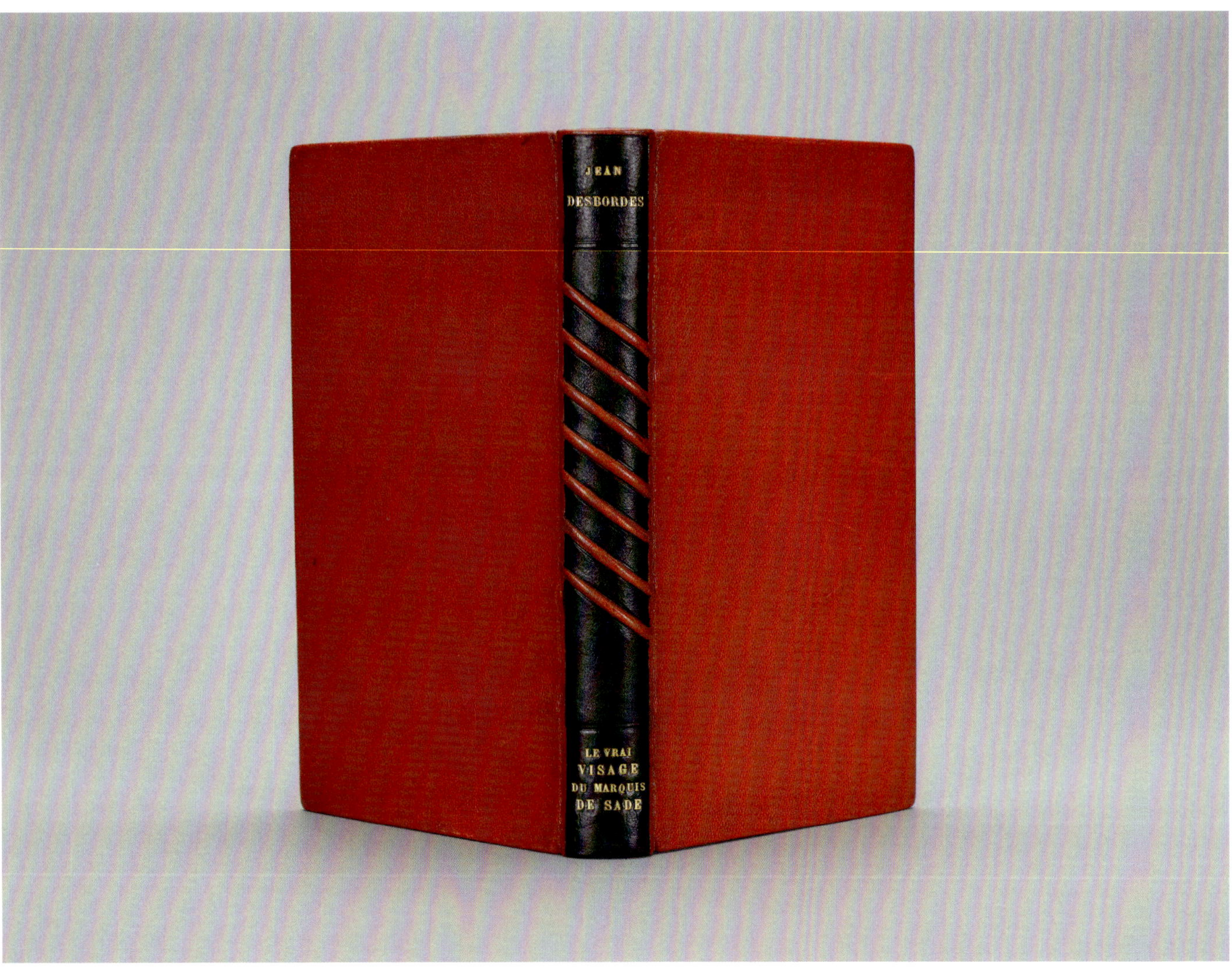

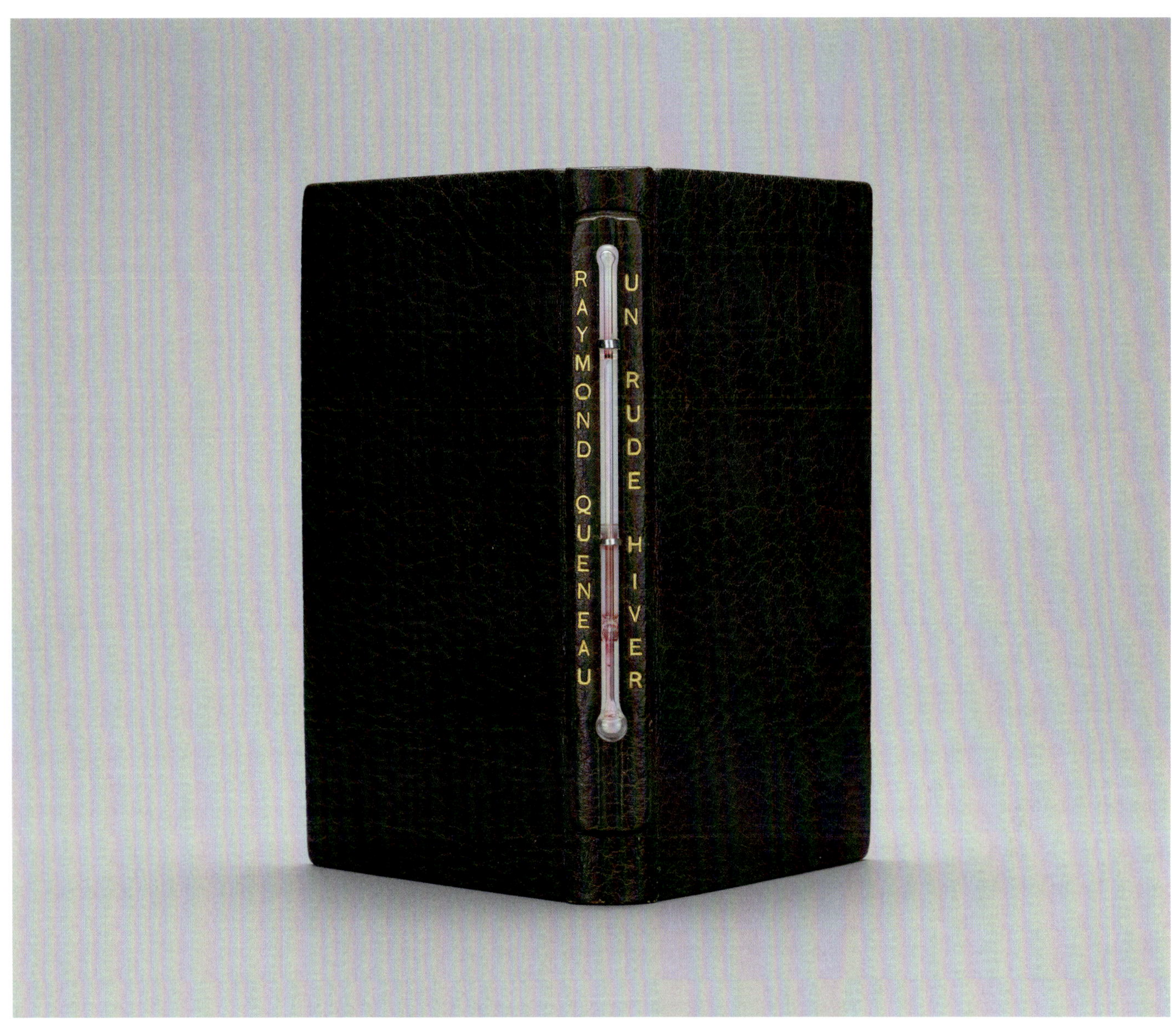

"It had never been so cold outside."

—Raymond Queneau

Fig. 77 Mary Reynolds (American, 1891–1950). *Un rude hiver* (*A Hard Winter*) by Raymond Queneau (Paris: Gallimard, 1939), 1939–42 or 1945–50.

Full goatskin with leather-covered, raised panel; inset glass thermometer; and gold stamping. Ivory Japanese endpapers, goatskin doublures with blue- and red-goatskin onlays, top edge gilt; 19 × 13 × 2.5 cm (7½ × 5⅛ × 1 in.). The Art Institute of Chicago, Ryerson and Burnham Libraries, Mary Reynolds Collection, 2019.931.

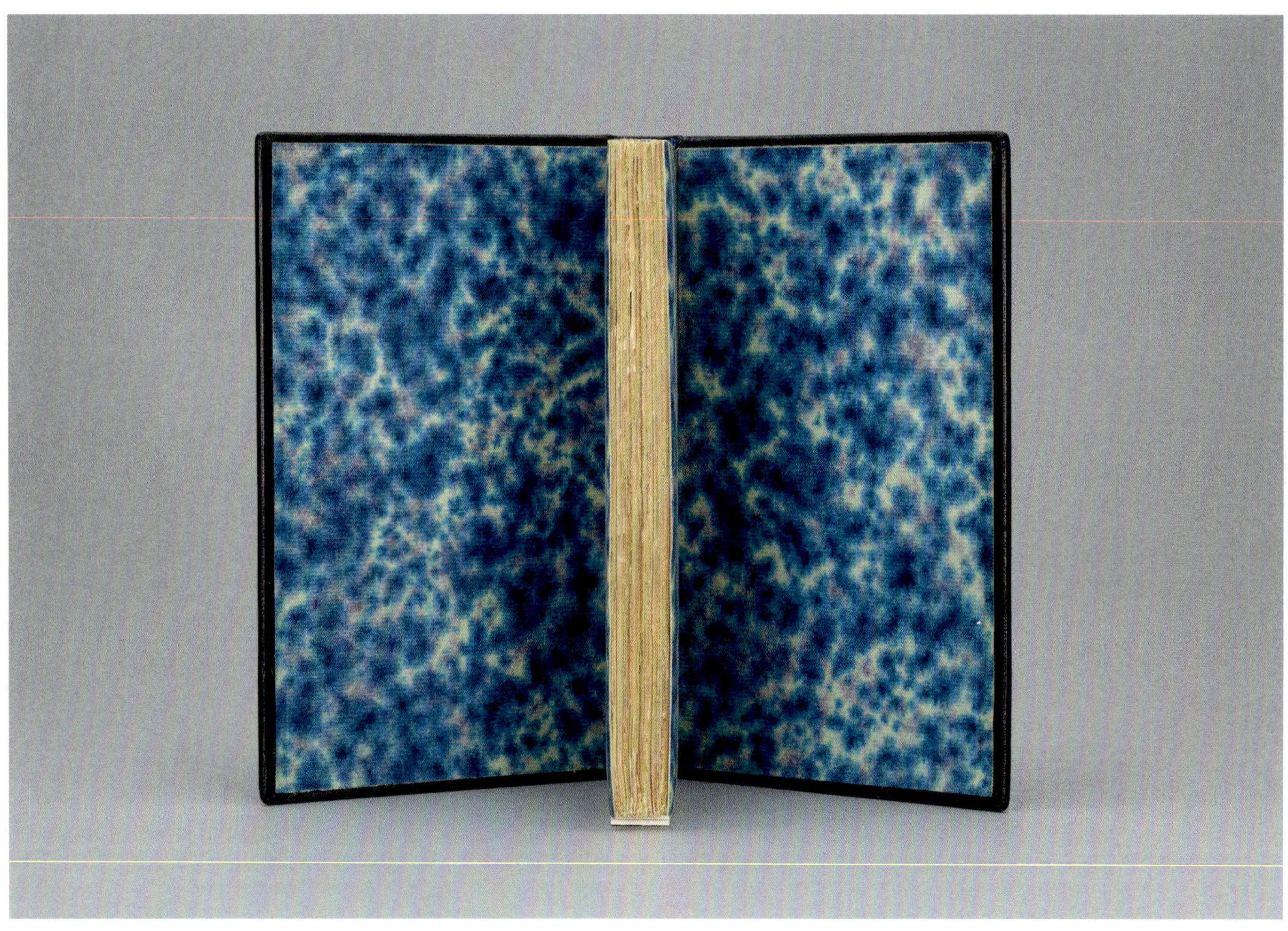

"Better a mad life than a reasonable death!"
"Oh, you know, your paradoxes don't impress me."

—Raymond Queneau

Fig. 78 Mary Reynolds (American, 1891–1950). *Les derniers jours* (*The Last Days*) **by Raymond Queneau (Paris: Gallimard, 1936), 1936–42 or 1945–50.**

Full black calfskin with raised bands and gold stamping. Agate-marbled laid-paper endpapers; 19.2 × 12.3 × 2.7 cm (7½ × 4¹³⁄₁₆ × 1¹⁄₁₆ in.). The Art Institute of Chicago, Ryerson and Burnham Libraries, Mary Reynolds Collection, 2024.855.

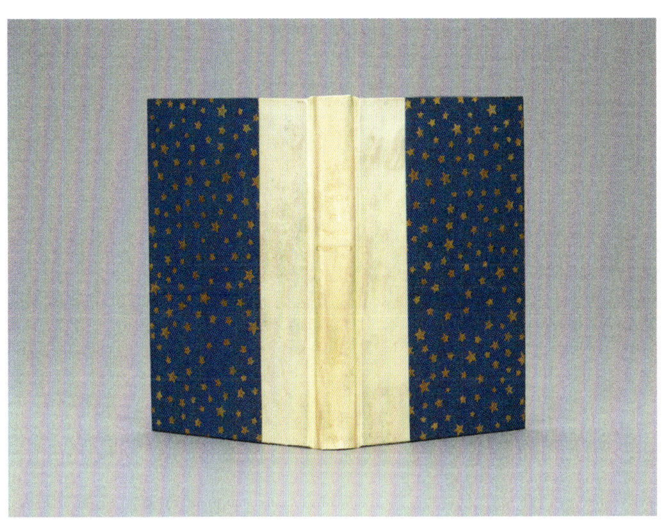

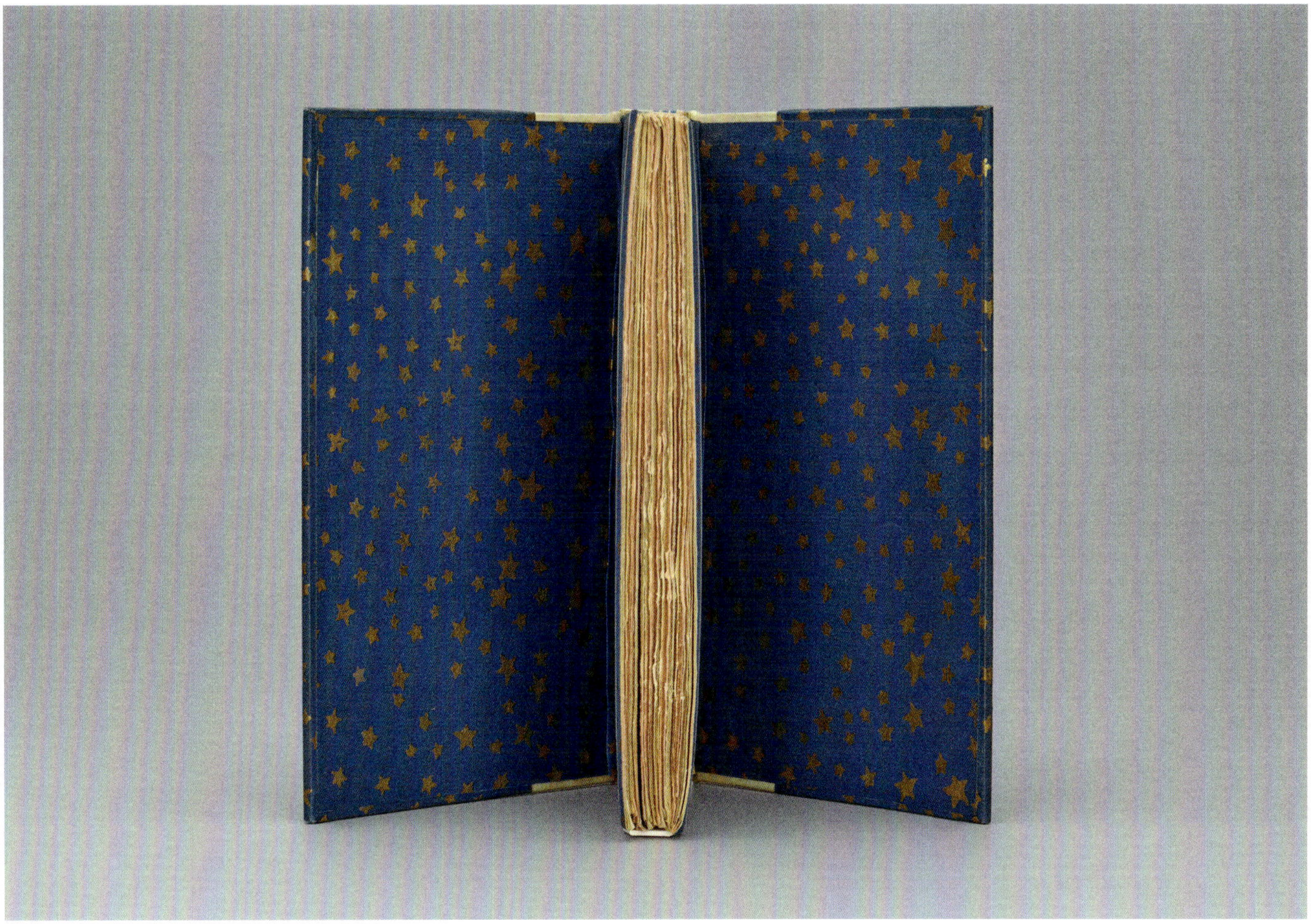

Fig. 79 Mary Reynolds (American, 1891–1950). *Thomas l'imposteur* **by Jean Cocteau (Paris: Librairie Gallimard, Éditions de La Nouvelle Revue Française, 1923), 1930–42.**

Quarter vellum with blue-paper sides and endpapers decorated with gold stars; 19 × 12 × 2.7 cm (7½ × 4¾ × 1¹⁄₁₆ in.).
The Art Institute of Chicago, Ryerson and Burnham Libraries, Mary Reynolds Collection, 2024.863.

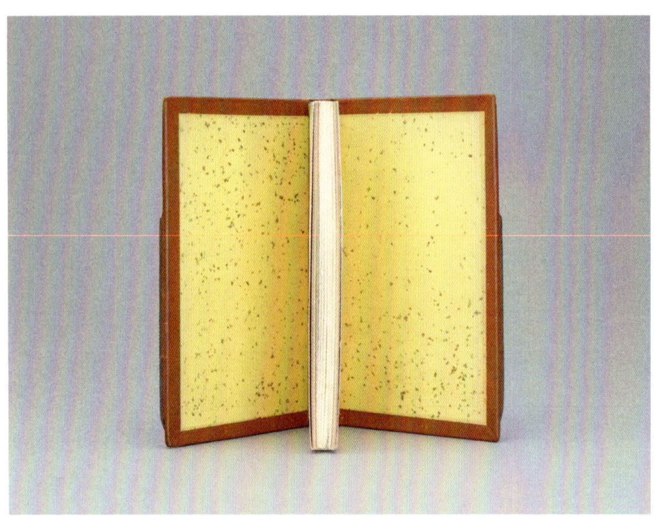

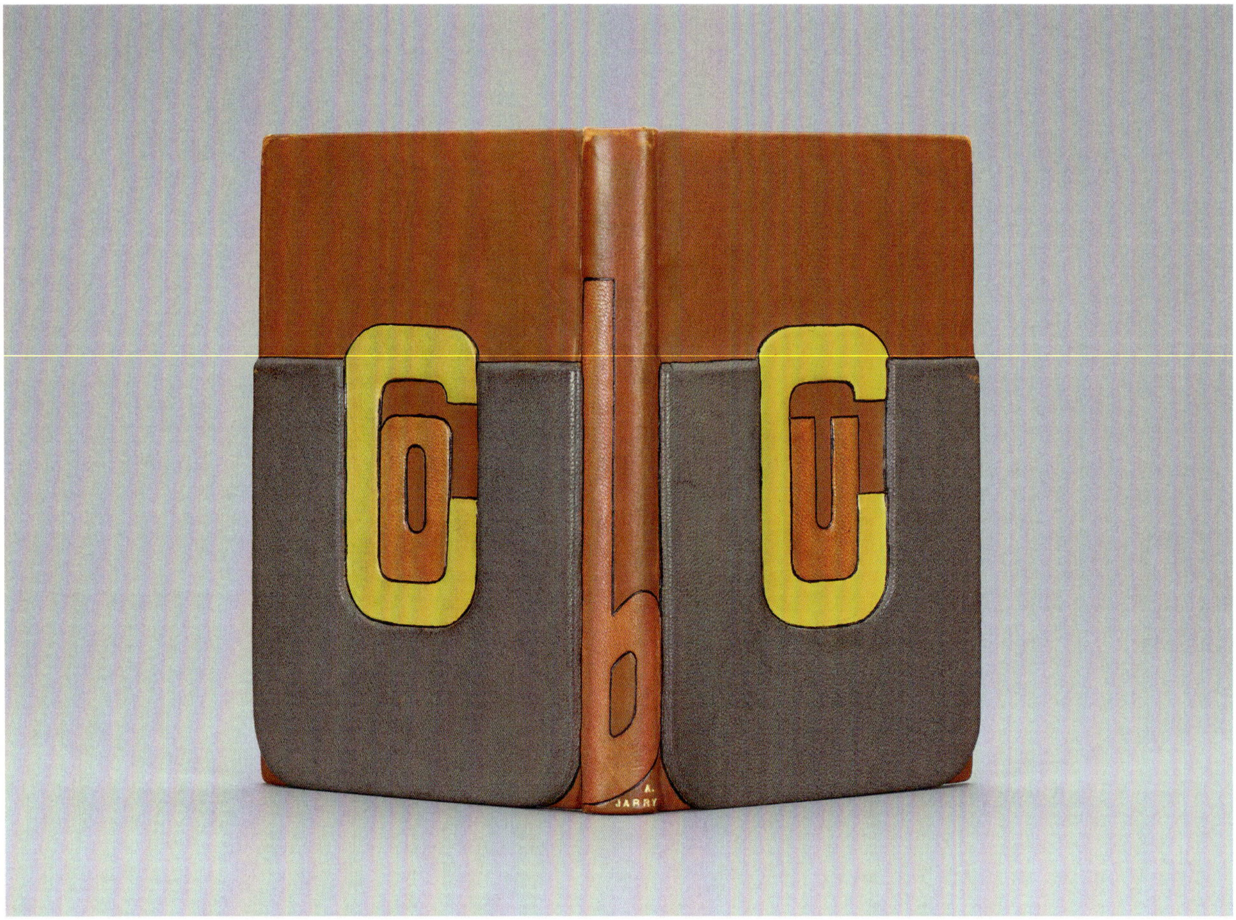

Fig. 80 Mary Reynolds (American, 1891–1950). *Ubu cocu (Ubu Cuckolded)* **by Alfred Jarry (Paris-Genève: Éditions des Trois Collines, 1944), 1945–50.**

Full tan calfskin with leather-covered cutouts, goatskin onlays spelling *Ubu* and *Cocu*, and gold stamping. Gold-speckled, yellow endpapers; 19 × 12.2 × 2.2 cm (7½ × 4¹³⁄₁₆ × ⅞ in.). The Art Institute of Chicago, Ryerson and Burnham Libraries, Mary Reynolds Collection, 2019.181.

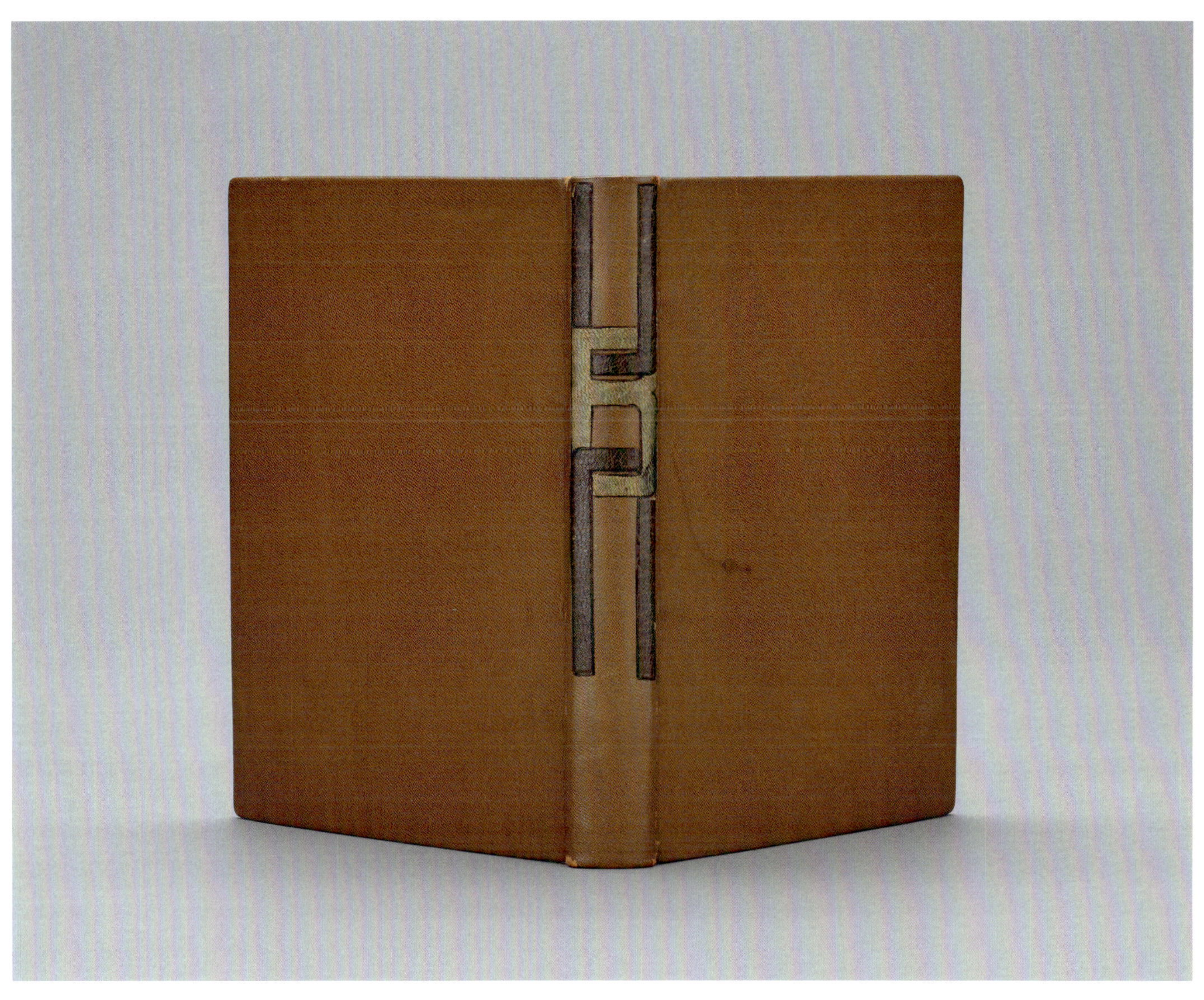

Fig. 81 Mary Reynolds (American, 1891–1950). *Ubu enchaîné* (*Ubu in Chains*) **by Alfred Jarry (Paris: Imprimerie de Rocroy, 1937), 1937–42.**

Full tan calfskin with leather-covered cutouts, goatskin onlays spelling *Ubu,* and gold stamping. Gold-speckled, yellow endpapers; 19 × 12.2 × 2.2 cm (7½ × 4¹³⁄₁₆ × ⅞ in.). The Art Institute of Chicago, Ryerson and Burnham Libraries, Mary Reynolds Collection, 2019.182.

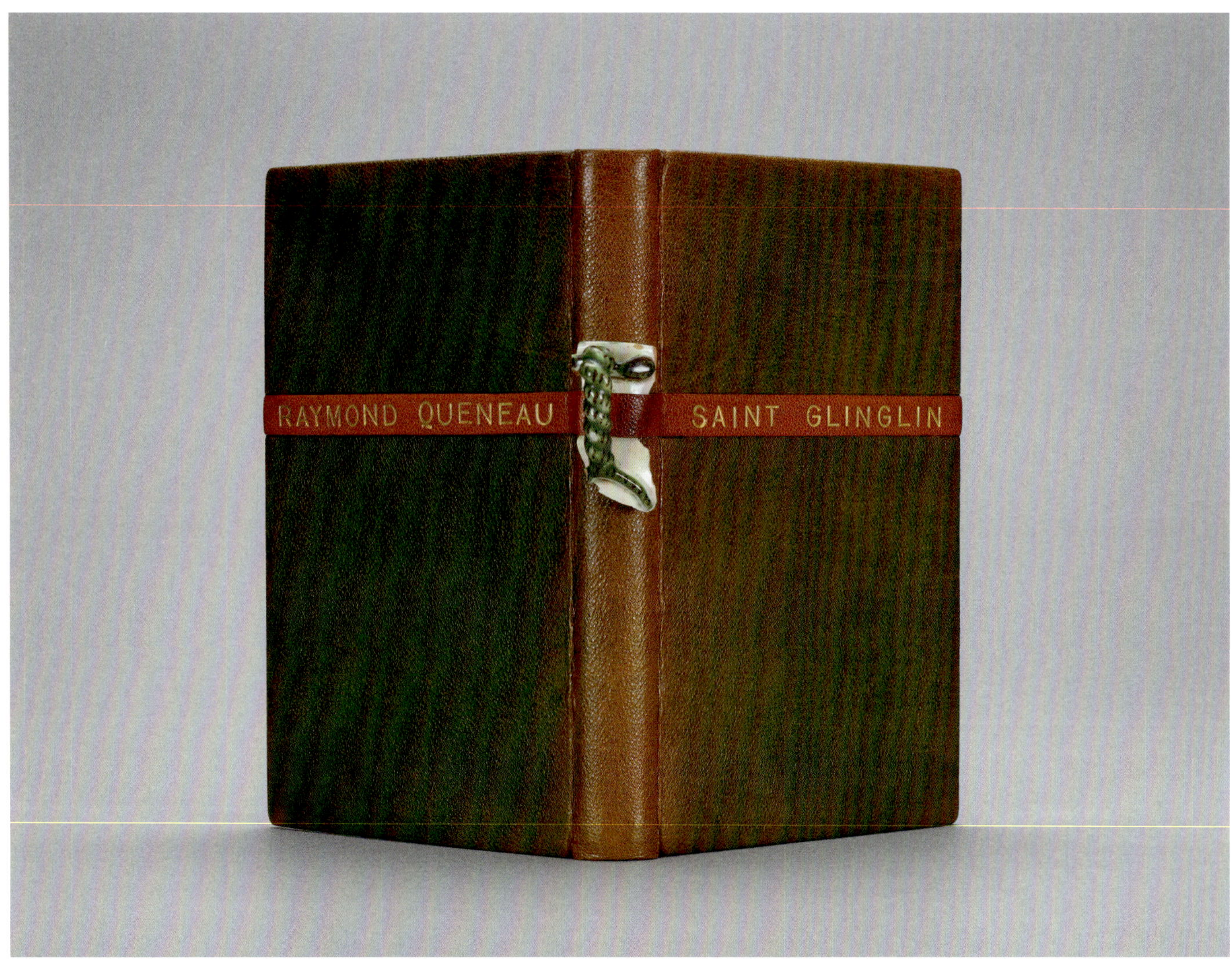

"Zostril raised his golf club and with a single vigorous blow smashed at least 203 plates."

—Raymond Queneau

Fig. 82 Mary Reynolds (American, 1891–1950). *Saint Glinglin* by Raymond Queneau (Paris: Gallimard, 1949), 1949–50.

Full green goatskin with tan horizontal goatskin onlay, gold stamping, and broken china-teacup handle. Marbled endpapers; 20 × 15 × 3 cm (7⅞ × 5¹⁵⁄₁₆ × 1³⁄₁₆ in.). The Art Institute of Chicago, Ryerson and Burnham Libraries, Mary Reynolds Collection, 2019.932.

Fig. 83 Mary Reynolds (American, 1891–1950) and Marcel Duchamp (American, born France, 1887–1968). *Anthologie de l'humour noir* (*Anthology of Black Humor*), **edited by André Breton (Paris: Sagittaire, 1940), about 1945.**

Full brown, embossed goatskin with brown, embossed calfskin strap and gold stamping on spine. Printed endpapers. Brown-leather slipcase with paper-thin red cedar wood; 22.8 × 15.7 × 2.5 cm (9 × 6³⁄₁₆ × 1 in.). The Art Institute of Chicago, Ryerson and Burnham Libraries, Mary Reynolds Collection, through prior gift of Robert A. Lewis; and anonymous gift, 2024.842.

"Mexico, moreover, with its splendid funeral toys, stands as the chosen land of black humor."

—André Breton

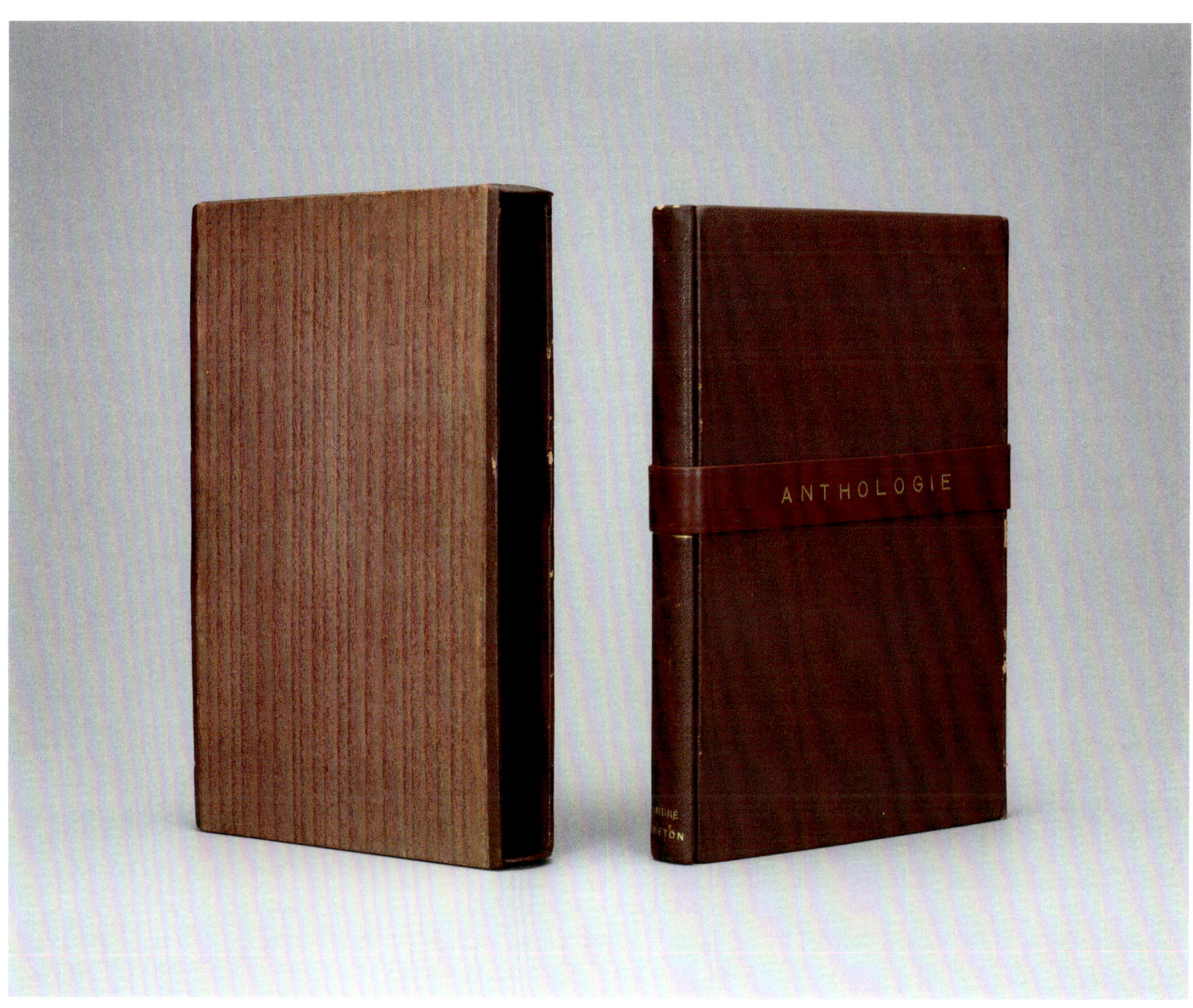

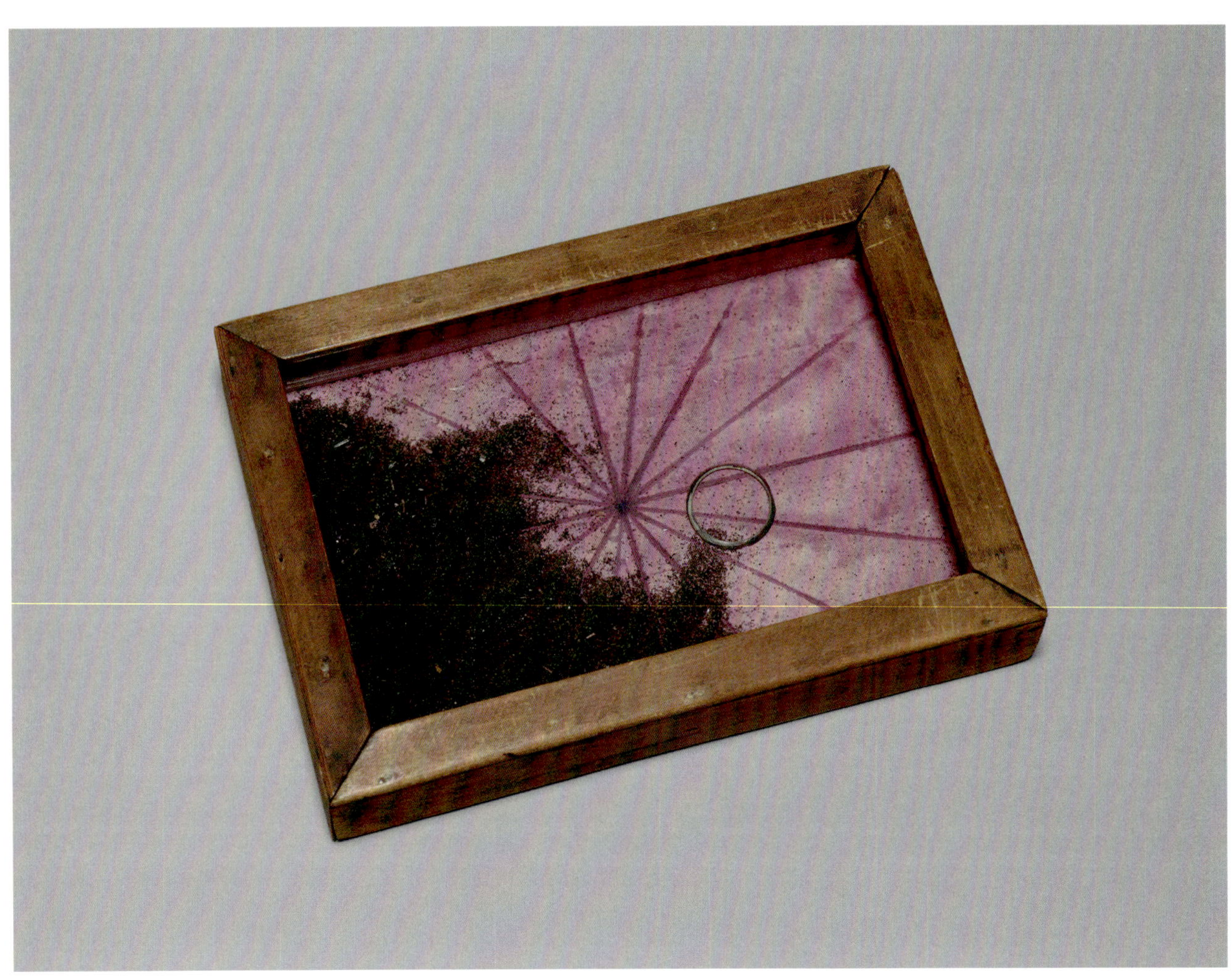

Fig. 84 Joseph Cornell (American, 1903–1972). *Untitled (Sand Box),* **about 1944.**

Glass-paned, painted-wood box with black sand, metal ring, and ball bearings; 26 × 18.1 cm (10¼ × 7⅛ in.). The Art Institute of Chicago, gift of Frank B. Hubachek, 1951.201.

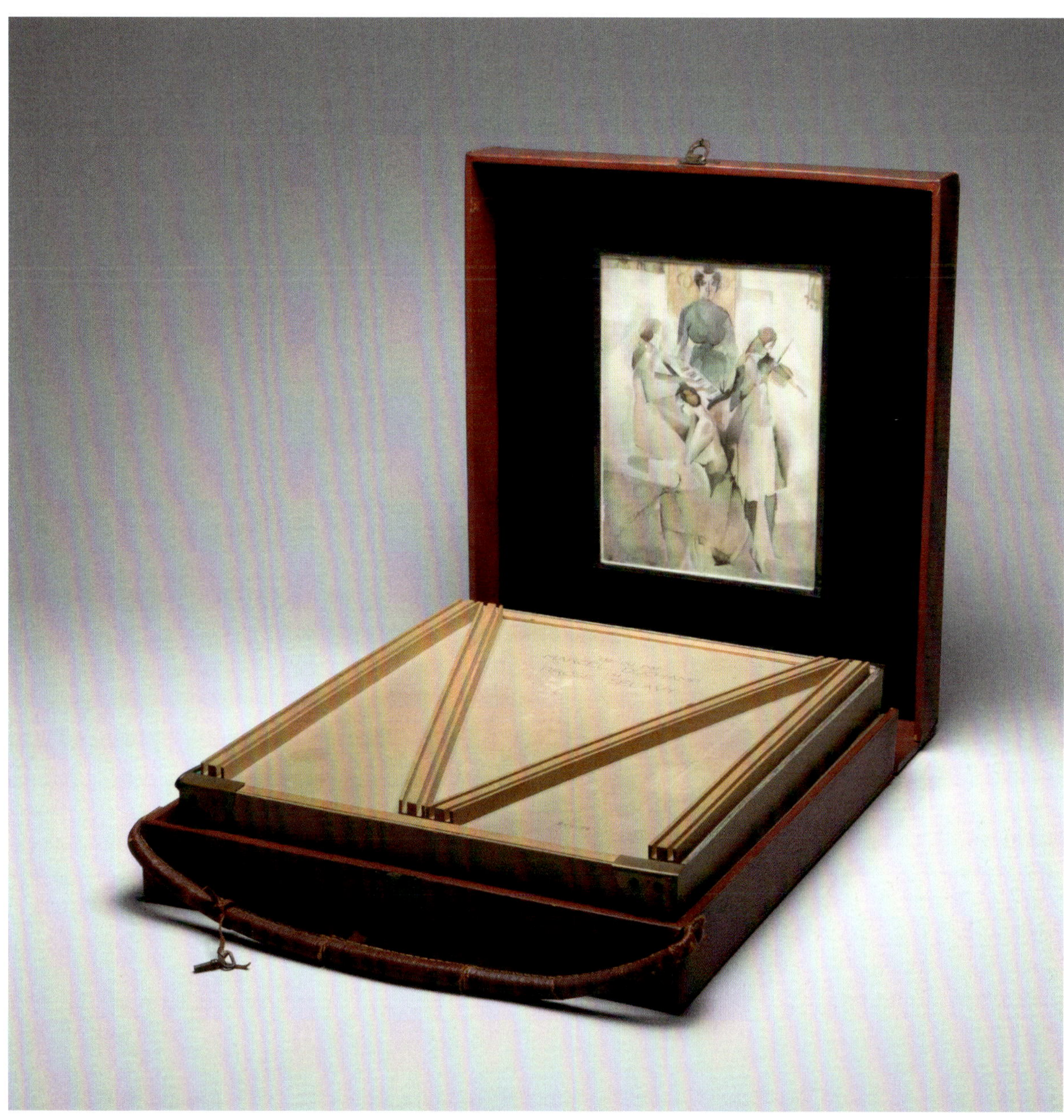

Fig. 85 Marcel Duchamp (American, born France, 1887–1968). *From or by Marcel Duchamp or Rrose Sélavy (The Box in a Valise)*, **Series A, 0/XX, 1941.**

Brown-leather valise with handle. Miniature replicas, printed reproductions, and one original, hand-colored collotype, *Sonate*, 1938. Dedication to Mary Reynolds, May 1941; case (closed): 9.4 × 38.5 × 41.2 cm (3¹¹⁄₁₆ × 15³⁄₁₆ × 16¼ in.); overall (opened): 40 × 38.5 × 91.7 cm (15¾ × 15³⁄₁₆ × 36⅛ in.). The Art Institute of Chicago, Ryerson and Burnham Libraries, Mary Reynolds Collection, 2019.158.

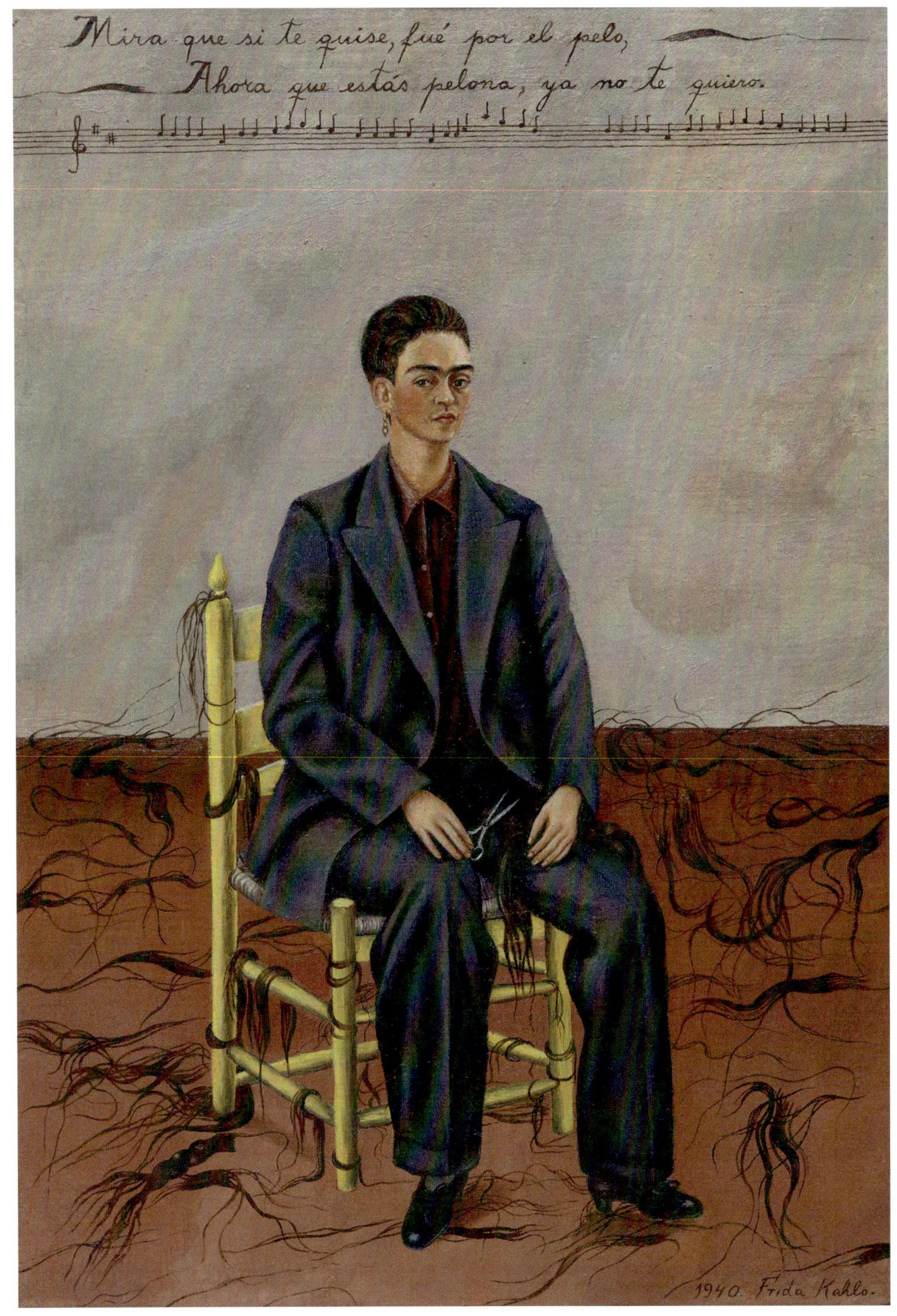

Fig. 86 Frida Kahlo (Mexican, 1907–1954). *Self-Portrait with Cropped Hair,* **1940.**

Oil on canvas; 40 x 27.9 cm (15¾ x 11 in.). The Museum of Modern Art, New York, gift of Edgar Kaufmann, Jr., 1943.

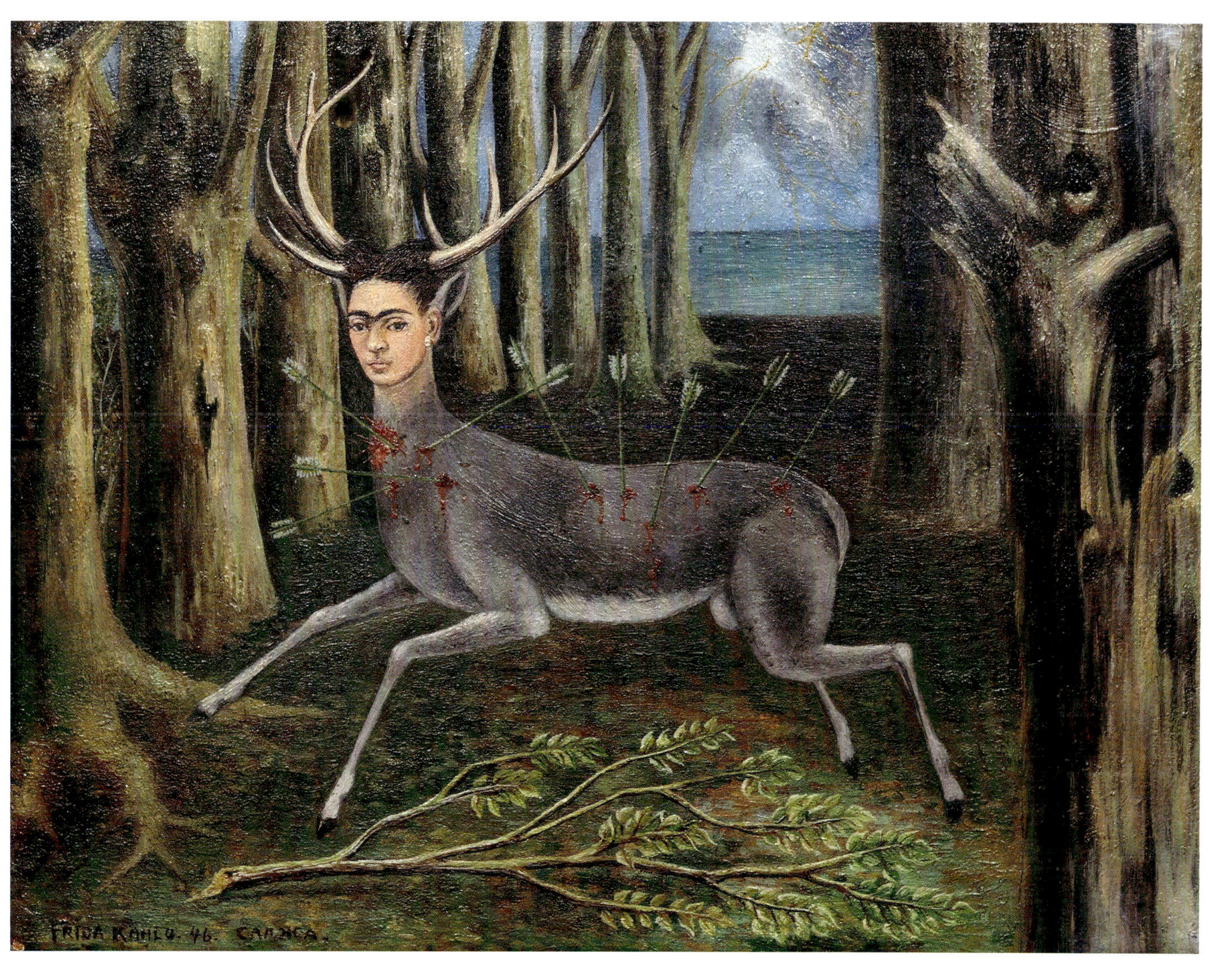

Fig. 87 Frida Kahlo (Mexican, 1907–1954). *The Wounded Deer*, 1946.

Oil on hardboard; 22.4 cm × 30 cm (8¹³⁄₁₆ in × 11¹³⁄₁₆ in.). Private collection.

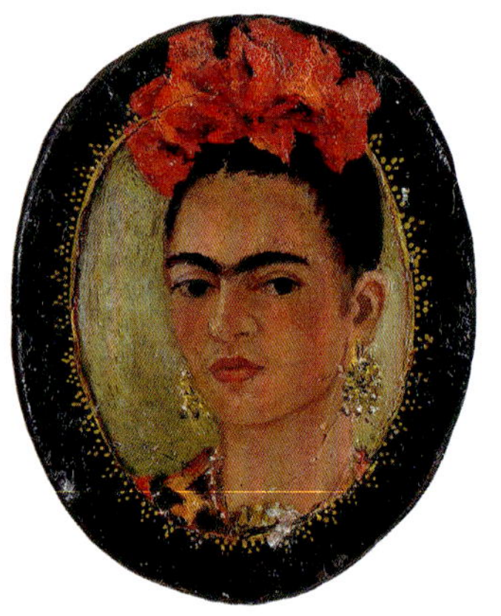

Fig. 88 Frida Kahlo (Mexican, 1907–1954).
Self-Portrait in Miniature, **about 1938.**

Oil on wood panel; 5 cm × 4 cm (2 × 1⅝ in.). Private collection.

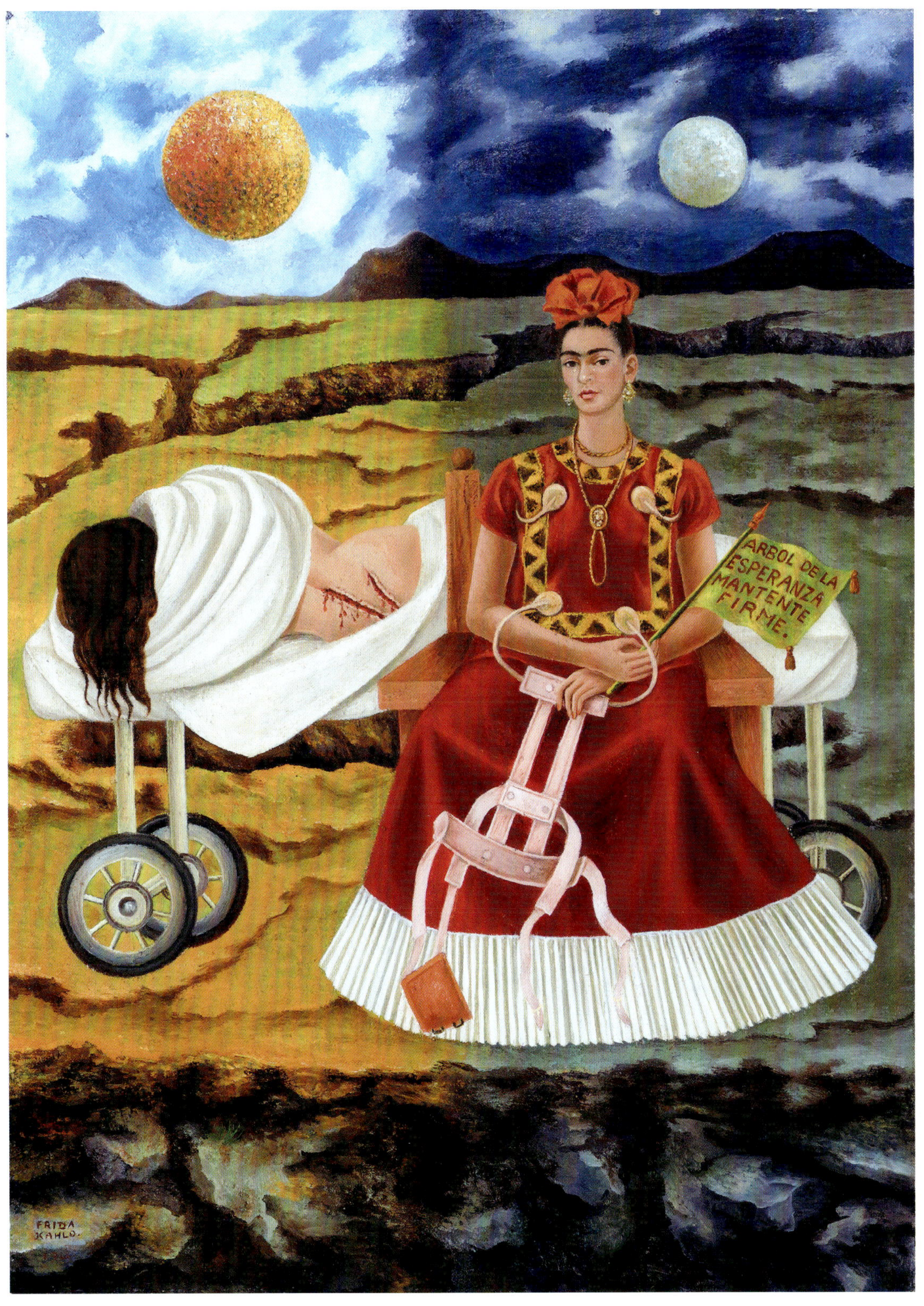

Fig. 89 Frida Kahlo (Mexican, 1907–1954). *Tree of Hope, Remain Strong, 1946.*

Oil on hardboard; 56 × 40.6 cm (22¹⁄₁₆ × 16 in.). Private collection.

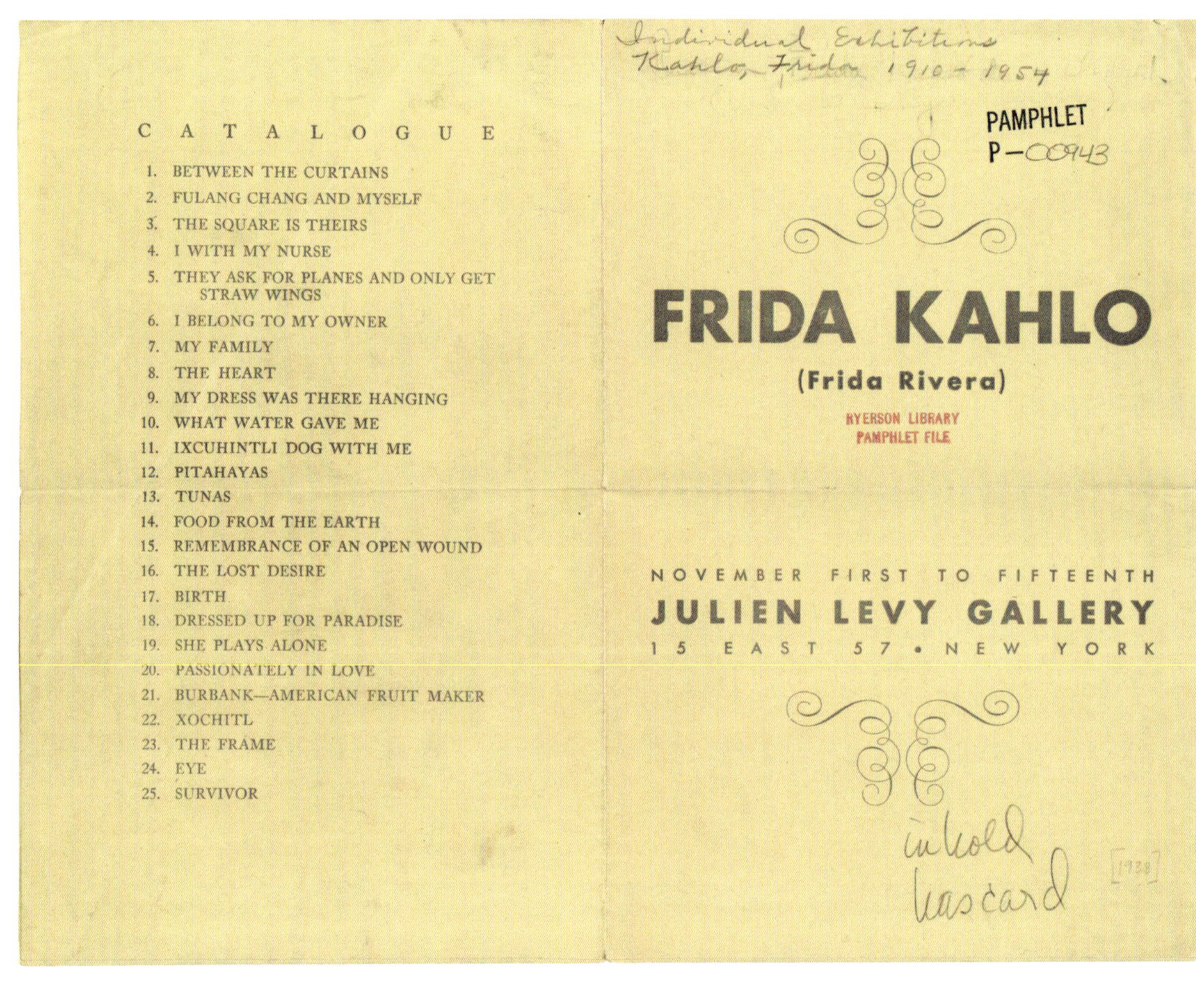

Fig. 90 Brochure for *Frida Kahlo (Frida Rivera)* at Julien Levy Gallery, New York, 1938.

The Art Institute of Chicago, Ryerson and Burnham Libraries.

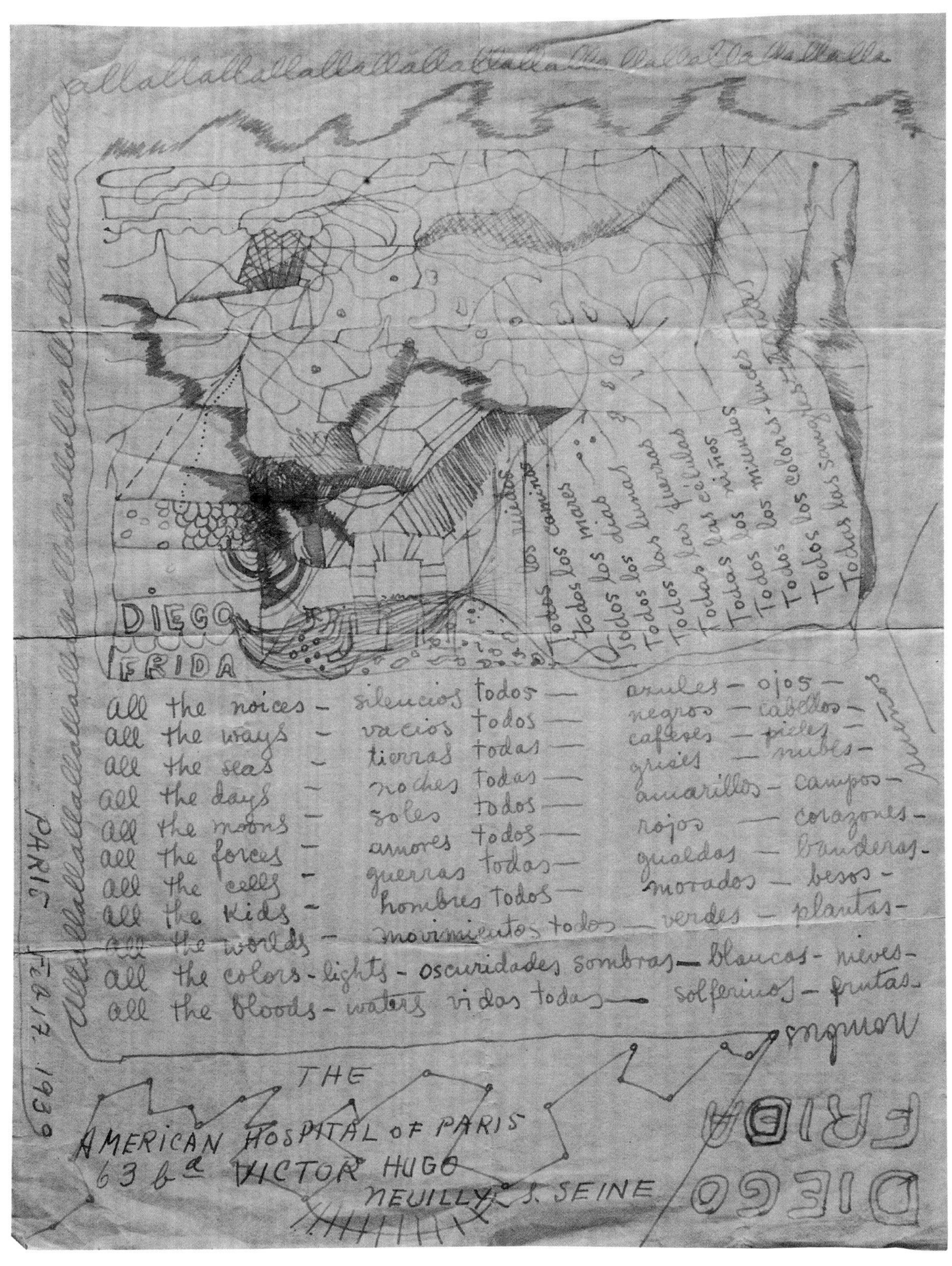

Fig. 91 Frida Kahlo (Mexican, 1907–1954). *Drawing of Paris Made at the American Hospital,* 1939.

Ink on paper; 26.7 × 20.9 cm (10½ × 8¼ in.). Museo Frida Kahlo, Mexico City.

— 65 —

*scram from here.

My ticket will last for a long time but I already have acomodations for the "Isle de France" on the 8 of March. I hope I can take this boat. In any case I won't stay here longer than the 15th of March. To hell with the exibition in London. To hell with every thing concerning Breton and all this lousy place. I want to go back to you. I miss every movement of your being, your voice, your eyes, your hands, your beautiful mouth, your laugh so clear and honest. YOU I love you my Nick. I am so happy to think I love you — to think you wait for me — you love me. —

My darling give many kisses to Mam on my name, I never forget her. Kiss also Aria and Lea. For you, my heart full of tenderness and caresse. One special kiss on your neck. Your

Xochitl. —

give my love to Mary. I swear if you see her and to Ruzzy

at the sculpture near the ~~kissing~~ fire place.
I see clearly, the spring jumping on the air,
and I can hear your laugh – just like a
child's laugh, when you got it right. Oh
my darling Nick I adore you so much. I
need you so, that my heart hurts.

I imagine Blanche will be here the first
week of March. I will be so happy to see
her because she is a real person, sweet
and sincere, and she is to me like a part
of yourself.

How ~~are~~ Aria and Lea? Please give my love
to them. Also give my love to the Kid Ruzzi,
tell him that he is a ~~swell~~ swell guy.

My darling, do you need any thing from Paris?
please tell me, I will be so happy to get you any
thing you may need.

If Eugenia phones you, please tell her that I
lost her adress and that is why I didnt write.
How is that wench?
If you see Rosemary give her lots of kisses. She
is O.K. To Mary Sklar lots of love. I miss
her very much.

To you, my loveliest Nick, all my heart. blood
and all my being. I adore you. Frida.

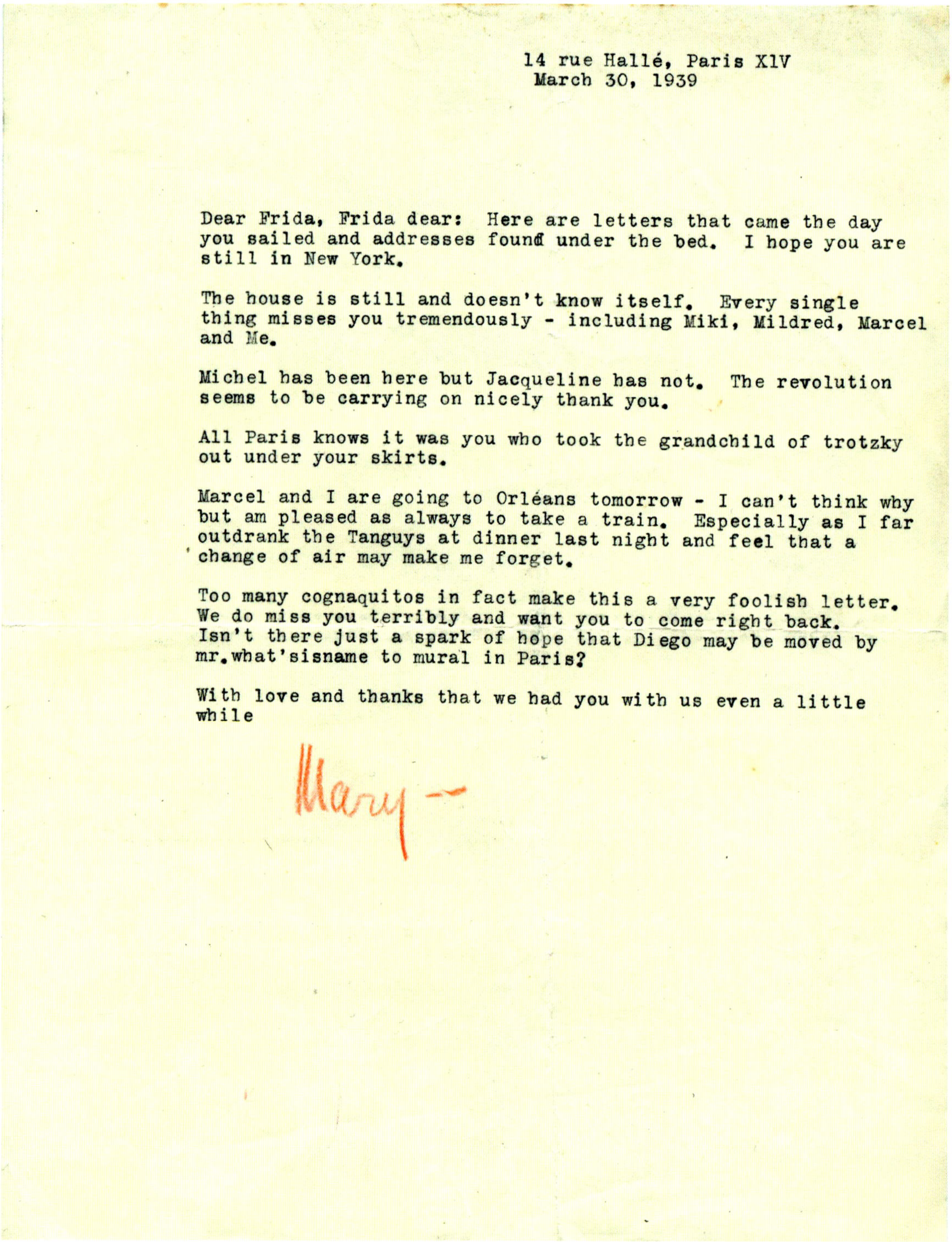

                                        14 rue Hallé, Paris X1V
                                        March 30, 1939

        Dear Frida, Frida dear: Here are letters that came the day
        you sailed and addresses found under the bed. I hope you are
        still in New York.

        The house is still and doesn't know itself. Every single
        thing misses you tremendously - including Miki, Mildred, Marcel
        and Me.

        Michel has been here but Jacqueline has not. The revolution
        seems to be carrying on nicely thank you.

        All Paris knows it was you who took the grandchild of trotzky
        out under your skirts.

        Marcel and I are going to Orléans tomorrow - I can't think why
        but am pleased as always to take a train. Especially as I far
        outdrank the Tanguys at dinner last night and feel that a
        change of air may make me forget.

        Too many cognaquitos in fact make this a very foolish letter.
        We do miss you terribly and want you to come right back.
        Isn't there just a spark of hope that Diego may be moved by
        mr. what'sisname to mural in Paris?

        With love and thanks that we had you with us even a little
        while

                        Mary -

Fig. 94 Mary Reynolds to Frida Kahlo, March 30, 1939.

Museo Frida Kahlo, Mexico City, Archivo Diego Rivera y Frida Kahlo.

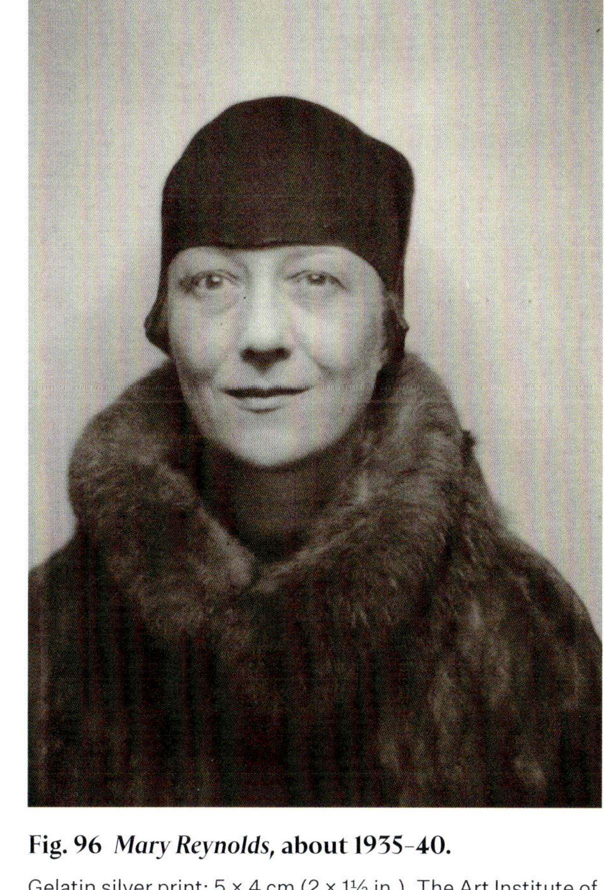

Fig. 96 *Mary Reynolds,* **about 1935–40.**

Gelatin silver print; 5 × 4 cm (2 × 1½ in.). The Art Institute of Chicago Archives, Mary Reynolds Collection, gift of Marjorie Watkins, October 1992.

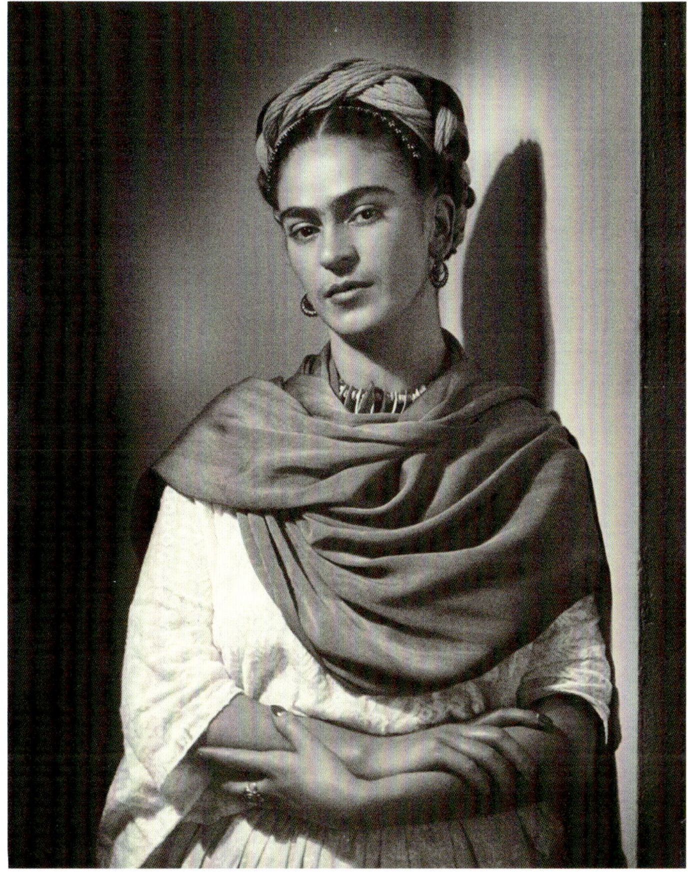

Fig. 95 Nickolas Muray (American, born Hungary, 1892–1965). *Frida Kahlo,* **1938.**

Gelatin silver print; 24.1 × 19.1 cm (9½ x 7½ in.). Private collection.

Lives in Parallel: A Chronology, 1891–1954

Tamar Kharatishvili and Alivé Piliado Santana

Frida Kahlo (1907–1954)		**Mary Reynolds (1891–1950)**
	1891	On October 19 Mary Louise Hubachek is born in Minneapolis. Her father, Frank Rudolph Hubachek, is a lawyer, her mother, Nellie Brookes Hubachek, a homemaker.
	1894	On August 10 Reynolds's brother, Frank Brookes Hubachek, is born in Minneapolis. Known as "Brookes," he is Reynolds's only sibling.
On July 6 Magdalena Carmen Frida Kahlo y Calderón is born in Coyoacán, Mexico City. Her father, Guillermo Kahlo, is a photographer, her mother, Matilde Calderón y González, a homemaker. Kahlo is the couple's third daughter.	**1907**	Reynolds attends Minneapolis public schools.
On June 7 Kahlo's youngest sister, Cristina, is born.	**1908**	
On November 10 the Mexican Revolution begins.	**1910**	
Although Kahlo's father is a former employee of the deposed president Porfirio Díaz, her mother supports the revolutionaries and welcomes them into the family home.	**1913**	Reynolds graduates with a bachelor of arts degree from Vassar College in Poughkeepsie, New York, having completed courses in art, chemistry, English, French, geology, German, mathematics, and psychology.
Kahlo becomes familiar with the work of José Guadalupe Posada, whose prints she encounters in the Coyoacán market.	**1914**	Reynolds enrolls in postgraduate courses at the University of Minnesota in Minneapolis, where Brookes is also a student at the time.
Due to the revolution, Kahlo's father loses his government photographic contracts, and the family struggles financially.	**1916**	Reynolds designs her own woodblock bookplate with a pastoral vignette. On July 24 Mary weds Matthew Givens Reynolds. Although Matthew is from St. Louis, the couple decides to move to Greenwich Village in New York, where Matthew accepts a position with an English insurance company specializing in ocean shipping.

| | 1917 | In November Matthew enlists in the US Army and is deployed to the Western Front of World War I. Stationed in France, he commands a field artillery unit with the Thirtieth Infantry Division. |

Kahlo contracts polio. One of her legs is left weaker than the other, affecting her mobility and causing chronic pain for the rest of her life.

1918

1919 On January 10 Matthew dies of pneumonia while in Luxembourg. Reynolds returns to Minneapolis and enters a period of mourning. Her parents encourage her to remarry and start a family. Instead, she moves back to New York and from there decides to travel to Europe.

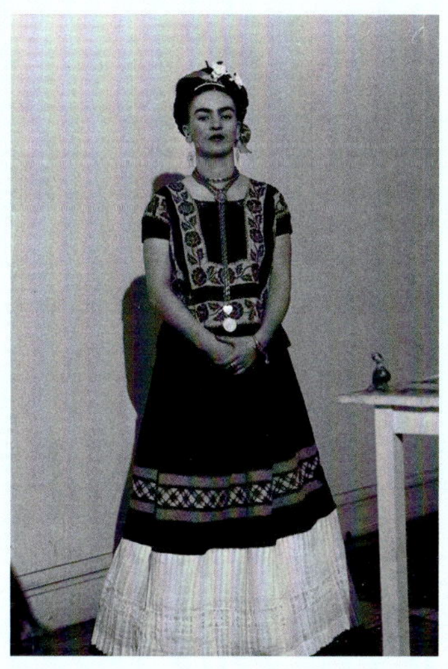

Fig. 97 Dora Maar (French, 1907–1997). *Frida Kahlo*, 1939. Gelatin silver negative on glass support; 12 × 9 cm (4¾ × 3⁹⁄₁₆ in.). The Centre Pompidou, Paris, Cabinet de la photographie, AM 2004-0163 (187).

1921 On April 22 Reynolds applies for a US passport. In the application, she lists her profession as "decorator" and notes a desire to study art in Italy.

In November Reynolds arrives in Paris and rents an apartment at 14 rue de Montessuy, near the Eiffel Tower. She lives on her pension as a "war widow" and on the income from a modest trust established by her parents. She spends much of her time in Montparnasse, becoming active in the neighborhood's artistic circles. She meets American artist Man Ray, who had arrived in the French capital that summer, and the two become close friends.

Kahlo enrolls at the Escuela Nacional Preparatoria in downtown Mexico City, aspiring to study medicine. At the time, Diego Rivera is completing his first mural, *La Creación*, in the school's amphitheater.

On November 30 Kahlo's poem "Recuerdo" appears in the newspaper *El Universal Ilustrado* as her first publication.

1922 Reynolds meets American art collector Peggy Guggenheim.

1923 Reynolds and Guggenheim tour Egypt and Italy together.

On May 15 Reynolds travels to London and is present for the birth of Guggenheim's first child, Michael Cedric Sinbad Vail.

Reynolds begins a relationship with French artist Marcel Duchamp.

While Rivera works on his mural cycle for the Ministry of Public Education in Mexico City, Kahlo frequently visits the adjacent Ibero-American Library to read.

1924 In May Reynolds begins spending time with French author Henri-Pierre Roché, who introduces her to Constantin Brancusi at the sculptor's studio at the Impasse Ronsin. Roché becomes Reynolds's confidant, supporting her through Duchamp's dalliances with other women.

1925

In September Kahlo is riding in a bus when it collides with a streetcar. She is grievously injured, and the accident affects her physical health for the rest of her life. After a month recovering in the hospital, Kahlo spends three months in bed at home and is forced to abandon her studies. Her mother places a mirror above her bed and installs a custom easel so that Kahlo can look at herself and make self-portraits. Using this contraption, Kahlo first begins to paint.

Man Ray takes the first of many photographs of Reynolds.

1926

In September Kahlo completes her first self-portrait, *Self-Portrait in a Velvet Dress* (1926; private collection, Mexico City).

1927

On June 7 Duchamp marries Lydie Sarazin-Levassor. The marriage is short-lived, ending in divorce in January the following year. After the divorce, his relationship with Reynolds resumes and becomes public.

1928

Kahlo joins the Mexican Communist Party.

Kahlo meets Rivera and begins visiting him while he works on murals, seeking his opinion on her paintings and drawings.

1929

On August 21 Kahlo and Rivera marry in Coyoacán. Later that year she sells her first painting when US industrialist and collector Jackson Cole Phillips buys *Two Women* (1928; Museum of Fine Arts, Boston).

Kahlo distances herself from the Mexican Communist Party after it expels Rivera.

Kahlo becomes pregnant for the first time. She loses the pregnancy in the first trimester.

Reynolds begins studying bookbinding in the atelier of Pierre Legrain. Legrain works with Reynolds for a year, imparting an interest in bookbindings that incorporate animal skins, patterns, and prints.

1930

In November Kahlo accompanies Rivera to San Francisco, where he is commissioned to paint murals for the California School of Fine Arts and the Pacific Stock Exchange. They both engage with the Bay Area arts community. Kahlo meets Dr. Leo Eloesser, who diagnoses her with lumbar scoliosis. He continues to treat Kahlo and remains a close friend for the rest of her life.

1931

In May Kahlo returns to Mexico while Rivera remains in San Francisco. She meets Hungarian-born American photographer Nickolas Muray through their mutual friend, Mexican artist Miguel Covarrubias. Kahlo and Muray begin an intermittent affair that lasts until 1940.

Later that year Kahlo returns to San Francisco and paints *Frieda and Diego Rivera* (p. 45, fig. 41), her first self-portrait with Rivera. She exhibits the work at the *Sixth Annual Exhibition of the San Francisco Society of Women Artists*. The work is given to Albert M. Bender.

In September Reynolds rents Villa Marguerite in Villefranche-sur-Mer on the French Riviera, where she stays with Duchamp. Brancusi joins them and brings his camera, and the trio appear in numerous photographs from the trip (see p. 4, fig. 1, and p. 37, fig. 32).

By the end of the year, Kahlo and Rivera go to New York for the first time on the occasion of Rivera's retrospective at the Museum of Modern Art.

1931

On April 21 Kahlo and Rivera travel to Michigan, where he is engaged to paint a mural cycle at the Detroit Institute of Arts.

During this time, Kahlo continues to create small-scale works that she does not exhibit. She also suffers another pregnancy loss, impacting both her physical and mental health.

In September Kahlo returns to Mexico to be with her mother as she nears death.

In October Kahlo rejoins Rivera in Detroit before they head together to New York, where Rivera has secured a commission at Rockefeller Center.

1932

Reynolds, Duchamp, Brancusi, pianist Vera Moore, and writer Ezra Pound are photographed at a gathering celebrating Brancusi's new fireplace at Impasse Ronsin (p. 46, fig. 42). A short film reel Brancusi made during the party is the only extant moving image of Reynolds.

In autumn Reynolds moves to a home at 24 rue Hallé in the fourteenth arrondissement.

On December 20, following the destruction of Rivera's mural in the lobby of the RCA Building at Rockefeller Center, Kahlo and Rivera move back to their house in San Ángel, Mexico City.

1933

Reynolds and Duchamp travel widely in Europe throughout the year.

Reynolds and Duchamp spend August and September in Spain, renting a house in Cadaqués to be near Portlligat, where their friends Salvador and Gala Dalí reside.

Kahlo moves out of the home she shares with Rivera after she discovers his affair with her sister Cristina.

In July Kahlo travels to New York with Anita Brenner. Upon her return, she undergoes another operation on her right foot, having had one the previous year.

By the end of the year, Kahlo reconciles with Rivera.

1935

Reynolds and Duchamp make their first collaborative binding, for Alfred Jarry's *Ubu roi* (*King Ubu*; p. 21, fig. 14).

Duchamp devises the designs that will lead to his Rotoreliefs. Reynolds uses trial printings of a cover for the Surrealist magazine *Minotaure* featuring these images as endpapers in two bindings, for Raymond Queneau's *Loin de Rueil* and Antoine de Saint-Exupery's *Night-Flight* (p. 53, figs. 50–51).

Together with Rivera, Kahlo participates in an anti-fascist demonstration in Mexico City.

Art collector Albert M. Bender gives the painting *Frieda and Diego Rivera* (p. 45, fig. 41) to the San Francisco Museum of Art, making it the first of Kahlo's works to enter a US museum collection.

1936

In February or March Reynolds exhibits bindings in London. She eventually has business cards made that read MARY REYNOLDS / RELIURE / 24, R. HALLÉ, PARIS XIV (p. 16, fig. 7).

Reynolds and Duchamp begin collaborating on a binding for *Hebdomeros* (p. 56, fig. 54), Giorgio de Chirico's only literary work.

On January 9 Kahlo travels to Tampico to meet Leon Trotsky and his wife, Natalia Sedova, who had arrived in Mexico as exiles with help from Rivera. They are hosted at Kahlo's family home in Coyoacán.

In September Kahlo exhibits her work for the first time in Mexico. The exhibition is a group show at the art gallery of the Social Action Department at the Universidad Nacional Autónoma de México in Mexico City.

1937

Reynolds and Duchamp travel to London and are photographed by Constantin Achillopoulos (p. 44, fig. 40).

On July 29 Reynolds and Duchamp travel to Copenhagen to buy leather, presumably for bookbindings.

Reynolds has kidney problems and is operated on at the American Hospital in Paris.

Kahlo paints *Pitahayas* (p. 72, fig. 72) and *The Frame* (p. 68, fig. 67).

From April to August Kahlo and Rivera host André Breton and Jacqueline Lamba in Mexico City. Breton delivers lectures at the Universidad Nacional and the Palacio de Bellas Artes.

In November, having been invited by Julien Levy to exhibit work at his gallery, Kahlo travels to New York for her first solo exhibition. During the run of the show, Levy makes a series of photographs of Kahlo (see p. 15, fig. 6). After seeing her work in the exhibition, collector A. Conger Goodyear commissions *Self-Portrait with Monkey* (p. 69, fig. 68).

1938

On January 17 Reynolds and Duchamp travel to London for the inaugural exhibition at Guggenheim Jeune, Peggy Guggenheim's gallery. They help install the show, which is dedicated to drawings by Jean Cocteau.

Reynolds begins renting a second property at 14 rue Hallé, a two-story home with a quiet back garden. She and Duchamp collaborate on the décor, and the home becomes a hub for their community of artists.

On January 14 Kahlo travels from New York to France aboard the SS *Paris*, disembarking in Le Havre on January 21.

In early February Kahlo develops a kidney infection. She spends three weeks in the American Hospital in Paris. Having met Reynolds just days before becoming ill, Kahlo accepts an invitation to stay at her home at 14 rue Hallé.

On March 10 the exhibition *Mexique*, featuring Kahlo's paintings, opens at Galerie Renou et Colle in Paris to great acclaim.

On March 25, having arranged for her paintings to be deinstalled before the close of *Mexique*, Kahlo sets sail for New York aboard the SS *Normandie*.

On April 6 Kahlo returns to Mexico City. Muray visits her in the following months.

In September Kahlo welcomes Alice Rahon and Wolfgang Paalen to Mexico City, as Paalen begins to organize the *International Exhibition of Surrealism*.

After a tumultuous period in their relationship, Rivera and Kahlo divorce on November 6.

1939

In February Reynolds and Duchamp meet Kahlo through Walter Pach. Duchamp assists André Breton with preparations for Kahlo's participation in the exhibition *Mexique* at Galerie Renou et Colle.

On February 2 Reynolds helps Kahlo obtain treatment at the American Hospital in Paris.

On February 22 Reynolds begins hosting Kahlo at 14 rue Hallé while she prepares for the exhibition *Mexique*.

Reynolds sends a farewell letter to Kahlo on March 30, after Kahlo leaves Paris (p. 94, fig. 94).

In January the *International Exhibition of Surrealism* opens at Galería de Arte Mexicano in Mexico City. Kahlo exhibits two monumental works, *La Mesa Herida* (1940; location unknown) and *Las dos Fridas* (1940; Museo de Arte Moderno, Mexico City).

On December 8 Kahlo and Rivera remarry at San Francisco City Hall, shortly after he completes the mural *The Marriage of the Artistic Expression of the North and of the South on this Continent*, known as *Pan American Unity*, created for the Golden Gate International Exposition. As part of this world's fair, Kahlo exhibits *Food from the Earth* (p. 73, fig. 73) in the *Contemporary Mexican Painting and Graphic Art* show at the Palace of Fine Arts.

1940

On May 10 Germany invades France.

On June 14 the Nazi occupation of Paris begins.

As Reynolds's and Duchamp's friends begin to leave Paris, Reynolds stays behind. From October her home is used for the safekeeping of artworks, especially those by Man Ray and Brancusi.

Reynolds begins work on a binding for Duchamp's *Rrose Sélavy* (p. 48, fig. 44) using trial blind stamps of a letterpress block he made for his *Box in a Valise* (p. 85, fig. 85).

Kahlo continues to work on commissions from US-based collectors. Her work is exhibited in the group exhibition *Modern Mexican Painters* at the Institute of Modern Art in Boston.

In October Kahlo takes part in the exhibition *First Papers of Surrealism*, organized by Breton and designed by Duchamp, at Madison Avenue Gallery in New York.

Kahlo is invited to join the founding group of Seminario de Cultura Mexicana. On November 20 her work is displayed in the group's inaugural exhibition at Palacio de Bellas Artes.

In December Kahlo's *Self-Portrait with Braid* (1941; The Jacques and Natasha Gelman Collection of Twentieth-Century Mexican Art) is included in the exhibition *20th Century Portraits* at the Museum of Modern Art in New York.

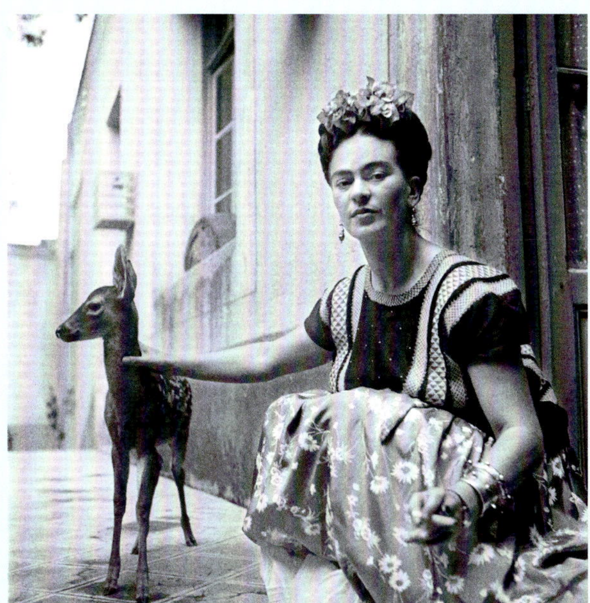

Fig. 98 Nickolas Muray (American, born Hungary, 1892–1965). *Frida with Granizo*, 1939. Platinum print; 27.9 × 26.7 cm (11 × 10½ in.). Private collection, Dallas.

1941

In an April 22 letter to Brookes, Duchamp announces that he has managed to procure a permit allowing him to travel into the Unoccupied Zone, valid for three months and multiple trips. He intends to return to Paris whenever possible to visit Reynolds, lamenting her stubborn refusal to leave 14 rue Hallé. Reynolds adds a few lines to the letter, explaining her position: "Don't worry, no torture, no boats for six months. . . . Conditions acceptable here."

On May 29 Reynolds sends the following message to Brookes: "Could not cross ocean, too scared, very comfortable here."

Reynolds joins the French Resistance with the code name *Douce Mary* (Gentle Mary).

1942

Reynolds still refuses to leave Paris, despite Duchamp's repeated attempts to have her join him in various cities in the Unoccupied Zone.

In a November letter to Brookes, Reynolds describes life as "reduced to its most primitive form." She spends her time tracking down food and offering aid. Her home becomes a hiding place for documents related to the French Resistance.

Reynolds ceases her work as a bookbinder, not to resume until 1945.

Artist Jean Hélion, who had recently escaped from a Nazi prisoner of war camp, hides for ten days at 14 rue Hallé.

By spring 1942 it is apparent that 14 rue Hallé is under Gestapo observation. According to Brookes, several of Reynolds's compatriots active in the French Resistance are caught and killed. Brookes describes Reynolds witnessing "two carloads of armed Gestapo soldiers" surrounding her house.

In September Reynolds escapes to Lyon, France, illegally crossing the Line of Occupation. She spends eight weeks there, waiting for her exit visa. She eventually makes her way to Pau, France, from where she hopes to reach Spain. Alongside two Jewish men, one Jewish boy, and a mountain guide, Reynolds traverses the Pyrenees on foot, carrying only essentials. Two of the refugees are arrested at the Spanish border, and Reynolds is held for questioning for six days.

Reynolds arrives in Madrid on December 14 and cables her brother to inform him of her escape. Relaying the news to Duchamp, Brookes describes receiving the cable as "getting her back from the dead." Reynolds begins arrangements to fly to New York.

Edgar Kaufmann Jr. gives Kahlo's painting *Self-Portrait with Cropped Hair* (p. 86, fig. 86) to the Museum of Modern Art, New York.

Kahlo exhibits her work in multiple group exhibitions in Mexico City, at the Ministry of Agriculture and Development, the Palacio de Bellas Artes, and the Benjamin Franklin Library. She also participates in *Mexican Art Today* at the Philadelphia Museum of Art and in *Exhibition by 31 Women* at the Peggy Guggenheim's Art of This Century Gallery in New York.

Kahlo teaches at the Escuela de Pintura y Escultura la Esmeralda, a public, federally funded art school in Mexico City that offers classes to a wide sector of the population.

1943

On January 6 Reynolds arrives in New York physically depleted. She briefs the Office of Strategic Services, forerunner of the Central Intelligence Agency, on French Resistance activities and the locations of Nazi border guards.

The New Yorker publishes "The Escape of Mrs. Jeffries," a thinly veiled account of Reynolds's escape from Europe. Written by Reynolds's longtime friend Janet Flanner, it is serialized across three issues from late May to early June.

1944

In July Reynolds applies for a job with the Office of Strategic Services. She is ultimately not offered a position.

Kahlo and Rivera participate in the inaugural exhibition at the short-lived Galería de Arte Maupassant in Mexico City.

Kahlo declines a commission to paint a mural at the Posada del Sol Hotel. She offers the opportunity to her students, known as "Los Fridos."

On June 24 Kahlo writes to Dr. Eloesser, expressing her distress over intense spinal pain. Dr. Alejandro Zimbrón prescribes complete rest and designs a steel corset to keep her back in a fixed position.

1945

Six weeks after the Allies declare victory in Europe, Reynolds returns to her home at 14 rue Hallé. She begins working as the Parisian correspondent for the avant-garde magazine *View*, which she continues to do until the end of the magazine's run in 1947. Although Duchamp does not accompany Reynolds back to Paris, they collaborate on projects for the magazine.

Calder agrees to a major exhibition at Galerie Louis Carré to open the next year. In September Reynolds begins acting as Calder's agent, assisting in planning the show.

Kahlo paints *The Wounded Deer* (p. 87, fig. 87) before traveling to New York to undergo an operation to treat her spine, having been bedridden for four months. Upon her return to Mexico in July, she paints *Tree of Hope, Remain Strong* (p. 89, fig. 89), depicting her painful recovery.

1946

Duchamp briefly joins Reynolds in Paris.

From late July to the start of September, Reynolds and Duchamp spend time in Switzerland.

Kahlo exhibits her paintings in two shows at the Palacio de Bellas Artes: *45 Autorretratos de pintores mexicanos del siglo XVII al XX* and the inaugural exhibition of the Museo Nacional de Artes Plásticas, housed in the same venue.

1947

In January Duchamp moves back to New York.

Kahlo rejoins the Mexican Communist Party and becomes more active in the organization.

1948

Kahlo takes part in the inaugural exhibition of the Salón de la Plástica Mexicana in Mexico City.

1949

Never having fully recovered from the deprivations of the war and the hardships of her escape, Reynolds's precarious health begins to decline quickly.

Reynolds creates one of her last bookbindings for Queneau's *Saint Glinglin* (p. 82, fig. 82).

Kahlo's health worsens, and she is admitted to the hospital for nearly the entire year, undergoing seven operations on her spine.

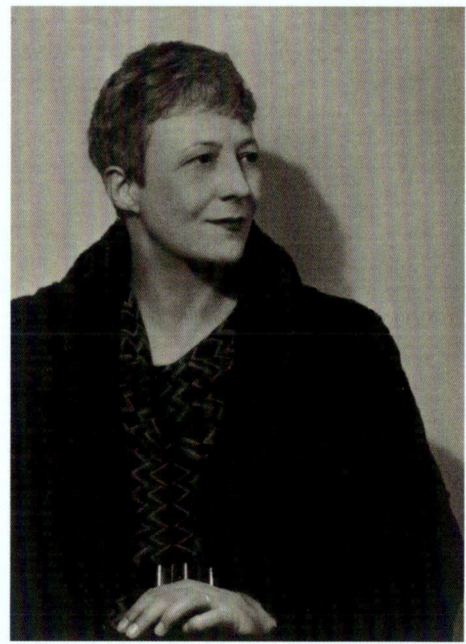

Fig. 99 Man Ray (American, 1890–1976). *Mary Reynolds*, 1930. Gelatin silver print; 35.2 × 25.2 cm (13⅞ × 9¹⁵⁄₁₆ in.). Museo Frida Kahlo, Mexico City, Archivo Diego Rivera y Frida Kahlo.

1950

In April, amid her friends' growing concern for her health, Reynolds checks into the American Hospital, where it is discovered that she has cancer. Duchamp is acutely worried, and queries their friends for information about her condition.

With a ticket purchased by Brookes, Duchamp sails to France in September on the RMS *Queen Mary*. Four days after he arrives at Reynolds's bedside in Paris, she falls into a coma.

On September 30 Reynolds dies at her home on 14 rue Hallé, with Duchamp at her side.

On October 3 Reynolds's funeral is held in Paris at the American Cathedral on the Avenue Georges V.

Duchamp begins inventorying Reynolds's possessions at 14 rue Hallé, including her bookbindings, library, and art collection, assembled during her three decades in Paris.

1951

Brookes begins working with the Art Institute of Chicago to create a permanent home for the Mary Reynolds Collection, which is ultimately established in 1955. He commissions drawings in memory of Reynolds from Calder (p. 18, fig. 10), Cocteau, and Jacques Villon.

Duchamp designs the bookplate (p. 8, fig. 2) for the Mary Reynolds Collection, based on a black-and-white photograph of Reynolds taken by Man Ray (p. 17, fig. 8). He works with Brookes over several months to arrive at the final version.

In May Kahlo's work is shown for the second time in Paris, featured in the exhibition *Art mexicain du précolombien à nos jours* at the Musée National d'Art Moderne. In September the exhibition travels to the Liljevalchs Gallery in Stockholm.

1952

On April 13 Kahlo holds her first and only solo exhibition in Mexico City at the Galería de Arte Contemporáneo, managed by Lola Álvarez Bravo. Despite her deteriorating health, she attends the opening lying in a hospital bed on wheels.

1953

On July 2, with her health continuing to decline, Kahlo demonstrates her political commitments by participating in a march protesting the overthrow of the democratic government in Guatemala.

On July 13 Kahlo dies at her family home in Coyoacán. The official cause of death is listed as pulmonary embolism. Rivera arranges a service at the Palacio de Bellas Artes, where more than six hundred people gather to pay tribute to her.

1954

Notes

All translations are by the authors unless otherwise noted.

FRIDA KAHLO AND MARY REYNOLDS: A SURREALIST DRAMA IN FIVE ACTS

I thank Tamar Kharatishvili and Alivé Piliado Santana for essential aid in researching this essay. Conversations with Rachel Cohen, Anne Collins Goodyear, and Hannah B Higgins informed and improved this text at several stages.

1. Janet Flanner, "Reporter at Large: The Escape of Mrs. Jeffries—I," *New Yorker*, May 22, 1943, 23.

2. On the exchange of ideas between France and Mexico during the global rise of Surrealism, see, among others, Whitney Chadwick, *Women Artists and the Surrealist Movement* (London: Thames and Hudson, 1985); Matthew Affron, Mark A. Castro, Dafne Cruz Porchini, and Renato González Mello, eds., *Paint the Revolution: Mexican Modernism, 1910–1950* (Philadelphia: Philadelphia Museum of Art, 2017); Ilene Susan Fort, Teresa Arcq, and Dawn Ades, eds., *In Wonderland: The Surrealist Adventures of Women Artists in Mexico and the United States* (Los Angeles: Los Angeles County Museum of Art, 2012); and Stephanie D'Alessandro and Matthew Gale, *Surrealism Beyond Borders* (New York: Metropolitan Museum of Art, 2021).

3. "Tout porte à croire qu'il existe un certain point d'esprit d'où la vie et la mort, le réel et l'imaginaire, le passé et le futur, le communicable et l'incommunicable, le haut et le bas cessent d'être perçus contradictoirement." André Breton, "Second manifeste du surréalisme," *La Révolution surréaliste* 12 (December 15, 1929): 1.

4. On this topic, see, for example, Rita Eder, "Surrealism in Mexico: Tensions and Encounters," in Affron et al., *Paint the Revolution*, 359–69; and Tere Arcq, "In the Land of Convulsive Beauty: Mexico," in Fort et al., *In Wonderland*, 65–87.

5. See, for example, Geoffrey T. Hellman and Harold Ross, "Ribbon Around Bomb," *New Yorker,* November 12, 1938, 19; Walter Pach, "Frida Rivera: Gifted Canvases by an Unselfconscious Surrealist," *Art News*, November 12, 1938, 13; "Bomb Beribboned," *Time*, November 14, 1938, 29; and Bertram D. Wolfe, "Rise of Another Rivera," *Vogue*, November 1, 1938, 64–65, 131.

6. Julien Levy Gallery, press release for the exhibition *Frida Kahlo (Frida Rivera)*, late October 1938, quoted in Beth Gates Warren and Marie Difilippantonio, eds., *Julien Levy: The Man, The Gallery, The Legacy*, vol. 3 (Newtown, CT: Jean and Julien Levy Foundation for the Arts, 2023), 1461. The same statement by Kahlo was quoted in Wolfe, "Rise of Another Rivera," 64.

7. While Maar's presence cannot be definitively documented, it is suggested in several sources that she was there to help with translation if the need arose. Although Kahlo was fluent in Spanish and English, she commented at several points during her stay in Paris on her lack of proficiency in French.

8. See Frida Kahlo to Diego Rivera, January 28, 1939, Archivo Diego Rivera y Frida Kahlo, Museo Frida Kahlo, Mexico City, quoted in Jaime Moreno Villarreal, *Frida en París, 1939* (Mexico: Turner Noema, 2021), 42.

9. For some of Kahlo's complaints regarding Breton and Lamba's accommodations, see Moreno Villarreal, *Frida en París*, 53, 55. Lamba later regretted the house's condition and the decision not to offer Kahlo hotel accommodations.

10. Frida Kahlo to Nickolas Muray, February 16, 1939, Nickolas Muray Papers, 1910–1992, Archives of American Art, Smithsonian Institution, Washington, DC.

11. See Moreno Villarreal, *Frida en París*, 70, which refers to an invoice of February 14, 1939, in Archivo Diego Rivera y Frida Kahlo, Museo Frida Kahlo, Mexico City, showing an incorrect application.

12. "Un joto chingado casado con Carmen Corcuera, de lo más antipático y pesado que he visto en mi vida. Es el marchand de Dalí, pero su galería vale mierda pues es una covacha infecta llena de mugre." Frida Kahlo to Diego Rivera, January 28, 1939, Archivo Diego Rivera y Frida Kahlo, Museo Frida Kahlo, Mexico City, reproduced in Moreno Villarreal, *Frida en París*, 69.

13. Kahlo to Muray, February 16, 1939.

14. Frida Kahlo to Nickolas Muray, February 27, 1939, Nickolas Muray papers, 1910–1992, Archives of American Art, Smithsonian Institution, Washington, DC.

15. Sometime in 1937 (before November), Reynolds had kidney problems and was treated at the American Hospital in Paris. See Paul B. Franklin, ed., *Étant donné no. 8: Marcel Duchamp and Mary Reynolds* (Paris: Association pour l'Etude de Marcel Duchamp, 2007), 74, 101n4.

16. Kahlo to Muray, February 27, 1939.

17. Mary Reynolds to Man Ray, August 18, 1948, reproduced in Franklin, *Étant donné*, 198.

18. Man Ray, *Self-Portrait* (Boston: Little Brown, 1963), 238–39.

19. See Susan Glover Godlewski, "Warm Ashes: The Life and Career of Mary Reynolds," in "Mary Reynolds and the Spirit of Surrealism," special issue, *Art Institute of Chicago Museum Studies* 22, no. 2 (1996), 104.

20. See "Matthew G Reynolds Junior," March 17, 1921, Form No. 84c-8, New York State Abstracts of World War I Military Service, 1917–1919, Series B0808, Adjutant General's Office, New York State Archives, Albany, New York.

21. "Marcel knows a lot of people, journalists, etc., who could be useful to you for your exhibition, Marcel speaks perfect English." Walter Pach to Frida Kahlo, December 25, 1938, quoted in Moreno Villarreal, *Frida en París*, 52.

22. See Moreno Villarreal, *Frida en París*, 109.

23. See Marjorie Hubachek Watkins, interview by Paul B. Franklin, in Franklin, *Étant donné*, 9.

24. Jean Suquet quoted in Franklin, *Étant donné*, 202.

25. Man Ray, *Self-Portrait*, 238–39.

26. See Watkins, interview by Franklin, *Étant donné*, 9. The glass pieces on the banister are also recounted by photographer Florence Henri; see Paul B. Franklin, "De ou par Mary Reynolds: The Making of a Collection," in Franklin, *Étant donné*, 76, 102n24.

27. Henri-Pierre Roché, journal entry, June 9, 1924, reproduced in Franklin, *Étant donné*, 229. On the display of earrings, see also Anaïs Nin, *The Diary of Anaïs Nin, 1931–1934* (New York: Gunther Stuhlmann, 1969), 356.

28. On the Calder mobiles installed outdoors, see Hélène Hoppenot, journal entry, January 1, 1948, reproduced in Franklin, *Étant donné*, 125. On the installation of Brancusi's *Two Penguins*, see Henri-Pierre Roché, journal entry, June 27, 1935, reproduced in Franklin, *Étant donné*, 237.

29. Godlewski, "Warm Ashes," 108.

30. Reynolds and Duchamp's collaborative work started with Duchamp's *Bride Stripped Bare by Her Bachelors, Even* (*The Green Box*; p. 54, fig. 52) in 1934 and continued with books they jointly designed, like the bindings for Giorgio de Chirico's *Hebdomeros* (p. 56, fig. 54) and Alfred Jarry's *Ubu roi* (*King Ubu*, p. 21, fig. 14). Reynolds would have also been involved in the making of the housing for Duchamp's *Box in a Valise* (p. 85, fig. 85). See Janine Mileaf, "Boxes, Books, and the *Boîte-en-valise*," in Sophie Lévy, ed., *A Transatlantic Avant-Garde: American Artists in Paris, 1918–1939*, exh. cat. (Giverny, France, and Berkeley, CA: Musée d'Art Américain Giverny and University of California Press, 2003), 168. See also Ecke Bonk, "Delay Included," in *Joseph Cornell/Marcel Duchamp . . . in Resonance*, exh. cat. (Houston and Philadelphia: Menil Collection and Philadelphia Museum of Art, 1998), 101.

31. On the contents of Reynolds's library, see Hugh L. Edwards, *Surrealism and Its Affinities: The Mary Reynolds Collection, a Bibliography* (Chicago: Art Institute of Chicago, 1956).

32. Mary Reynolds to Hélène Hoppenot, November 4, 1947, Bibliothèque littéraire Jacques Doucet, Paris, quoted in Page Dougherty Delano, "Kay Boyle and Mary Reynolds: Friendship Intensified by War," *Revue életronique d'études sur le monde anglophone* 10, no. 2 (2013), https://doi.org/10.4000/erea.3132.

33. On Reynolds's use of readymade elements and the haptic nature of her oeuvre, see Jenny Harris, "Object Study: Binding Saint Glinglin," *Journal of Surrealism in the Americas* 12, no. 1 (2021): 60–77.

34. As noted above, Kahlo's first solo exhibition took place in 1938. On Kahlo's relatively limited exhibition practice prior to 1940, see the chronology in this volume, 96–103.

35. Kahlo to Muray, February 16, 1939.

36. "La peinture de Frida Kahlo de Rivera est un ruban autour d'une bombe." André Breton, "Préface," in *Frida Kahlo (Frida Rivera)*, exh. cat. (New York: Julien Levy Gallery, 1938), n.p.

37. Frida Kahlo to Ella and Bertram Wolfe, March 17, 1939, reproduced in Martha Zamora, *The Letters of Frida Kahlo: Cartas Apasionadas*, trans. Jorge Gonzalez Casanova with Daniela Garaiz (San Francisco: Chronicle Books, 1995), 96.

38. See Hayden Herrera to Albright-Knox Art Gallery, April 20, 1977, object file for *Self-Portrait with Monkey* (p. 69, fig. 68), Buffalo AKG Art Museum, New York.

39. Kahlo to Muray, February 27, 1939.

40. See Kahlo to Muray, February 27, 1939.

41. Kahlo to Wolfe, March 17, 1939.

42. See Moreno Villarreal, *Frida en París*, 179. Kahlo wrote to Rivera on March 16, 1939, that Duchamp "colocó mis cuadros tal como si tú mismo los hubieras puesto" (installed my paintings as if you had installed them yourself), while "el pobre de Tanguy" (poor Tanguy) directed the installation of the rest of the exhibition.

43. Kahlo to Wolfe, March 17, 1939.

44. Kahlo to Wolfe, March 17, 1939.

45. See Moreno Villarreal, 188–90. Kahlo was also concerned about those fleeing the ongoing Spanish Civil War; see Marcel Petitjean, *The Heart: Frida Kahlo in Paris*, trans. Adriana Hunter (New York: Other Press, 2020), 78–79.

46. The acquisition of *The Frame* led Kahlo to be remembered in her *New York Times* obituary as "the first woman artist to sell a picture to the Louvre"; see "Frida Kahlo, Artist, Diego Rivera's Wife," *New York Times*, July 14, 1954, 27. While this was the first purchase of Kahlo's work by a museum, her painting *Frieda and Diego Rivera* (p. 45, fig. 41) had been in the collection of the San Francisco Museum of Art since 1936, a gift from Albert Bender.

47. Quoted in Petitjean, *The Heart*, 164. See also Moreno Villarreal, *Frida en París*, 183.

48. On this exhibition, see *Alexander Calder: Mobiles, Stabiles, Constellations*, exh. cat. (Paris: Galerie Louis Carré, 1946).

49. Marcel Duchamp, foreword to *Surrealism and Its Affinities*, 6.

50. "Mexican Autobiography," *Time*, April 27, 1953, 90.

51. Mary Reynolds to Frida Kahlo, March 30, 1939, Archivo Diego Rivera y Frida Kahlo, Museo Frida Kahlo, Mexico City (p. 94, fig. 94).

CAST OF CHARACTERS

1. See Ingrid Schaffner, "Alchemy of the Gallery," in Ingrid Schaffner and Lisa Jacob, eds., *Julien Levy: Portrait of an Art Gallery* (Cambridge, MA: MIT Press, 1998), 20.

2. Julien Levy, *Memoir of an Art Gallery* (New York: Putnam's Sons, 1977), 17.

3. Levy, *Memoir of an Art Gallery*, 22. Duchamp's studio was very near the Grande Mosquée de Paris.

4. See Julien Levy Gallery, *Frida Kahlo (Frida Rivera)*, exh. cat. (New York: Julien Levy Gallery, 1938).

5. Beth Gates Warren and Marie Difilippantonio, eds., *Julien Levy: The Man, The Gallery, The Legacy*, vol. 3 (Newtown, CT: Jean and Julien Levy Foundation for the Arts, 2023), 1458, 1466.

6. Quoted in English translation in André Breton, *Surrealism and Painting*, trans. Simon Watson Taylor (New York: Icon, 1972), 144.

7. "México tiende a ser el lugar surrealista par excelencia." André Breton, interview by Rafael Heliodoro Valle, "Diálogo con André Breton," *Mensual de cultura popular* 5, no. 29 (1938): 6.

8. Breton went to Mexico to deliver five conferences at the National University of Mexico. See André Breton, *Las Conferencias de México, 1938*, trans. Jaime Moreno Villarreal (Ciudad de México: Auieo, 2015).

9. See Jaime Moreno Villarreal, *Frida en París, 1939* (Mexico: Turner Noema, 2021), 35.

10. This language comes from a manuscript Breton wrote about the exhibition sometime between February and March 1939. André Breton, unpublished manuscript, Association Atelier Andre Breton, Paris, quoted in Moreno Villarreal, *Frida en París*, 178.

11. The book is listed among the works in André Breton's collection by the Association Atelier Andre Breton, andrebreton.fr/en/work/56600100687511. See Hugh L. Edwards, *Surrealism and Its Affinities: The Mary Reynolds Collection, a Bibliography* (Chicago: Art Institute of Chicago, 1956).

12. Jaqueline Lamba to Diego Rivera, April 30 and 31, 1939, Archivo Diego Rivera y Frida Kahlo, Museo Frida Kahlo, Mexico City, quoted in Moreno Villarreal, *Frida en París*, n.p.

13. See Salomon Grimberg, *I Will Never Forget You: Frida Kahlo to Nickolas Muray: Unpublished Photographs and Letters* (Munich: Schirmer/Mosel, 2004), 32.

14. Lamba to Rivera, April 30 and 31, 1939, quoted in Moreno Villarreal, *Frida en París*, 71.

15. Lamba to Rivera, April 30 and 31, 1939, quoted in Moreno Villarreal, *Frida en París*, 178.

16. Rosalind Krauss, *Bachelors* (Cambridge, MA: MIT Press, 2000), 24.

17. See Abigail Solomon-Godeau, "*Bande à part:* Jacqueline Lamba, Dora Maar, and the Surrealists' Women's Network," in Damarice Amao, Amanda Maddox, and Karolina Ziebinska-Lewandowska, eds., *Dora Maar* (Los Angeles: J. Paul Getty Museum, 2019), 133.

18. Solomon-Godeau, "*Bande à part*," 133.

19. Marcel Petitjean, *The Heart: Frida Kahlo in Paris*, trans. Adriana Hunter (New York: Other Press, 2020), 17. See also Moreno Villareal, *Frida en París*, 44.

20. Petitjean, *The Heart*, 106.

21. Diego Rivera with Gladys March, *My Art, My Life: An Autobiography* (New York: Citadel Press, 1960), 224.

22. See Frida Kahlo to Diego Rivera, January 28, 1939, Archivo Diego Rivera Frida Kahlo, Museo Frida Kahlo, Mexico City, quoted in Moreno Villarreal, *Frida en París*, 157.

23. See Moreno Villarreal, *Frida en París*, 125.

24. Nickolas Muray to Frida Kahlo, February 6, 1939, in Catalina Museum, "Catalina Island Museum presents En Garde! A Virtual Exploration of Frida Kahlo and Nickolas Muray," streamed live on August 22, 2020, YouTube video, posted January 20, 2023, 1:05:36, youtube.com/watch?v=py2kaU4Gfns&t; the letter appears at 6:48.

25. Muray wrote to Kahlo of the Surrealists, "They live in an imaginary circus, taking their lives and their fucking art extremely seriously, but wishing and waiting for someone else to come along and do something for them." Nickolas Muray to Frida Kahlo, February 6, 1939, Archivo Diego Rivera y Frida Kahlo, Museo Frida Kahlo, Mexico City, quoted in Moreno Villarreal, *Frida en París*, 105.

26. See Grimberg, *I Will Never Forget You*, 16.

27. See Grimberg, *I Will Never Forget You*, 20.

28. These photographs taken in New York and sent to Breton in Paris are referenced in Frida Kahlo to Nickolas Muray, February 27, 1939, Nickolas Muray Papers, 1910–1992, Archives of American Art, Smithsonian Institution, Washington, DC.

29. According to the story, these were gouaches by artist and poet Max Jacob, a lifelong friend of Colle's. Linda Lachgar, "À propos de Pierre Colle," in *Max Jacob dans tous ses états* (Paris: Éditions du Canöe, 2019), 62.

30. See Julia Drost, "Le surréalisme et le commerce de l'art parisien dans l'entre-deux-guerres," in Denise Vernerey-Laplace and Hélène Ivanoff, eds., *Les artistes et leurs galeries, Paris-Berlin 1900–1950*, vol. 1, *Paris* (Rouen and Le Havre, France: Presses universitaires de Rouen et du Havre, 2018), 296.

31. Renou had made a name for himself dealing works by Pierre-Auguste Renoir and Paul Cezanne. Renou was close to Renoir's family, having by chance in his youth spent a summer in a house next to the artist's in Cagnes-sur-Mer, France. See Marianne Feilchenfeldt Breslauer, *Bilder meines Lebens: Erinnerungen* (Wädenswil, Germany: Nimbus Kunst und Bücher, 2009), 212–13.

32. Frida Kahlo to Nickolas Muray, February 16, 1939, Nickolas Muray Papers, 1910–1992, Archives of American Art, Smithsonian Institution, Washington, DC.

33. See Warren and Difilippantonio, *Julien Levy*, 1476.

34. Henri-Pierre Roché, "Souvenirs of Marcel Duchamp," trans. William Copley, in Robert Lebel, ed., *Marcel Duchamp* (New York: Paragraphic Books, 1959), 87.

35. Susan L. Glover, "Cendres chaudes: vie et carrière de Mary Reynolds," in Paul B. Franklin, ed., *Étant donné no. 8: Marcel Duchamp and Mary Reynolds* (Paris: Association pour l'Etude de Marcel Duchamp, 2007), 21.

36. See Janine Mileaf, "Boxes, Books, and the *Boîte-en-valise*," in Sophie Lévy, ed., *A Transatlantic Avant-Garde: American Artists in Paris, 1918–1939*, exh. cat. (Giverny, France, and Berkeley, CA: Musée d'Art Américain Giverny and University of California Press, 2003), 168.

37. Man Ray photographed Duchamp posing as Rrose Sélavy in 1920–21.

38. On Duchamp's non-artistic work, especially as an agent, artistic advisor, and curator, see Elena Filipovic, *The Apparently Marginal Activities of Marcel Duchamp* (Cambridge, MA: MIT Press, 2016).

39. See Christine M. Fabian and Jack Perry Brown, "Never Judge a Book by Its Cover: Mary Reynolds's Binding for *Night-Flight*," in "Art through the Pages: Library Collections at the Art Institute of Chicago," special issue, *Art Institute of Chicago Museum Studies* 34, no. 2 (2008): 56.

40. Man Ray's dedication to Reynolds in her copy of *Revolving Doors, 1916–1917* (1926), a collection of his prints.

41. Man Ray, *Self-Portrait* (Boston: Little Brown, 1963), 236.

42. In her 1921 application for a US passport, Reynolds noted that she intended to leave the United States from the port of New York aboard the SS *Patria* on May 12, 1921, with Italy as her first destination. She spent some time in Rome before arriving in Paris in November. Mary Reynolds passport application, April 23, 1921, Roll 1579 (Certificates: 23626–23999, 23 April 1921), *NARA Series: Passport Applications, January 2, 1906–March 31, 1925*, National Archives and Records Administration, Washington, DC. See also Glover, "Cendres chaudes," 19.

43. Man Ray, *Self-Portrait*, 236.

44. Man Ray had also described his own hands as "dreaming" as he executed the book's drawings. Glover, "Cendres chaudes," 28.

45. See Glover, "Cendres chaudes," 33. See also Man Ray, *Self-Portrait*, 256–58.

46. Virginia M. Dortch, *Peggy Guggenheim and Her Friends* (Milan: Berenice, 1994), 10.

47. Peggy Guggenheim, *Out of This Century: Confessions of an Art Addict* (New York: Universe Books, 1987), 50.

48. Michael Cedric Sinbad Vail was born in London on May 15, 1923. Reynolds proposed the middle name "Cedric" in honor of her artist friend Cedric Morris. Guggenheim, *Out of This Century*, 40.

49. Guggenheim, *Out of This Century*, 50.

50. See Guggenheim, *Out of This Century*, 163.

51. See Guggenheim, *Out of This Century*, 163.

52. Frida Kahlo to Diego Rivera, February 13, 1939, Archivo Diego Rivera y Frida Kahlo, Museo Frida Kahlo, Mexico City, quoted in Moreno Villarreal, *Frida en París*, 141.

53. Guggenheim wrote to Kahlo: "Dear Frida, the earrings are beautiful, I love them. I am very sorry that you did not come to London and declined having an exhibition here. What a pity! Thank you and have a good trip. Affectionately, Peggy." Peggy Guggenheim to Frida Kahlo, undated, Archivo Diego Rivera y Frida Kahlo, Museo Frida Kahlo, Mexico City, quoted in Moreno Villarreal, *Frida en París*, 142.

54. Walter Pach to Frida Kahlo, December 25, 1938, Archivo Diego Rivera y Frida Kahlo, Museo Frida Kahlo, Mexico City, quoted in Moreno Villarreal, *Frida en París*, 51.

55. Pach to Kahlo, December 25, 1938, quoted in Moreno Villarreal, *Frida en París*, 51.

56. Diego Rivera to Walter Pach, October 11, 1938, box 2, folder 49 (Rivera, Diego and Lupe de Rivera, 1922–1942), Walter Pach Papers, 1857–1980, Archives of American Art, Smithsonian Institution, Washington, DC.

57. See Bennard B. Perlman, *American Artists, Authors, and Collectors: The Walter Pach Letters, 1906–1958* (Albany, NY: State University of New York Press, 2002), 20.

58. Paul B. Franklin, "Henri-Pierre Roché, a General Introducer," in Paul B. Franklin, ed., *Brancusi and Duchamp: The Art of Dialogue*, exh. cat. (New York: Kasmin, 2018), 123.

59. Henri-Pierre Roché, journal entry, May 21, 1924, reproduced in Franklin, *Étant donné*, 228.

60. Henri-Pierre Roché, journal entry, May 24, 1924, reproduced in Franklin, *Étant donné*, 228.

61. Henri-Pierre Roché, journal entry, February 17, 1937, reproduced in Franklin, *Étant donné*, 237.

62. See, for example, Henri-Pierre Roché, journal entries, June 27, 1935; February 17, 1937; and August 10, 1937, reproduced in Franklin, *Étant donné*, 237–38.

63. Henri-Pierre Roché, journal entry, August 15, 1937, reproduced in Franklin, *Étant donné*, 238. Roché is referring either to his *Fragments sur Don Juan* (1916) or his *Don Juan et . . .* (1921).

64. Mary Reynolds to Alexander Calder, November 23, 1945, reproduced in Franklin, *Étant donné*, 212. Reynolds was acting as Calder's agent for his upcoming show with the gallerist Louis Carré.

65. See Alexander Calder, *An Autobiography with Pictures* (New York: Pantheon Books, 1966), 126.

66. See Franklin, *Étant donné*, 212.

67. Alexander Calder to Frank B. Hubachek, July 13, 1955, Mary Reynolds Collection, Ryerson and Burnham Art and Architecture Archives, Art Institute of Chicago.

68. Mary Reynolds and Marcel Duchamp to Constantin Brancusi, postmarked August 10, 1946, reproduced in Franklin, *Étant donné*, 71.

69. Duchamp and Brancusi met in Paris sometime between 1904 and 1912; see Franklin, *Brancusi and Duchamp*, 6.

70. See Henri-Pierre Roché, journal entry, June 9, 1924, reproduced in Franklin, *Étant donné*, 229.

71. Duchamp eventually ceded his share of the Brancusi works to Roché to repay his friend for various debts. See Franklin, *Brancusi and Duchamp,* 147–48, 228.

72. See Henri-Pierre Roché, journal entry, May 25, 1940, reproduced in Franklin, *Étant donné*, 238.

73. See Franklin, *Brancusi and Duchamp*, 149; and Franklin, *Étant donné*, 62.

74. *Gallina* is also the Italian word for "chicken"; Franklin suggests that the nickname may have had something to do with Reynolds's close ties to Italy. See Franklin, *Étant donné*, 62.

75. Mary Reynolds and Marcel Duchamp to Constantin Brancusi, mid-September 1933, reproduced in Franklin, *Étant donné*, 69.

76. See Ariane Coulondre, Julie Jones, and V. Loth, eds., *Brancusi: L'art ne fait que commencer* (Paris: Centre Pompidou, 2024), 86.

77. Frank B. Hubachek conveyed Cocteau's remarks in English in a letter he wrote to Carl O. Schniewind, February 14, 1957, Mary Reynolds Collection, Ryerson and Burnham Art and Architecture Archives, the Art Institute of Chicago.

78. See Guggenheim, *Out of This Century*, 161. The exhibition ran from January 24 to February 12, 1938.

79. See Kenneth E. Silver, *Jean Cocteau: The Juggler's Revenge*, exh. cat. (Venice: Marsilo Arte and Peggy Guggenheim Collection, 2024), 60.

80. "À Mary Reynolds / pour distraire son exil / avec les hommages de Queneau." Queneau's dedication to Reynolds in her bound copy of his 1942 novel *Pierrot Mon Ami.*

81. See Raymond Queneau, *Œuvres complètes*, vol. 1, ed. Claude Debon (Paris: Gallimard, 1989), i. With his 1928 marriage to Janine Kahn, Queneau was briefly Breton's brother-in-law, until Breton's separation from Simone Kahn in 1929. Queneau was eventually one of the signatories of Georges Bataille's 1930 anti-Breton pamphlet, *Un Cadavre.*

82. For instance, Queneau's novel *Saint Glinglin*, as Jenny Harris has pointed out, is written entirely without the letter *x* and features comical, phonetic renderings of words like *eggzistence* (existence). See Jenny Harris, "Object Study: Binding *Saint Glinglin*," *Journal of Surrealism and the Americas* 12, no. 1 (2021): 60–77.

83. *Odile* featured thinly fictionalized portraits of key Surrealist figures, and mathematics play an important thematic role in the book. See Chris Andrews, "Surrealism and Pseudo-Initiation: Raymond Queneau's 'Odile,'" *Modern Languages Review* 94, no. 2 (1999): 377–94.

84. See Daniel Levin Becker, *Many Subtle Channels: In Praise of Potential Literature* (Cambridge, MA: Harvard University Press, 2012), 142–45.

85. Alfred Jarry, *Ubu roi,* in Alfred Jarry, *Œuvres complètes*, vol. 4 (Monte Carlo: Éditions du Livre, 1948), 35.

86. See Sheelagh Bevan, ed., *Alfred Jarry: The Carnival of Being* (New York: Morgan Library and Museum, 2019), 1.

87. See Katie L. Price and Michael R. Taylor, eds., *'Pataphysics Unrolled* (University Park: Pennsylvania State University Press, 2022), 2–3.

88. See Alastair Brotchie, *Alfred Jarry: A Pataphysical Life* (Cambridge, MA: MIT Press, 2015), 165.

89. See Price and Taylor, *'Pataphysics Unrolled*, 3. See also Brotchie, *Alfred Jarry*, 27–35.

90. André Breton, *Mexique*, exh. cat. (Paris: Renou et Colle, 1939), n.p., quoted in Ian Walker, "Manuel Álvarez Bravo, Surrealism and Documentary Photography," *Journal of Surrealism and the Americas* 8, no. 1 (2014): 13.

91. See Lucrecia Martín, "El ejercicio de lo diverso. Entrevista con Manuel Álvarez Bravo," *Revista de la Universidad de México* 2–3 (October 1978): 32.

92. See André Breton, Mauruce Heine, and Pierre Mabille, *Minotaure: revue artistique et littéraire* 12-13 (Paris: Skira, May 1939), 32.

93. Álvarez Bravo's comment began, "Many times my work, taken as a whole, has been related to Surrealism. I believe that this is an equivocation." Manuel Álvarez Bravo, untitled text, in Jain Kelly, ed., *Nude: Theory* (New York: Lustrum Press, 1979) 9–12, quoted in Walker, "Manuel Álvarez Bravo," 14.

94. See Beth Gates Warren and and Marie Difilippantonio, "Documentary and Anti-Graphic Photographs by Cartier-Bresson, Walker Evans and Álvarez Bravo," in Warren and Difilippantonio, *Julien Levy*, vol. 3, 1050–88.

95. In a letter to Muray, Kahlo stated that Breton was planning to include in the Paris exhibition "about 32 photographs of Álvarez Bravo." Kahlo to Muray, February 16, 1939.

96. "J'aime et j'admire Frida plus encore qu'à Paris." Wolfgang Paalen to André Breton, November 7, 1939, Association Atelier Andre Breton, Paris, andrebreton.fr/en/work/56600101001897.

97. In the summer of 1938, on Breton's recommendation, Paalen opened a solo exhibition at Galerie Renou et Colle in Paris. Subsequently, with Duchamp's support, he exhibited in early 1939 at the Guggenheim Jeune in London and in 1940 at Julien Levy Gallery in New York. See Andrea Neufert, *Wolfgang Paalen: Scenes for a Sorcerer*, exh. cat. (San Francisco: Rowland Weinstein and Weinstein Gallery, 2023), 86.

98. Frida Kahlo to Diego Rivera, January 28, 1939, Archivo Diego Rivera y Frida Kahlo, Museo Frida Kahlo, Mexico City, quoted in Moreno Villarreal, *Frida en París*, 89. Frida Kahlo to Ella and Bertram Wolfe, March 17, 1939, reproduced in Martha Zamora, ed., *The Letters of Frida Kahlo: Cartas Apasionadas* (San Francisco, Chronicle Books, 1995), 96.

99. See Alice Rahon to Frida Kahlo, July 1, 1939, Series 1: Correspondence, Nelleke Nix and Marianna Huber Collection: The Frida Kahlo Papers, Archives of Women Artists, Betty Boyd Dettre Library and Research Center, National Museum of Women in the Arts, Washington, DC.

100. See Dafne Cruz Porchini and Adriana Ortega Orozco, "The 1940 *International Exhibition of Surrealism*: A Cosmopolitan Art Dialogue in Mexico City," *Dada/Surrealism* 21, no. 1 (2017): 1–23.

101. Wolfgang Paalen continued to reside in Mexico, apart from a period between 1948 and 1954 when he lived in San Francisco and Paris. See Neufert, *Wolfgang Paalen*, 88.

102. See Annette Leddy and Donna Conwell, *Farewell to Surrealism: The Dyn Circle in Mexico* (Los Angeles: Getty Research Institute, 2012).

103. Frank Brookes Hubachek to Elizabeth M. Hilles, November 5, 1963, quoted in Paul B. Franklin, "De ou par Mary Reynolds: The Making of a Collection," in Franklin, *Étant donné*, 98.

104. Kenan Heise, "Lawyer Frank Hubachek, 92," *Chicago Tribune*, December 10, 1986, A14.

105. Marjorie Hubachek Watkins quoted in Paul B. Franklin, "Remembering Aunt Mary: An Interview with Marjorie Hubachek Watkins and Frank Brookes Hubachek Jr.," in Franklin, *Étant donné*, 10.

106. See Franklin, "De ou par Mary Reynolds," 12.

107. See Michael R. Taylor, "Duchamp in the Wilderness: *Moonlight on the Bay at Basswood* and the Landscape Backdrop of Étant donnés," in Franklin, ed., *Étant donné* no. 8, 44, 47.

CHRONOLOGY

Hugh L. Edwards, *Surrealism and Its Affinities: The Mary Reynolds Collection, a Bibliography* (Chicago: Art Institute of Chicago, 1956).

Paul B. Franklin, ed., *Étant donné no. 8: Marcel Duchamp and Mary Reynolds* (Paris: Association pour l'étude de Marcel Duchamp, 2007).

Susan Glover Godlewski, "Warm Ashes: The Life and Career of Mary Reynolds," in "Mary Reynolds and the Spirit of Surrealism," special issue, *Art Institute of Chicago Museum Studies* 22, no. 2 (1996): 102–29.

Hayden Herrera, *Frida: A Biography of Frida Kahlo* (New York: Harper and Row, 1983).

Luis-Martín Lozano and Marina Vázquez Ramos, "Biography 1904–1954," in *Frida Kahlo: The Complete Paintings*, ed. Luis-Martín Lozano (Cologne, Germany: Taschen, 2021) 386–407.

Jaime Moreno Villarreal, *Frida en París*, 1939 (Mexico: Turner Noema, 2021).

Christine Oddo, *Mary Reynolds: Artiste surréaliste et amante de Marcel Duchamp* (Paris: Tallandier, 2021).

Helga Prignitz-Poda, Salomón Grimberg, and Andrea Kettenmann, eds., *Frida Kahlo: Das Gesamtwerk* (Frankfurt: Verlag Neue Kritik, 1988).

Notes on Mary Reynolds's Bindings

TITLES

The captions for most of the bindings illustrated in this publication include a direct English translation of the French book title. When Reynolds bound books that were published in English under a different title (rather than a translation of the French title), they are listed in the caption. When the book is a translation of a work originally published in another language, the caption provides the original-language title. We have not provided an English translation of French titles when cognates are obvious or when no meaningful translation is possible. Translated titles are styled like titles (i.e., capitalized and italicized) only if the book was published in English under that title.

DATES

When the specific date of a binding is unknown, we have made every effort to place it in one of two categories: 1930–42 or 1945–50, based on the understanding that Reynolds was not actively binding between 1942 and 1945, during the period of World War II when she was not living at 14 rue Hallé. For bindings of books published after 1930, we have listed the publication year as the earliest possible date.

MEDIUM DESCRIPTIONS

Medium descriptions for Reynolds's bindings are in the following order: The first sentence describes exterior binding components, like the type of leather, and notes any inlaid or onlaid materials and stamping. The second sentence lists information about the binding's interior materials, such as endpapers and the presence of gilt edges. Additional sentences describe any slipcases or other housings as well as any inscriptions or drawings.

Contributors

Caitlin Haskell is the Gary C. and Frances Comer Senior Curator of Modern and Contemporary Art at the Art Institute of Chicago, where she has worked since 2018. A scholar of twentieth-century painting and sculpture, her research and writing address the production, critical reception, and legacies of the art of the historical avant-gardes in Europe and the Americas.

Tamar Kharatishvili is the Daniel F. and Ada L. Rice Research Fellow in Modern Art at the Art Institute of Chicago, serving the departments of Modern and Contemporary Art and Provenance Research. Her dissertation, "Technology as Refuge: Sonia Delaunay-Terk's Collaborative Intermediality, 1913–1937" (2024), examined the relationship between art, technology, and migration in Paris.

Alivé Piliado Santana is the curatorial associate at the National Museum of Mexican Art in Chicago, as part of the Advancing Latinx Art in Museums initiative. Previously, she was a research associate in Modern and Contemporary Art at the Art Institute of Chicago. She has also worked as a curator at national art museums in Mexico City.

Photo Credits

Unless otherwise noted, photographs of artworks in the collection of the Art Institute of Chicago are copyrighted by the Art Institute of Chicago.

Every effort has been made to identify, contact, and acknowledge copyright holders for all reproductions; additional rights holders are encouraged to contact the Art Institute of Chicago. The following credits apply to all images in this book for which separate acknowledgment is due.

Front cover; p. 68, fig. 67: © Banco de México Diego Rivera Frida Kahlo Museums Trust, Mexico, D.F. / Artist Rights Society (ARS), New York. Photos © CNAC/MNAM, Dist. RMN-Grand Palais / Art Resource, NY. **Back cover (detail); p. 21, fig. 14; p. 57, fig. 43; pp. 49–52, figs. 45–49; pp. 55–58, figs. 53–56; pp. 62–65, figs. 60–64; pp. 74–82, figs. 74–83:** © Mary Reynolds. **P. 2; p. 29, fig. 23; p. 101, fig. 98:** Photos courtesy of the Nickolas Muray Estate. **P. 4, fig. 1; p. 19, fig. 12:** © Constantin Brancusi. **P. 12, fig. 4; 95, fig. 95:** © Nickolas Muray. Photo by Jamie Stukenberg. **P. 14, fig. 5:** © Banco de México Diego Rivera Frida Kahlo Museums Trust, Mexico, D.F. / Artist Rights Society (ARS), New York. **P. 17, figs. 8–9; p. 59, fig. 57:** © 2025 Man Ray Trust / Artists Rights Society (ARS), New York / ADAGP, Paris. **P. 18, fig. 10:** © 2025 Calder Foundation, New York / Artists Rights Society (ARS), New York. **P. 20, fig. 13:** © Yves Tanguy. **P. 22, fig. 16; p. 26, fig. 19; p. 91, fig. 91; p. 103, fig. 99:** Photos courtesy of the Museo Frida Kahlo, Mexico City. **P. 24, fig. 17:** © The Joseph and Robert Cornell Memorial Foundation / Licensed by VAGA at Artists Rights Society (ARS), New York. Photo courtesy of the Philadelphia Museum of Art. **P. 25, fig. 18:** © 2025 Man Ray Trust / Artists Rights Society (ARS), New York / ADAGP, Paris. Photo courtesy of the Museo Frida Kahlo, Mexico City. **P. 27, fig. 20:** © Dora Maar. Photo courtesy of the Metropolitan Museum of Art. **P. 27, fig. 21; p. 32, fig. 27:** © 2025 Man Ray Trust / Artists Rights Society (ARS), New York / ADAGP, Paris. Photos © CNAC/MNAM, Dist. RMN-Grand Palais / Art Resource, NY. **P. 28, fig. 22:** Photo courtesy of the Museo Casa Estudio Diego Rivera y Frida Kahlo, Mexico City. **P. 29, fig. 23:** © Nicholas Muray. Photo courtesy of the Nickolas Muray Estate. **P. 29, fig. 24:** © Miguel Covarrubias Estate. Photo courtesy of the National Portrait Gallery, Smithsonian Institution, gift of Mimi and Nicholas C. Muray. **P. 30, fig. 25:** © Henri Cartier-Bresson / Magnum Photos. Photo courtesy of Magnum Photos. **P. 31, fig. 26:** © 2025 Man Ray Trust / Artists Rights Society (ARS), New York / ADAGP, Paris. Photo courtesy of the Centre Pompidou, MNAM-CCI / Guy Carrard / Dist. RMN-Grand Palais. **P. 33, fig. 28:** © Estate of Berenice Abbott. Photo courtesy of the Amon Carter Museum of American Art. **P. 34, fig. 29:** © The Waintrob Project for the Visual Arts, Inc. **P. 35, fig. 30:** Photo © CNAC/MNAM, Dist. RMN-Grand Palais / Art Resource, NY. **P. 36, fig. 31:** Photo courtesy of Photography Collection, The New York Public Library. **P. 37, fig. 32:** © Marcel Duchamp. **P. 38, fig. 33:** © Dora Maar, ADAGP, Paris. Photo courtesy of the Centre Pompidou, MNAM-CCI / Georges Meguerditchian / Dist. RMN-Grand Palais. **P. 39, fig. 34:** Photo courtesy of photo collection succession Raymond Queneau/ Diffusion Gallimard. **P. 40, fig. 35:** Photo courtesy of Sotheby's. **P. 41, fig. 36:** © Lola Álvarez Bravo. Photo © Center for Creative Photography, The University of Arizona Foundation. **P. 42, figs. 37–38:** Photos courtesy of Florida Atlantic University. **P. 45, fig. 41:** © Banco de México Diego Rivera Frida Kahlo Museums Trust, Mexico, D.F. / Artist Rights Society (ARS), New York. Photo by Ben Blackwell. **P. 48, fig. 44; p. 53, figs. 50–51:** © Mary Reynolds. © 2025 Marcel Duchamp, New York / Artists Rights Society (ARS), New York. **P. 69, fig. 68:** © Banco de México Diego Rivera Frida Kahlo Museums Trust, Mexico, D.F. / Artist Rights Society (ARS), New York. Photo courtesy of the Buffalo AKG Art Museum / Art Resource, NY. **P. 70, fig. 69:** © Lola Álvarez Bravo / Artist Rights Society (ARS), New York. **P. 71, fig. 71:** © Diego Rivera. **P. 72, fig. 72:** © Banco de México Diego Rivera Frida Kahlo Museums Trust, Mexico, D.F. / Artist Rights Society (ARS), New York. Photo courtesy of the Madison Museum of Contemporary Art, Wisconsin. **P. 73, fig. 73:** © Banco de México Diego Rivera Frida Kahlo Museums Trust, Mexico, D.F. / Artist Rights Society (ARS), New York. Photo courtesy of the Banco Nacional de México Collection. **P. 86, fig. 86:** © Banco de México Diego Rivera Frida Kahlo Museums Trust, Mexico, D.F. / Artist Rights Society (ARS), New York. Photo © The Museum of Modern Art / Licensed by SCALA / Art Resource, NY. **P. 87, fig. 87:** © Banco de México Diego Rivera Frida Kahlo Museums Trust, Mexico, D.F. / Artist Rights Society (ARS), New York. Photo courtesy of the Museum of Contemporary Art Chicago. **P. 88, fig. 88:** © Banco de México Diego Rivera Frida Kahlo Museums Trust, Mexico, D.F. / Artist Rights Society (ARS), New York. Photo by Nicolas Pishvanov, courtesy of Weinstein Gallery. **P. 89, fig. 89:** © Banco de México Diego Rivera Frida Kahlo Museums Trust, Mexico, D.F. / Artist Rights Society (ARS), New York. Photo by Nathan Keay, courtesy of the Museum of Contemporary Art Chicago. **Pp. 92–93, fig. 92–93:** © Banco de México Diego Rivera Frida Kahlo Museums Trust, Mexico, D.F. / Artist Rights Society (ARS), New York. Photos courtesy of the Archives of American Art, Smithsonian Institution. **P. 94, fig. 94:** © Mary Reynolds. Photo courtesy of the Museo Frida Kahlo, Mexico City. **P. 97, fig. 97:** © Dora Maar. Photo © CNAC/MNAM, Dist. RMN-Grand Palais / Art Resource, NY.

Frida Kahlo's Month in Paris: A Friendship with Mary Reynolds was published in conjunction with an exhibition of the same title organized by the Art Institute of Chicago, March 29–July 13, 2025.

Major support for *Frida Kahlo's Month in Paris: A Friendship with Mary Reynolds* is provided by the Zell Family Foundation, Pat and Ron Taylor, Constance and David Coolidge, The Donnelly Family Foundation, and Natasha Henner and Bala Ragothaman.

Additional support is contributed by Kathy and Chuck Harper.

First edition
Printed in Canada

ISBN: 978-0-300-27966-5 (hardcover)

Library of Congress Control Number: 2025931129

Published by
The Art Institute of Chicago
111 South Michigan Avenue
Chicago, IL 60603-6404
artic.edu

Distributed by
Yale University Press
302 Temple Street
P. O. Box 209040
New Haven, CT 06520-9040
yalebooks.com/art

Edited by Kit Shields
Production by Elizabeth Upenieks and
    Lauren Makholm
Photography research by Josephine Maria
    Yanasak-Leszczynski
Proofreading by Sarah Robinson
Photography by Nathan Keay, Juan Molina
    Hernández, and Joe Tallarico
Postproduction by Hayley Hinsberger and
    Kaitlyn Fultz-Campion
Design and typesetting by Anjali Pala
Separations by Professional Graphics,
    Rockford, Illinois
Printing and binding by Friesens

Publishing, the Art Institute of Chicago
Katie Reilly, Associate Vice President
Lisa Meyerowitz, Editorial Director
Lauren Makholm, Director of Production

Imaging, the Art Institute of Chicago
Bonnie Rosenberg, Director of Imaging
Nathan Keay, Associate Director
    of Photography
Elyse M. Allen, Associate Director
    of Production

Front cover: Frida Kahlo, *The Frame* (p. 68, fig. 67)
Back cover: Mary Reynolds, *Les mains libres* (p. 58, fig. 56)

Authorized Representative in the EU: Easy Access System Europe, Mustamäe tee 50, 10621 Tallinn, Estonia, gpsr.requests@easproject.com

This book was made using paper and materials certified by the Forest Stewardship Council, which ensures responsible forest management.

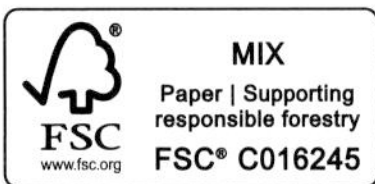